HOUSE OF DeWOLFF

A TRUE STORY OF CORRUPTION, KIDNAPPING, AND CONSPIRACY IN THE JUSTICE SYSTEM

BY

JOSEPH CHARLES WAIKSNIS

First Edition: October 2016

Book Cover Design by ebooklaunch.com

ISBN: 978-0-9977414-1-4

CONTENTS

Introduction 1

Chapter One 7

Chapter Two... 21

Chapter Three 32

Chapter Four... 44

Chapter Five... 59

Chapter Six... 66

Chapter Seven 77

Chapter Eight... 90

Chapter Nine... 96

Chapter Ten... 104

Chapter Eleven... 116

Chapter Twelve... 124

Chapter Thirteen.. 147

Chapter Fourteen... 156

Chapter Fifteen 162

Chapter Sixteen... 176

Chapter Seventeen 195

Chapter Eighteen 207

Chapter Nineteen.. 220

Chapter Twenty... 227

Chapter Twenty-One.. 236

Chapter Twenty-Two.. 252

INTRODUCTION

Most nightmares have a beginning and an end. Whether you experience them subconsciously, in the deepest of sleep, or consciously as you live through the hours, days, or even months of harrowing events, you tell yourself you can and will survive this bad dream. This too shall pass, you tell yourself. You keep faith in reality or in yourself, a friend, or a loved one. Perhaps you pray. At some point, you look forward to the day when the nightmare will be over and happiness and harmony are restored.

Sometimes, though, nightmares endure. They keep recurring. You find that a situation in your life is not so easily resolved.

In my own life, my nightmare has all but taken over. Once a respected, stable, family man, today I am a single father forced to live under constant harassment. To some degree, I write this to try to afford myself some respite from the ongoing drama.

Our legal system can be like a snare; once you are entangled, it is very difficult to get out. You are less and less "presumed innocent" with every brush with the courts. The system becomes more and more punitive toward you; fees and penalties escalate, even if your initial offense was relatively minor or even non-existent.

For example, if you have ever failed to appear in court for some reason, a bench warrant will be issued for your arrest. Your problem might have been a traffic violation, but if you fail to appear in court, you are suddenly considered a fugitive from the law. Things get very serious very fast. You may then experience a version of what I went through and am going through—the snare of the legal system. Often a person is unaware that the bench warrant has been issued. It happens with the almost automatic bang of a judge's gavel, and you may not even know it occurred until the next time you are pulled over. Then, suddenly, you are carted off to jail. The police and courts tend to get pretty draconian about such things.

There are many reasons why a well-intentioned, otherwise law-abiding citizen might miss a court date. Yet if you do, you may very quickly be relegated to the fearsome status of being a "fugitive from justice," which means whatever your legal problem was in the first place, you've got additional charges and a bench warrant to deal with now. Also, if they find you, you are going straight to jail.

Detectives may come to your last known address. Your relatives may wake up one fine day to find their front and back yards swarming with officers of the law, detectives ringing their doorbell and standing there with a photo of you. You may have to go through the embarrassment of trying to explain to your neighbors why your house became the center of a dragnet. The police act as if you were a dangerous criminal by standing around points of exit, just waiting to apprehend the escaping you. They may be brusque with your relatives and seem to doubt their veracity when they say they don't know where you are. They stiffly warn your relatives that if they are harboring a fugitive from justice, they are going to be in big legal trouble too.

It is not a pretty scene. I know because I have been there, and my family has been there, in this kind and other kinds of legal snafus that never seem to get straightened out but haunt your days, nights, footsteps, and finances for years on end. A small legal difficulty can snowball from a minor incident until you find yourself in prison.

So many lawyers these days advise their clients just to plead guilty to a lesser charge to get out of the legal snare. Yes, American citizens are being encouraged to give up their right to a fair trial to plead guilty to crimes they did not commit just to get out of the grasp of the justice system.

My legal nightmare started in 1993. In 1993 I was declared guilty of a crime I did not commit. Prior to the conviction, I was brutally apprehended and held in police custody without any reference to the basic procedures of law.

As a result of this arrest, I was later forced to relocate and to give up a valuable property I had inherited from my maternal grandfather, located in a small Pennsylvania town. The home built upon that property was coveted by the people responsible for my persecution and was, I believe, a key part of why I was targeted in the first place.

It is difficult to imagine that the authorities of a small town would persecute a man for a piece of land in the United States. Home ownership and property rights are part of the American Dream. Voting rights were originally based on property ownership. The lyrics of the second verse of "The Star-Spangled Banner" speak about people's rights to "stand between their loved homes and the war's desolation." The right to private property was a key part of our democracy. Protecting one's home and property is, it seems to me, a basic American right.

Yet people coveted my property, and the upshot of it is that to this day, although I am an ordinary, hardworking, law-abiding citizen, I am treated like a criminal. My own experience exposes the corruption that can and does exist in the very system designed and pledged to protect this country's citizens—me and my family, and you and yours.

I know we would all like to believe that our justice system has the best intentions toward citizens and that our police officers don't abuse their power. How we all wish this were so. To paraphrase Winston Churchill, I'm going to say that we have the worst justice system in the world—unless you count all the others. That backhanded compliment is not saying much, though, in what is supposed to be the land of the free and the home of the brave.

My story spans such a long time period and such a range of prosecutorial efforts against me that I honestly find it hard to believe myself. I might chalk it up to a bad dream, if it were not for the evidence, the cold, hard facts, that stand before me every minute. If it were not for the truth I know, I might think all this was impossible.

Much of my story comes down to money. My family's persecution has been fueled by monetary greed. We have, perhaps, been targeted with such furious persistence because we are of limited means—we cannot fight fire with fire; we cannot fight back at the highest level. Thus, we are perhaps ready targets for a system more powerful and with more resources than we have. I think we all know that he who hires the best lawyer wins, and hiring the best lawyer takes big bucks—bigger bucks than I or my family had.

The monetary greed part, I suppose, is not unusual. It has been part of the human condition for a long time. Yet this is America, the land of the free, where we suppose truth and justice should prevail in our justice system. Yet I was falsely arrested, threatened, roughed up, extradited, and pulled before countless courts to defend myself against charges that were not only trumped up, as they say, but were downright false and which escalated punitively as time went on. That is all part of the nightmare I am living.

I address myself to those seeking justice. I call to all people for whom justice, truth, and freedom are fundamental human rights.

I am not a professional writer. I never went to law school. I understand the justice system from the perspective of one of its victims, not one of its educated advocates. Yet, with the help of ordinary people, I have been able to tell my story, and I hope it will be instructive for others. All the documentation, photos, and evidence are on my website.

For those who believe that every policeman and figure of authority in the justice system is trustworthy, I offer two instructive examples of legal corruption. In recent years, the ex-police chief of Suffolk County, New York, one James Burke, has pled guilty to violating a citizen's rights and conspiring to obstruct justice over it. Burke spent 46 months behind bars for his brutal treatment of a young man who broke into Burke's police car and stole a bunch of pornography and sex toys Burke had there. When he caught the perpetrator, Burke beat him and made death threats. Why did he do this? Possibly because Burke didn't want anyone to know about his porn habit. So he abused his power and authority to intimidate this poor, hapless person—a detainee who had certain rights, no matter what he had done—and then tried to obstruct justice to keep it from being discovered. The judge described Burke as a "dictator" whose actions involved the "whole police department". (Please see http://www.nytimes.com/2016/02/27/nyregion/james-burke-ex-suffolk-county-police-chief-guilty-plea.html) As such, the entire police department and district attorney's office came under investigation too, leading to the convictions of former DA Thomas Spota and former anti-corruption czar Christopher McPartland for conspiracy, obstruction of justice, witness tampering, and accessories to the deprivation of civil rights. After much delay, Spota and McPartland were each sentenced to five years in federal prison.

In the wake of these revelations, another development has been uncovered in neighboring Nassau County: nine whole cases that have been sealed from the public record without any given reason, together dubbed the "secret docket," that show a callous lack of regard for civil liberties on the part of Nassau's authorities. My case in Suffolk has received similar treatment, so I have had my suspicions raised by the Newsday report on these cases, and Suffolk Deputy County Chief Clerk Chris Como's denials that a similar docket exists in Suffolk in spite of my experience.

So it does happen. Police and other representatives of the law sometimes abuse their power. Personally, even I find it hard to believe, even now, that in the United States the police sometimes can operate as if we are in a dictatorship, as if ours was a regime that condones violence against other human beings and interference with the basic freedoms of the citizens of the nation. Yet that sorry reality is confirmed by my story, among so many others.

I come forward now after years of work and a light at the end of the tunnel for the unjustly treated. The downfall of Spota – who as DA quietly kept his thumb on my case and countless others like it – has given me the breathing room and spotlight to finally bring my story to my fellow citizens after countless attempts over the years. We are also in a time where the ways in which the brutality, callousness, and corruption the legal system has wrought in particular on our nation's most disadvantaged and discriminated against denizens, Black and indigenous, are finally getting the attention they deserve. To a significant extent my tale is like theirs, those who are more likely to suffer indignities like these and worse. I hope that telling my story can help them find justice and peace too.

Although names and details have been changed or omitted, the following events are my true story, starting in small town America and detailing the abuse of power by local authorities that ensnared my life and my freedom in an ever larger and more strangling net of incompetence, corruption, and bureaucratic callousness as I fought to clear my name of a crime of which I was not guilty.

Welcome to my nightmare.

CHAPTER ONE

Even as a young boy, my grandfather, Johannes Reinier De-Wolff, dreamed of being a sailor. After finishing eight years of grammar school in Holland, at the young age of 14, he apprenticed as a deck boy on board the German built 20,000-ton triple screw luxury liner SS Reliance, which was owned at the time by Hamburg American Lines. It was 1925. When the ship docked in New York, John met his parents, who had emigrated from Holland the following year, and visited them in their home—one of the many brownstones that shaped the Brooklyn skyline. Then he would head back to the ship.

John and his younger sister Josephine, in Holland, date unknown. Shades of things to come: He was wearing a sailor suit!

Letter address to John from his parents on his maiden voyage to America "John DeWolff Deck boy SS Reliance Pier 86" dated October 28 1925

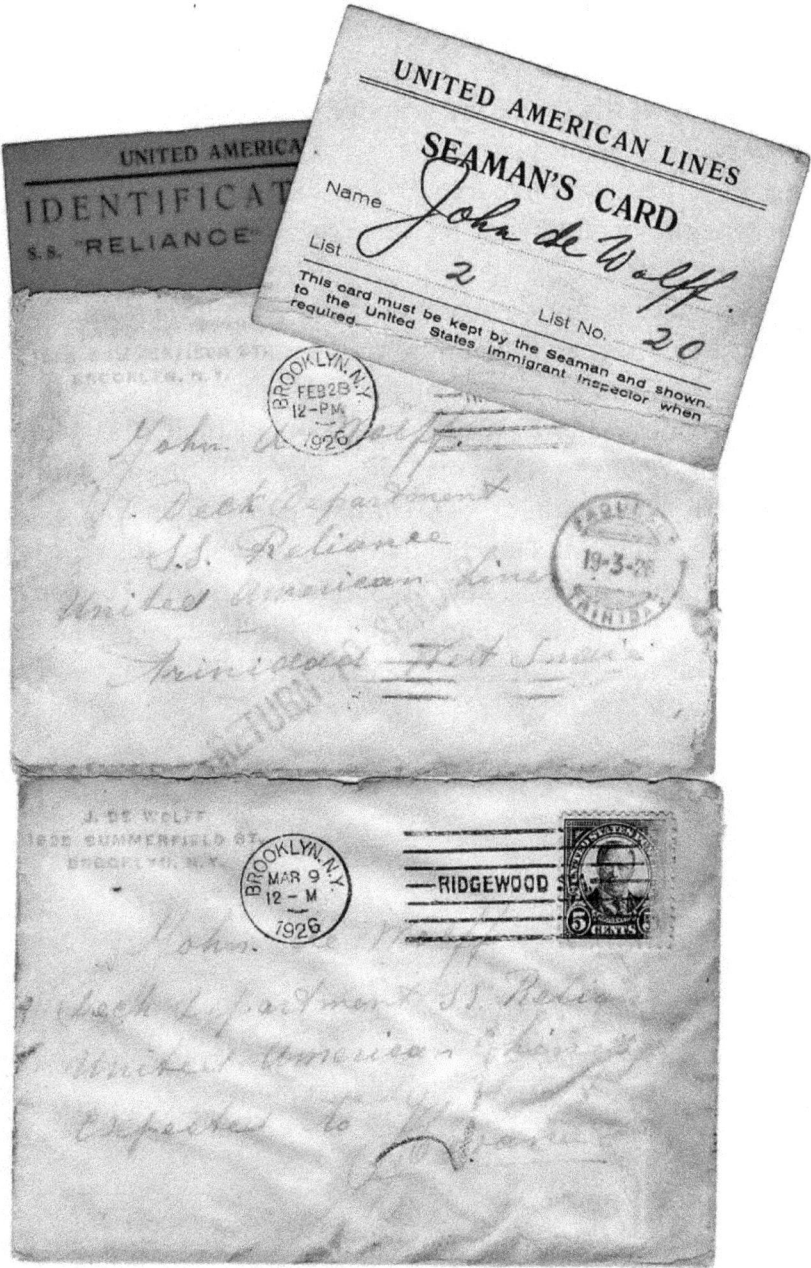

**Letters to my grandfather while he was serving on the
SS Reliance in the Caribbean**

In one of the ironies of life, two of the few letters my family has from that time period in our family's history are dated February 28th and March 9th. These two dates were to figure prominently in the life of my grandfather's descendant—me. On February 28th, many years later, I left my grandfather's home, never to return, and on March 9th I was abducted by the police in what was the beginning of my bizarre, Herculean struggle with the justice system.

John's father, my great grandfather, Joseph DeWolff, was an electrical engineer in Holland by trade, and he managed to get a job at Con Edison as a chief engineer. Having a good paying job and job security, the DeWolff family bought their first house in Baisley Park, Queens, New York. They lived only three doors away from my future grandmother, Regina Popko. Regina and John became good friends and started dating in the early '30s during his visits to his parents. One day, upon docking in New York, my future grandfather jumped ship, giving up his life at sea so he could stay with his love, Regina. They married in 1937.

Photo to the left: my grandfather John lived with his parents and his younger siblings in their new home in Baisley Park. Photo to the right: my grandmother lived three houses down on the same block.

John and Regina DeWolff, my grandparents

August 1937
Geneva – Seneca Lake

My grandmother and grandfather shared a love story that
started in the 1930s and, even after separation and divorce,
only ended upon John's death in 1988.

They honeymooned in upstate New York, traveling in their new sedan to Niagara Falls and Seneca Lake, where my grandfather fell in love with the countryside. He would yearn to return there later.

My mother, Veronica, was born to the couple in November of 1939, not long after John and Regina bought their first house in Jamaica, New York. Because of the Depression, work was hard to find, but John was able to find a job in Long Island City working for the Silvercup Bread Company maintaining their fleet of vehicles.

**My grandfather holding my mother,
and a shot of their first home.**

John always had his eyes and ears open for opportunities to earn a better living. Because of this, my grandfather was able to find a better job as a carpenter's apprentice sometime in 1940, but he had to travel out of state, sometimes as far away as Maine, working on big commercial projects. Sometimes he was away from home for as long as two months at a time. That must have put a strain on their marriage, although he sent a lot of money home to pay the bills. What was more, John entered a trade school around this time to learn steel plate printing; this would enable him to become a jeweler later in life.

Once World War II started, my grandfather's number came up from the Selective Service Board of Registration. John was visited at his home by two immigration officers who gave him two choices: join the United States Armed Forces or be deported. It didn't matter that John had married a U.S. citizen and had a child. This was war, and the country needed him.

Because of his background with ocean-going vessels, John joined the United States Navy; he was inducted on May 23, 1944. To his surprise, he was sent to the lovely Seneca Lake area where he and my grandmother had gone on their honeymoon. This time, however, he was going to be staying at the newly built Sampson Naval Training Station for basic training. At the same time John became a naturalized citizen of the United States.

After completing basic training John headed back home on leave to spend some time with his wife and daughter before heading on to Davisville Naval Construction Battalion Center on Rhode Island.

**John with his family, his fellow servicemen,
and alone in his uniform.**

John received special training by joining the 3rd U.S. Navy Construction Battalion, with "Construction Battalion" often called "CB." They are often fondly called the "Seabees," and in WWII, they were known as "The Fighting Seabees."

In 1945 my grandfather took part in one of the bloodiest assaults of the entire war: the Battle of Okinawa. It was the largest amphibious assault in the Pacific theater, lasting some eighty-two days. To strengthen his resolve, he always carried his Navy-issued Bible, family photos, and a lock of my mother's hair.

John received the Asiatic Pacific Ribbon, the American Theatre Ribbon, Expert Rifleman, Victory Medal, and an Honorable Discharge after the war. He was very proud of his record of service, and it entitled him to further his education under the GI Bill.

**John DeWolff, my grandfather,
in proud service to his country, 1945**

CHAPTER TWO

Times were hard on the home front, though; bills were adding up, and the mortgage was overdue on my grandparents' house. The bank foreclosed, and while John was away fighting the war, Regina and my mother had to move in with her parents. So much separation, plus the new living situation, must have put even more strain on my grandparents' relationship. Unfortunately, my grandmother met another man, Bill, with whom she became friends and, over time, more than friends. There are many such wartime stories. While my grandfather did not receive the infamous "Dear John" letter while he was serving in the navy, in fact, his wife had met someone else with whom she was more compatible.

When he returned after the war, the couple had no place to stay together, so they stayed with their respective parents while they figured out what to do. John remembered how much he had loved the area near Seneca Lake. In 1946 John headed upstate to the Finger Lakes Region and got a job with the Corning Glass Works in Corning, New York, not far from Seneca Lake. He had a few navy buddies in Pennsylvania, near the New York State line, so he was able to stay there inexpensively in the town of Oliverville, Pennsylvania. He was hoping to build a house so that Regina would join him there, but it did not happen. Regina wanted a separation.

I've mentioned that they were rather incompatible. My grandfather was a perpetual joker, and my grandmother was a serious, responsible woman. In fact, my grandfather was passed up for a Good Conduct medal in the armed forces, probably because of this jokester mentality. They realized they were very poorly matched sometime after the war, and certainly the long separation they had when John was away working and during the war cannot have been easy. There were other people they felt closer to—Bill, for my grandmother Regina, and a teacher named Mary Moore, who lived in Oliverville, for my grandfather.

In 1948 John granted my grandmother's wishes and Bill paid for the divorce. Both my grandparents remarried soon after. Of course, there were bad feelings among family members, as there so often are in a case of divorce. Over time, distance, and negative emotions, the families drew apart, and I rarely saw my grandfather.

John eventually purchased a home in Oliverville, Pennsylvania, at 72 Market Street, right in the heart of the little town. It was a very large house, with two stories and seven bedrooms, a full basement, and a stand-up attic. The property came with a two-story, three-bay barn and garage, where John kept one of the many boats he had over the years. The original house was built in 1905 when such outbuildings were common.

A large, friendly, versatile house, 1988

Large three door garage barn with loaf me standing in the doorway "1988

Close-up of me standing in the barn doorway, 1988

It was a spacious, multi-use place

Working on my auto while one of John's boats sits in the barn, 1990

My mother strolls down the driveway while visiting her father

It was a large, spacious property, well-suited to multi-purpose use. It was a valuable property too. The house was heated with gas, but there was a beautiful fireplace in the living room, adding to the value of the place.

The main house had an extension added on in the rear at some point, too, designed to accommodate a business. My grandfather turned the front of their home into a store and set up shop so he could make a living doing watch and jewelry repairs, which he had trained for under the G.I. Bill. He also set up to sell giftware and jewelry to the township.

Extension added on in the rear with two doors

My grandfather with his house front jewelry and gift shop

The drama that began brewing in Oliverville surrounding this desirable property took several decades to explode. Before this, my grandfather and his second wife Mary simply settled down into their new home in 1949. Not long after that, Mary's mother and father moved in with them. Although it is not always the case in such arrangements, this wasn't at all a bad thing for my grandfather and his new wife. Mary's father took to raising chickens, using a small area of the barn. He also grew row upon row of sunflowers, some of which reached more than six feet and added to the charm of the place.

Mary's mother brought her own energy to the house, too, preparing meals for the busy family day after day.

Sometime in the mid-1950s, John's father Joseph moved in when John's mother, my maternal great grandmother Jante, passed away. Joseph lived out the rest of his life with his son and his new family.

Although they remained close, my mother and my grandfather saw each other only very rarely during this period. My mother was still attending school at John Adams High School in Queens, and Oliverville was too far away for frequent trips.

When she did get to see my grandfather, it was usually because my grandfather's younger brother, known then as Uncle Joe, would take her along with him and his own children for a family reunion. My grandfather's second wife, Mary, was a wonderful woman and very kind to my mother. She was used to dealing with children, too, being a teacher, so it was almost second nature to be supportive and motherly. Mary's mother, though, was a different story. Maxine was apparently less than thrilled to have her son-in-law fawning and fussing over a child that was not her daughter's.

Still, the Oliverville home was a very exciting house back in the fifties, when my mother used to visit my grandfather there. John at times would take my mother water skiing on Seneca Lake. He never lost his love for boating and fishing. Because of the way the house was designed and the need to support my grandfather and his wife and relatives, the house was used in many ways to make money. In fact, it had been a funeral home before my grandfather bought it too. Its versatility was one of its extremely attractive features.

On one of her visits to the home, my mother found a hidden skeleton key. She tried the skeleton key in a door that was always locked, and it worked. That door led into the new addition in the back of the house. There were two small rooms, one leading into the other.

The first room had wooden wall cabinets filled with cosmetics, brushes, wigs, and old photography equipment, including vases and baskets that may have served as "props" in a photographer's studio. In the other room beyond that, which was part of the back wall of the house, a large white cast iron sink stood next to a long marble slab table that had a huge copper cylinder next to it. Beside another gas stove there were open wooden cabinets built into the wall and filled with bottles, jars, and what looked like surgical tools. They were embalming tools. Much of this stuff was still there when I moved in years later. The previous family had turned the original house into a funeral home back in the days when they still used gas lighting and horse-drawn carriages. My mother thinks the funeral home went belly up during the Depression, and that is why my grandfather was able to buy the house at a discount.

My mother's memories of the house were rather distant recollections by the time I heard them. At some point, while she was growing up, my mother lost contact with her father for a time. We believe this might have been due to Maxine's influence. Though sad, it didn't stop my mother from enjoying her youth.

My mother in the passenger seat with her high school friends, holding a doll, Coney Island, 1957

CHAPTER THREE

My mother moved on with her life. She married my father, Joseph, a U.S. Marine, on March 5, 1962 at Naval Air Station, Pensacola, Florida. I was born the following year in January at the St. Albans Naval hospital in Queens, New York.

Dad, 1962 Me, 1964

Waiksnis family, Queens, New York 1966

While my grandfather still resided in Pennsylvania with his "other family," he was not aware of my mother's marriage or of my birth since communication had fallen off. Then on Sunday November 13, 1966, my mother returned to her mother's home in Queens to find her father, John, sitting at the kitchen table with her mother, Regina, and stepfather Bill. Grandpa John was heading back from Maine to Pennsylvania, looking for another boat, when he decided to make a detour to wish my mother a happy birthday. There my grandfather and my mother reunited for the first time in years. He learned that my mother had married, and he discovered and met me, his only grandchild. I still have a vivid memory of sitting on his lap as a child.

John told of his beloved Mary's passing from cancer in September 1966, of his sadness over her loss, and of his new love, a bigger boat. My mother questioned her father as to why he hadn't answered any of the letters she had sent him over the years. It turned out that Maxine must have intercepted the letters at the Post Office, because my grandfather never received them, and Maxine picked up the mail on a daily basis. The photos John had of my mother and of the two of them from the 1950s went missing as well. He advised us that Mary's father had passed away, and that Maxine was living with her other daughter nearby. In fact, he had evicted Maxine from his Oliverville home after Mary's death due to the problems she caused him.

From that time onward, my mother and grandfather stayed in touch, but I was kept out of the equation on my maternal grandfather's side. A family breakup can be downright cruel when one side of the family wants no ties with the other because of some sense of betrayal. There are such secrets in every family, and it is sad when they cause people to be estranged from one another.

My mother remarried in 1972 and occupied much of her time raising me and taking care of the home on Long Island, but she kept up with my grandfather. She heard from him that year, 1972, when tremendous rains in upstate New York had caused major flooding, affecting areas of northern Pennsylvania, including Oliverville.

Flooding surrounds the family home in Oliverville

My Grandpa John

The garage was flooded

The house was flooded too

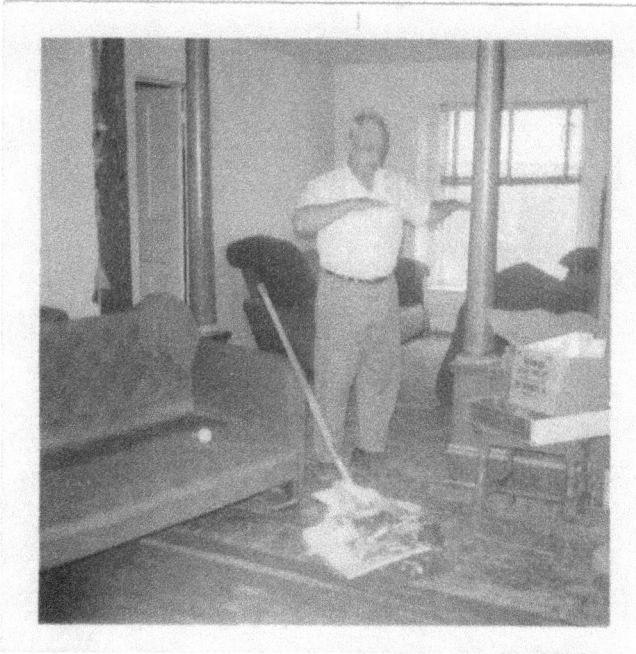

My grandfather describes the water levels

Front Store

Old embalming room

The Army Corps of Engineers had the task of cleanup. Some homes had been swept off their foundations by the volume of water that passed through the Oliverville area. Flooding was an issue again three years later. My grandfather's home was safe, as well as many others that were located on the west side of Main Street. We were very fortunate.

In the early eighties, my mother and stepfather visited Oliverville a few times and saw the aftermath of the floods there still. A good portion of the homes and stores on the east side of Main Street were gone; only foundations remained as a sort of testimony to what once had been. My mother didn't realize it at the time (neither did my stepfather) but what they saw on those visits would allow us all to understand later why my grandfather's home was so valuable.

My parents sitting with my grandfather in his home

One day in July of 1988, my mother learned that her father was in a VA hospital in Bath, New York. How my mother found out was very upsetting. Because of John's health problems, my mother would call him every weekend to see how he was doing, but one weekend there was no answer.

At the time John had a lady friend in town who was helping him out around the house. My mother and stepfather had met her on one of their visits, and they were very grateful that her father had someone to help him out and keep him company. Her name was Colene.

John explained to my mother that he had known Colene for some time and trusted her, so he added her to his checking account so she could deposit his Social Security check and write out bills for him. His eyesight was very poor because of his diabetes. John also gave Colene some of the furniture that she liked from his house as gratitude for how much she had helped him out. My mother felt there was no problem with this. My mother and Colene got to know each other while she was there, and they exchanged phone numbers in case of an emergency or if Colene needed anything in regard to my grandfather's care.

After not hearing from her father over the weekend, my mother tried calling Colene but to no avail. That Monday, my mother tried calling John again, with no luck. She finally got through to Colene and was told by her that her father was in the VA hospital in Bath, New York and had been there for a week.

My mother asked Colene why she had not contacted her, and Colene said it was because John hadn't wanted my mother to worry because it wasn't anything serious. My mother had to call information to get the number for the VA hospital because Colene didn't have it in front of her and she said she was running late for an appointment and had to go.

My mother called the VA hospital and identified herself as John's daughter. She was quickly connected to John's social worker, Joyce Roma, who was unaware that John had any children or living family at all. Colene had never mentioned it. What's more, Colene had put herself in charge of all of John's affairs.

Miss Roma told my mother, "If you don't take legal charge of your father, we will."

My mother and stepfather left for Bath, New York the following morning, arriving that afternoon. My mother entered John's room and saw him on a ventilator. She introduced herself to the staff as John DeWolff's daughter, and the staff actually burst into spontaneous applause. They had seen how my father was being railroaded, and these altruistic people had been hoping a relative would come. My mother was told her father had been admitted to the hospital because of breathing problems from bronchitis. He was doing well, they assured her, but he needed his rest what with all the commotion going on.

"What commotion?" my mother asked.

"It's a circus in your father's room," the staff told her. "We've had to ask people to leave."

It turned out that between Colene and the mayor of Oliverville, my grandfather was being put under a lot of pressure to sign papers having to do with his will and the donation of his house. The staff said they had never seen anything like it—people pressuring a man when he was ill to do their bidding.

The doctors explained that John was in no condition to go to his home alone, since he needed care around the clock. My mother got together with Joyce, his social worker, to see what her options were, with the thought to move John to Long Island so she could be there for him. My mother wasted no time getting power of attorney either. While the paperwork was being drawn up, my mother and stepfather went back home to get things ready for the arrival of my grandfather.

For the first time I became involved with my maternal grandfather's life. My mother and stepfather had kept silent all these years when they were visiting him, keeping me in the dark. I was shocked to learn that Grandpa John was still alive. It had been many years since I had seen him and now I had my chance to have a relationship with my grandfather. I didn't hesitate to go on the next trip to see him. The three of us hurried to make that long trip to Bath, New York. Along the way my mother brought me up to speed about my grandfather.

My grandfather's eyesight was severely compromised by diabetes, so when I met and talked to him for the first time, I sat close to him so that he could reach out and hold my hand and touch my face. At the touch of my grandfather, whom I had hardly known, my eyes welled with tears, and I got a lump in my throat. It was the same for him. There are times when words cannot express the longing for a relationship between two blood relatives. We had nothing to say, but our touch was enough to tell each other that in spite of all the distances and gulfs, emotional and physical, over the years, we loved one another and were grateful for these moments together.

My mother was caring for my grandmother, Regina, on Long Island, so in 1988, they moved my grandfather to the same hospital where I was born in 1963, in the area. It was originally the St. Albans Navy Hospital but in time it became the St. Albans VA Nursing Home. It was a good place for my grandfather, because he needed care 24/7. He was in his last days.

With my grandfather nearby, the trip to see him took minutes instead of hours, and much family reconciliation went on. My grandmother's second husband, Bill, had passed away in 1986, and my mother and I brought my grandmother Regina along on a visit to see my grandfather at the nursing home. We noted that they were holding hands together in no time, reminiscing about their lives together and apart all those years.

With my grandfather dying, the serious business of managing his property needed to be undertaken. The house in Oliverville was vacant. My mother and her father had to decide what to do with the place.

In January of 1989 the house in Oliverville was bequeathed to me with the blessing of my grandfather John. My mother told me later how he took her hand and said that this one wish would make him happy. He wanted me to own and live in the house he had owned. He hoped it would make up for the time we had lost, my mother told me. She recalled that my grandfather had tears in his eyes as he expressed his wishes.

Neither Colene nor the mayor of Oliverville would have the house, much as they might have wanted it; the house would no longer be vacant. I had hopes of starting a new life in Pennsylvania; in January 1989 I traveled there with my mother and stepfather. We went to check on the house and turn on the heat and water again. Everything had been shut down since my grandfather had gone into the hospital.

I stayed behind at the house on that visit, and my mother and stepfather headed back to Long Island. I set about getting to know the house. I checked around to see just what work I could do to improve the place immediately, as well as what might have to be fixed up later on.

The weather was bad in February of 1989. My grandfather's condition deteriorated and he passed on February 24. I made a return visit to Long Island for my grandfather's funeral. He was buried out on Long Island at Pinelawn Memorial Park.

I was grateful I'd had some time with him, and that he had died at peace with our side of the family. In the end, all the troubles of the past melted into love.

**My grandfather's headstone
highlights his service to our country**

CHAPTER FOUR

Not long after the funeral, I returned to Oliverville in the midst of a Pennsylvania winter. I was no stranger to the cold, of course, growing up in New York, but it was somehow a lot more challenging to be in a strange place. It was also a lot harder to try to wait out a winter in a house that needed work, in a new town where I still barely knew my way around.

Soon I received a life changing visit. The ex-mayor of Oliverville stopped by. He introduced himself as Cameron Wainwright and asked who I was and what had happened to John. I explained who I was and told him about my grandfather's death.

The ex-Mayor said, "John and I go way back. He was a lot of fun. I'm going to miss him."

Then he came to what I sensed was the real purpose of his visit.

He said that the old house was way too big for me to be living there all alone. The town would like to buy it. I asked why, and he said it was because of the flood. So much was lost, the water borough authority worked out of the main office in the fire house where the fire chief was supposed to be. John's house had many rooms, so they could have an office. The chief of police could have his office there too, plus the huge barn would be perfect for a town hall. It would be a great piece of property for the township.

I listened as he talked, surprised that so many plans for my new home had already been imagined, but my mind was already made up. Mr. Wainwright told me not to tell anybody about our deal. I wondered what he meant; I hadn't made any deal. I just told him I would keep it in mind and he would be the first one to know if I ever decided to sell the old place.

In addition to apparently knowing Wainwright, my grandfather had also known the police chief, Robert Frist. This fact remained unknown to me for a while, but it was the root of the borough's campaign to seize the house.

I later learned after my encounter with the chief of police from my next-door neighbor that Frist had hassled my grandfather over an extended period; arresting and charging him with false charges that were eventually dismissed. He tormented the old man and bullied him in this fashion in a bid to have him give up the Oliverville house. Apparently 72 Market Street was a particularly valuable and coveted property in that part of town. I was about to find out just how much the town wanted it.

However, I had obtained employment at Sears Roebuck in Horseheads, New York. In 1992, I met another Sears employee, Dawn; we started dating and became engaged in 1993. She would move in with me to Oliverville and start planning for the wedding. If I'd had incentive before, with Dawn in my life I was determined to really give the house the TLC it needed.

**Me in the house I owned
and planned to live happily ever after in**

My wife, Dawn, in the Oliverville home

In March, 1993, I was working on the Oliverville property, trying to make some headway so the place would be livable when Dawn arrived. Spending a lot of time in town, I was also getting to know my way around and, as part of that, I guess I was also becoming aware of the attention I was getting from the locals, the police in particular, which had me feeling a little funny.

The morning of March 9th, though, started like any other day since I had started working at Sears. I woke up at 5:00 a.m., made coffee, made a quick bite to eat, and was off to work. Although it involved interstate travel, I always arrived at work by 6:00 a.m.

That morning Dawn and I made plans to go to her place after work. We had spent some time dividing up her belongings, with some boxes of personal items and cookware already waiting for me to take to Oliverville.

After work that evening, I followed her to her parents' house. I was having some trouble with my rusty red GMC S15 pickup. I had bought it for the sole purpose of using it to fix up the house, gathering material as well as cleaning out the house and barn. It was quite a truck. I had the only pickup in town with Mountain

Dew bumper stickers on the back and sides around the wheel wells to cover up the rust holes. It would stall at times when I tried to accelerate from a dead stop, and I was hoping it wouldn't give me any trouble on the way back to Oliverville. We then loaded some of Dawn's boxes into my pickup and kicked back in front of the TV for a while, ordering some takeout from a local Chinese restaurant.

In the background is my red GMC S15 pickup truck. Notice the Mountain Dew bumper sticker on the rear quarter panel. I'm working on Dawn's blue Ford Escort in front of the old barn. This is the same blue Ford Escort that Chief Frist rifled through in order to appropriate our mail

By eight o'clock, I was tired and wanted to get home. I decided to take a secondary route as a short cut to Oliverville in case my truck decided to break down. My pickup ran pretty well on my way home, and I felt confident I was going to make it home safe and sound. My only fear was that when I reached a certain intersection, where Frist and the township cops liked to hang out, setting up a kind of speed trap there for unsuspecting motorists, my truck might stall out.

I crossed my fingers and hoped that no police would be there, this being the first time I drove this route at night. They had stopped me on prior occasions, just to harass me, I thought, using the excuse of a "routine check." One of them had stopped me while I was jogging too, with quite a few questions about my house and who I was.

I continued driving, wondering to myself what the odds were of running into them that night. It was only a two-mile stretch of road before my driveway. But no sooner did I finish my thought than, after reaching the intersection, I was looking at an Oliver Township police car parked across from me and facing north.

I turned on my right turn signal and turned to head north. My headlights lit up the cop car, and I saw the passenger, Officer Thomas Penning, and the driver, Officer Blaine Hoover, looking at me as I made the turn. I increased my speed to the normal range, just within the speed limit, hoping they wouldn't bother me.

As I looked into the rearview mirror, I saw that the police car had started to follow me. It wasn't long before Officer Hoover pulled up close to the rear of my truck and started tailgating. They knew who I was: the new guy in town who now owned John's desirable house and property. The Mountain Dew bumper stickers must have been a dead giveaway.

Then the whole cab of the pickup lit up from the white flood lights on the roof of the cop car. However, there was no siren, no colored lights, just the flood lights. They'd bothered me before, either because I was "the new guy in town" or because I was from New York, or more probably, because they wanted to hound me out of town so the town could buy my house. Since they didn't flash the colored lights, I kept on driving, doing the speed limit. I could see the town just ahead on the other side of the bridge.

I drove the speed limit till I got to the bridge, then I slowed down to 35 mph. That's when they finally turned on the siren and colored lights. Once I crossed the bridge, I could see the only Oliverville borough cop car off to the side. I could see only one person in it: Frist.

Frist turned on his floodlight and pointed it right in the cab of my pickup. It was blinding.

All the previous stops by these local cops had taken place during the day. It was unnerving to have it happen at night, and I had fears for my own safety on the dark, isolated road outside of Oliverville.

All of a sudden, Blaine Hoover's police vehicle pulled up on the driver's side of my pickup and cut me off. His car then came to a stop, so I had no choice but to stop as well.

I could see in my side mirror that Frist was right behind me. Like clockwork, they all got out of their cars at once. Penning was right in front of me, pointing and saying to put my hands up while he ran over to my door with his other hand on his gun. Then I saw Frist running up alongside my pickup with his gun in his hand. Hoover stood wide-eyed, watching from his cop car, taking it all in.

"Why am I being stopped this time?" I cried out, but got no answer.

While my arms were up, I think it was Penning who swung my driver's side door open and grabbed my jacket. Frist then put his gun in my face and started to grab me too.

I can still remember that evil smile on his face, like he wanted to squeeze a shot off and kill me. Frist grabbed my left arm and tried to pull me out, hurting me.

I started to scream, "Watch my back; my seatbelt is on."

He kept pulling and pulling me by my arm, even with my seat belt secured around me.

Penning then jumped in, basically on top of me, trying to figure out how to unbuckle my seatbelt harness. Frist had his gun to my head, pressing hard on it. Wouldn't anyone say this was excessive force? I hadn't done anything dangerous or wrong. I was hardly someone dangerous enough to be held with a gun at my temple.

Hoover then came over and held the door, watching the whole thing. Once Penning figured out how to unbuckle the seatbelt harness, Frist once again pulled on my arm and dragged me out onto the road. He then twisted my arm, forced me to the ground, and put his knee in my back.

From that position, lying on the ground, I could see my pickup start to roll. Officer Penning jumped back in the pickup and put it in park. Both Penning and Hoover then turned and stood staring down at me from my pickup. It looked to me like they were waiting for Frist to make the next move or give an order. I could hear Frist breathing heavily over me.

Frist then pulled me up by my jacket, twisting my arm, and shoved me forward to the back of the cop car that was parked in front of my pickup. Robert Frist then slammed my body over the trunk of the cop car, pushing my face down into the trunk.

I was in a great deal of pain. I had just returned to work at Sears after several bolts of carpeting had come loose from a wall, pinning my body under them and damaging my back. I could feel that they had re-injured it. These officers did not give a damn, though. They just slammed both my body and my head into the metal of the police vehicle.

One of them was yelling, "You should have pulled over!"

I was yelling, "My back, my back!"

Frist pulled my other arm behind me and put the handcuffs on tight around my wrists. He then started to go through my jacket pockets, finding my wallet. He pulled me up by my jacket and pushed me over to the rear passenger door of Hoover and Penning's cop car, opening the door, shoving me in, and slamming the door behind me.

I sat up straight, looking around me to see if any other town folks were around to witness what these cops were doing to me. I saw a flashlight shine as Frist examined my wallet for a second or two, then turned it off.

Frist then opened my door and rolled down my window just a crack, slamming the door shut again. He bent down to the crack of the window and ordered me to spell my last name. I spelled it out loud, hoping someone else nearby might hear me. Frist repeated the spelling, and then added, "I'm taking him in for questioning."

He turned his back to me, calling Officer Hoover over as he walked to the rear passenger side of the cop car.

I heard through the crack in the door window: "What are we going to do with him, take him to Lackland?"

Lackland was a small town several miles away that had a real police department, but Frist responded, "No! Take him to the basement of the fire house."

"For real?"

"Yes! I'll have the pickup towed and meet you guys down there."

I turned my head and saw Hoover shining a flashlight on some keys. In the background, I could see Penning looking in the cab of my pickup.

I was driven past my grandfather's house. I could see my neighbor standing outside on their porch as we went by. At the stop light, Hoover turned right, drove about a hundred feet, and pulled in front of the Oliverville fire house, which is on the right side of the block.

Hoover turned the car off and looked at Penning, holding a key up in his hand. He smiled. Not one word was said for the whole thirty seconds it took to get there from where I was stopped.

The fire house was closed, and there was nobody around, and just an outside light on. Both of them got out. Penning opened my door and pulled me out of the car. The three of us walked over to a door in the fire house. Hoover used the key he had held up to open the door. He had trouble at first but he got it open.

Penning went in first and I followed. Hoover was behind me. The fire house itself was dark, and I could hardly see anything. He took hold of my jacket from behind and pushed me forward. I followed Officer Penning and almost fell when I started to go down some stairs.

Officer Penning turned a light on in a room at the bottom of the stairwell, and that's when I noticed I was heading down to the basement of the fire house. The first thing I remember seeing were the boxes of Christmas ornaments against the wall to the right of me. The basement looked to me like a small storage room, with a couple of small tables and a desk. Officer Hoover pushed me forward and told me to face the cinder block wall to the left of me.

Both my arms were cuffed behind my back, bringing back severe back pain from the accident I'd had at Sears. I was basically helpless and could not fight back. I couldn't protect myself, either, which I thought I might need to do, especially after being rough-housed and having Chief Frist hold a loaded gun to my head.

After standing there facing a cinder block wall for about ten minutes or so, I asked, "What now?" Hoover advised me to keep quiet, but I could hear movement behind me. Then I heard somebody coming down the stairs into the fire house basement. I looked over my shoulder and saw it was Frist coming in, holding a briefcase and looking quite happy. He glanced at me before saying, "Nice work, men."

Facing the cinder block wall again, I heard a chair being pulled out and keys and other items being laid on a table. I then heard Frist say, in a deep voice, "What do we have here?"

I turned to look and saw Frist sitting at a small desk with his arms on top of a briefcase. He was going through my wallet.

While going through my wallet, Robert Frist started to ask me personal questions about my parents.

There were many questions asked. I jotted down on paper those questions I could remember as soon as I got away. The following questions are the ones I remember...

- Whose blue car is that? (Referring to Dawn's blue Escort, which had been parked at 72 Market Street.)

    - Who's the girl? Who else lives with you?

    - What is your phone number?

    - What's your New York address?

    - Where is that?

    - What's your parents' address?

    - What do they do?

    - What's the phone number there?

    - Where do you work?

    - What is the work number?

- Whose cars are those in the barn? (Frist had been witnessed entering and exiting my barn many times, not only by me but by the next-door neighbors. He was certainly trespassing at the time, as he had no warrant and no probable cause to be entering parts of my property.)

- How good friends are you with the Gutierrezes? (My next door neighbors.)

- Are you running any kind of business?

- What's the name of your doctor? What's his address and phone number?

- Are you planning on moving? Do you deal in firearms or narcotics?

- You do know that your house is haunted?

To further intimidate me, Hoover stood with his one leg on a chair so I could see he had a large knife tucked in his boot. I felt he was warning me to answer all their questions or else.

"We don't like outsiders, especially New Yorkers," they said, adding, "We don't like you."

Another statement, one that sticks in my mind more than any other, was Robert Frist boasting, "I got your grandfather, and now I got you."

He was laughing about it. It was like a big joke to all three of them, me being down there. I kept my cool and told them what they wanted, although I never gave them the private phone numbers of my family.

Once the question game was over, Frist ordered me to turn around and pointed to the table Penning was leaning against.

"Sit," he said.

Thomas Penning stood up and walked behind me as I sat down at the table. I started to complain to him about the handcuffs cutting off the circulation to my wrists, but all I got out of him was the order: "Quiet."

I looked and saw that Frist had his briefcase open, and he was showing Officer Hoover some paperwork, talking to him in a very low voice. I noticed Frist handing out some pages and a pen. Hoover then walked over to the table and put one of the pages and a pen in front of me.

Penning ordered me to stand, and finally the cuffs came off. I sat back down, then Blaine Hoover ordered me to sign one page.

"What's this?" I asked. It was a routine check list, they told me, a form every driver must sign after being pulled over. What kind of a check list? Never mind; just sign it, I was told. I tried to read it first, knowing never to sign anything without first reading it, but then Hoover pulled it from me and said, "I'll read it to you." He started to read one of the pages in broken sentences.

It was something about waiving my rights in Pennsylvania to an attorney. I asked, "What kind of list is that?"

Hoover's reading didn't make any sense at all. The best Penning could say at the time was to repeat that I should have pulled over. They repeated that it was just a routine check list I had to sign before I could go home.

I could see Frist smiling, taking it all in while going through my wallet and writing down whatever personal information he could get from it. After several minutes of listening to Hoover and Penning talking amongst themselves, Frist sat back in his chair and said, "We have all night, you know." Then he went back to my wallet and I felt even more threatened and intimidated, wondering what the night had in store for me. Hoover laid that one page back in front of me again, but this time he held his right hand spread-eagled on top of it so I couldn't read it. I didn't say a word, staring at him while rubbing my wrists, trying not to think about the pain I was in, fearing that they were screwing with me, trying to trick me into signing something incriminating or that would compromise my rights or even my house.

After their ensuing threats failed to break me, Frist's smile disappeared. Frist then blared out for me to "Sign it!" as he leaned towards me. I just sat there, not saying a word, staring back at him.

Frist ordered me to stand and told his lackeys to search me again. I had to remove my winter jacket and put my hands above my head while Hoover patted me down. Penning went through my jacket pockets and found my glasses. I could see Frist was starting to get even more impatient as he ordered me to stand in front of that damn cinder block wall again.

"If you won't sign that form, we just have to go down the list and test you. Give him a field sobriety test."

Standing in front of me with his arms folded, Hoover ordered me to stand on one leg and count to thirty. I said I couldn't because they had aggravated my back injury, but Hoover kept ordering me to do it. Penning told me I'd better do it if I wanted to go home. Not knowing how long this list of tests was, I forced myself to take the pain and played Simon Says. I stood on one leg, then the other, both times counting to thirty. The next order was for me to touch my nose with my fingers; then I had to walk several paces from the basement door to the wall, turn, and walk back. Then Frist started with the personal questions again. At the same time Hoover and Penning were carrying on about me signing that form if I wanted to go home that night.

Once I was done with the paces, I was ordered to sit back at the table. Holding the form, Hoover said, "Are you ready to sign?" I sat there with my arms folded and said nothing, waiting for the next order. Frist was sitting and he said, "What's next?" looking at his check list of tests. "Oh, here's one."

Frist then ordered me to stand and put on my coat. Then he ordered for me to be handcuffed again. Then he again ordered me to stand facing that damn cinder block wall.

He got up from the desk and walked behind me; I was sure he was going to shoot me in the head and I started to pray. I then heard a click and flash of light that sounded like a Polaroid camera going off. My heart was pounding in my chest. Frist ordered me to turn around. As I turned, another flash of light went off. He was standing right in front of me, laughing and holding a Polaroid camera. "Let's see how a New Yorker looks." He then stared at me, reached for my glasses on the table, and put them on me, probably to hide the bruise he'd caused earlier.

Frist took two more Polaroid photos of me standing in front of that empty cinder block wall. They were all laughing, passing around the photos.

Once the charade was over, I stood there. I could see Penning yawning and getting tired. Was that it, then? Would they now let me go? No, Frist reached into his briefcase and pulled out a card.

"Fingerprint him," he ordered.

"Why am I being fingerprinted?"

Because I had refused to sign the form, they told me. Now I had given up my rights to drive home that night. They informed me that they had no choice but to impound my truck to do a thorough search.

I wasn't even given a paper towel to wipe the ink off my hands before Frist ordered the cuffs back on. Again, one of the minions asked if they were done for the night. It was getting late, after all. I guess Frist ran out of ideas this time though, because he said okay, give him a courtesy ride. He gave Hoover my wallet and stuck it back in my coat pocket. I then asked about my keys, since I needed them to get in the house. Frist ordered Hoover to call someone to get my keys back, and then spoke to him privately as he headed up the staircase.

My red GMC pickup, meanwhile, had been towed to the gas station right across the street. It was on a flatbed truck sitting in the garage.

Standing there, hands handcuffed behind my back, Frist ordered me to face the cinder block wall again, and both of them left the room and went topside talking quietly for several minutes before returning. Hoover returned a minute or two after that with some keys. With a loud voice, like he was in charge, Hoover ordered me to follow him up the stairs. Penning followed behind. Sitting in the back of the police car Hoover and Penning got in and drove me across the road, pulling around up in front of the gas station. I saw my pickup on the flatbed truck. From the looks of the station, it was closed for the night. Both got out, leaving me alone in the back of their vehicle. Looking over my shoulder out the back windshield, I saw Hoover let himself in the front entrance of the station before turning on a light in the shop area. I could see them through the bay door glass as both of them walked on over to where my pickup was at the end garage bay. Hoover climbed up on the flatbed to retrieve my keys from the cab. I could see them talking to one another for a brief moment. Hoover then jumped down and walked to the back end of the truck. From that angle it was hard to see what he was doing; part of the building's structure was blocking my view. Hoover then appeared at the rear gate of my pickup, standing on the flatbed, looking at something in his hands. It then appeared he unlocked the aluminum truck cap handle on the rear bed of my pickup. It held Dawn's belongings that I was bringing home that night.

I was watching to see what he was going to do next. He then came down and was back over talking to Penning. It didn't appear as though Hoover actually opened the rear tailgate at all so I figured he was just checking to see if it was locked.

Finally, they both came back with my keys and drove me across the street and past my house, at the same time advising me to go straight home and to keep off the street. Dropping me off near the corner entrance of the apartment complex by my home, Hoover removed the handcuffs from behind my back for the final time then threw my keys at me. I caught them as I turned around.

Not saying a word, I took off my eyeglasses, turned and hobbled down the sidewalk towards my home, trying to see if my one neighbor was still outside on their porch. No one was there, just a light on the second floor of their home. I made it down my driveway to my back porch, keys ready in hand. I could feel my heart pounding in my chest as I unlocked the door, slamming then relocking it. I finally felt somewhat safe being in my own home, yet my heart was beating something fierce.

Everything felt so surreal, but reality started setting in as I looked out the door window and saw the empty spot where I usually park my pickup in front of the barn.

All was quiet on the Western Front, as my grandmother use to tell me, just a barking dog off in the background and my heart still racing. The neighborhood was usually quiet this time at night, just broken by the occasional tractor trailers racing though town and the dog in the distance.

After calming down I went to the refrigerator that was kept back there to gulp down what milk I had left, leaning against the pile of firewood to steady myself.

Walking over the creaking trap door that led into the basement, I had to unlock the main backdoor that led into the kitchen. Turning on the light, I could see fingerprints from the ink they imprinted on the cardboard milk container still in my hand.

Feeling tired and dirty, I needed to go upstairs to wash up to get ready for bed. Heading out the kitchen and through the dining room, towards the double glass doors that led upstairs, I noticed the red blinking light coming from my answering machine that stood on top of the vintage telephone desk. Knowing it was most likely Dawn calling, I stood there for a moment and stared at the blinking light. I didn't bother to listen to any of the messages as I was thinking and wondering how I was going to explain this to my family and Dawn. Remembering how interested Frist was with all of his personal questions about me and her, I really didn't know what to expect next. I was exhausted.

My left leg was overwhelmed with shooting pain; my back hurt the worst since my workplace accident. I headed though the doors and up the wooden staircase one step at a time to the very top, then made my way down the long hallway through yet another glass door that divided the hallway to the end bathroom. Pulling on the light cord that hung down in front of the old wooden medicine cabinet, I turned up the gas heat and started filling the old rust-stained porcelain sink with both hot and cold running water from the antiquated double faucet.

Removing my jacket and shirts, I could see the black and blue bruises around my wrists from the handcuffs. Washing to remove the black ink from my hands, I could see the water starting to turn dark in color. Draining and refilling it, and using a washcloth to wash my face, I saw the damage to my left eye and a red mark on my left temple from Frist's pistol being pushed hard on me. Afterwards I took some aspirin and climbed into bed, falling asleep in no time.

CHAPTER FIVE

The following day, March 10, 1993, I woke up early, still bruised, aching, and shook up. My face, especially my hurt eye, had swelled up painfully from my injuries. My back still throbbed with almost the worst pain I'd ever suffered. My arms, especially my wrists, were also still aching from my cuffing.

Not wasting any time, I got ready and wearily made it over to the gas station to retrieve my pickup. The owner stated that I could only retrieve my vehicle after I paid him the towing bill. He was not pondering the reasons for my arrest or its legality as he was writing up the bill. He was quite content to play his part and charge me for the towing. The receipt for the payment of that bill is the only paper record related to what happened that night.

Towing bill receipt

I was in a state of horror and disbelief about the whole thing. Angry frustration had built up over those long hours in that basement, and I was extremely upset after seeing the condition of my pickup's interior. It was destroyed, and the upholstery was ripped to shreds. Every compartment in the interior had been torn open. The inside was trashed, and Dawn's possessions in the back of the pickup bed were strewn about.

It was clear that the boys or Frist had had their fun, tossing everything around, including her bras and panties. They had even placed her undergarments in a suggestive way. Horrified at the sight of this desecration, I straightened Dawn's boxes and garments so that I could close up my pickup to drive home.

It was difficult to know what to do next. My closest neighbors came over, seeing my battered face and the state of my pickup truck. My neighbor's son Richard said that his grandmother Adda had heard the whole conversation between the cops the previous night on her new police scanner, but they had never said what I was being pulled over for. She saw the Oliver Township police car turning towards the firehouse and my pickup truck being towed to the gas station. Richard asked what had happened.

"He's going to force you out of town, just like he did to my friend's family," he then said, explaining that a black family had moved into town and Robert Frist had intimidated them to a point that it wasn't safe for them to stay.

"If I was you," Richard added, "I'd check my pickup to see if they took or planted anything in there."

After hearing what Richard said, I took some photos as evidence. Richard helped me search my pickup. That's when I noticed two things were missing—a micro cassette recorder that I kept in my glove box, and a bottle of wine belonging to Dawn. These were nowhere to be found.

The day after the incident I was the talk of the town. It made no more sense to the people of Oliverville than it had made to me. People wondered what on earth two out-of-jurisdiction township officers were doing with me in a basement. Some town residents explained to me that normally, if you were arrested for a crime, they would bring you to the county seat or to Lackland; they both had police departments. There were also the State Police just down the road in Farmersfield.

After my so-called "arrest," I was hoping things would return to normal. I still felt as if all eyes were upon me, but I had plans of starting a new life with Dawn. There seemed too much to focus on beyond the trauma and injustice of that night. I was fearful of being out in the town, though, let alone out beyond its limits. I still felt like a marked man somehow, even in my own home.

Later that morning I spoke to Dawn on the phone and told her that I'd explain everything when she got here. Dawn showed up and saw the condition I was in. When I explained what had happened, she was shocked to hear it.

"So that's the reason why you didn't call me last night," she said. She was nervous being there and wanted to leave right away.

Dawn and I had been kicking around the idea of joining the naval reserves since the previous year. My neighbor Bob Gutierrez was in the navy at one time and gave us advice and said it wasn't a bad deal. Dawn wanted to better her education and take up nursing. The navy would pay for most of it. I liked to fix and build things, so I was thinking of joining the fighting CBs, as my grandfather had done back in World War II.

We planned that day to take a trip to the Naval Reserve Headquarters in Horseheads, New York, to meet with Petty Officer McGuire, who knew us pretty well.

When we arrived at his office, he saw the condition of my face and asked what had happened. After I explained, he asked what was I charged with and if I had any witnesses.

"No charges or tickets, just a $20 tow bill," I said, "but I do have witnesses. My neighbors heard and saw what happened to me that night, plus I have the bruises and photos to prove it."

Petty Officer McGuire wrote down the information I gave him, saying he had friends in the state police in Pennsylvania who could look into this and advise me what I could do about it. He thought I had grounds for a lawsuit against the county, "That's abduction," he said, "keeping you in the fire house basement all because the town wants your grandfather's property. You have rights, you know."

In the meantime, Dawn decided to sign up for full time active navy duty to become a Navy Corpsman (MEPS).

She had to drop off a copy of her school records and other forms with Petty Officer McGuire, so we met him the next day after work. He immediately told me he had heard from his friends in Pennsylvania and that I should forget about joining the reserves and should find myself a good lawyer because I had one hell of a lawsuit against those cops. They had no right, he said, to take me from my vehicle and keep me in that fire house basement against my will.

Dawn and I looked at each other.

"Let me call some law offices first and see what they have to say," I said, but I was still holding on to a faint hope that I would be left alone.

Once back in Oliverville I pulled out the only phone book I had and started looking up law offices. I spent time over the following two days calling them. It seemed that no attorney was interested in suing the local police. Only one took my name and number. His name was Lugosi, and he said he would look into my allegations. Little did I know, later on Lugosi would send a letter to my mother on behalf of Chief Robert Frist, threatening her with a lawsuit because she was trying to open an investigation as to what happened that March night. What I did learn from talking to one law office is that Oliverville didn't have a real police department, just one part time police officer. I looked in the phone book and found no listing for an Oliverville police department either.

I was still hoping that maybe all this would simply go away. I was not committed to pursuing a lawsuit. I was just gathering information to make a decision.

Meanwhile, things began to return to normal. The cops were keeping a low profile, and I was feeling somewhat better. I started working on my grandfather's house again. Dawn felt it might be safe to come over to visit and help me out.

Yet all my hopes of being left in peace were squashed when I received a certified letter from Lackland Court in Pennsylvania. Far from forgetting me or letting me be, the officers had charged me on five counts. The charges were DUI (driving under the influence), careless driving, reckless driving, eluding the police, and resisting arrest. Dated March 24th, the letter stated further that I must report to the Lackland court district for a preliminary hearing on April 20th. Closer reading revealed that the letter contained a notice demanding that I secure an attorney from "within the Horseboro Court district," which is the county seat.

I was shocked by all this. Were they afraid that, being from New York, I would hire a fancy, big city lawyer who would hopelessly defeat their local hicks? Not only was I facing five charges, I had to face them in a town I did not know, among people I did not know, being defended by one of their own. This was flabbergasting and terrifying all at once.

To make things worse, Dawn and I were to be married just a few days before the hearing, and this trip to Lackland would certainly be no honeymoon.

Mr. and Mrs. Waiksnis

**Dawn and I as pictured
in a newspaper marriage announcement**

Reading that letter, even just seeing the envelope among my papers, sent my heart racing. I suppose every person charged with a crime might say that at some point, but in my case, I had always tried to be a good person, a law-abiding citizen. I took things very seriously at that point in my life, too. I was about to get married and had a very clear sense of responsibility as to what it might mean to have another person so involved in my life. As soon as I received that paperwork, all I could think about was the need to go into court and let everyone know exactly what had happened to me that night.

The more closely I read the letter, the more worried I became. The letter indicated that the hearing was to be held before a Judge Sandringham, about whom I, of course, knew nothing. The stipulation that I had to have an attorney with me from that court district stung hard, particularly since no attorney from the area was interested in taking on the police. Lugosi, the only lawyer who had even taken down my name and number, had called again two days prior, saying, like all the others, that he didn't want to take on my case. He did recommend a Horseboro lawyer, though — one Marlin Bell.

I took down Marlin Bell's name and number for safe keeping. It looked like he was going to be my only choice. All my phone calls and the lawyers' responses pointed to that conclusion.

I wondered why he was the only one willing to take the case. Was there a conspiracy of silence among the other local lawyers? Was Marlin Bell their "go to" person when someone wanted to defend themselves against the police in court? If they required me to hire someone from that court district, why was there only one choice? Who was Marlin Bell, and was he any good? Or was he a bureaucrat deeply embedded in the system who would give me a half-hearted defense with a predictable outcome — guilty as charged? I had heard a New York police friend say that in small town justice systems the lawyers and judges "all drink tea together." Was this why I was being denied the right to find my own attorney outside their district?

Although my anxiety was building, Dawn and I went ahead and got married. We decided together that we would also try to settle into the Oliverville house, putting aside the legal issues, the dark cloud hanging over us. But it wasn't just the assault and the upcoming hearing that had left me feeling violated.

After all, the bruises had healed and my back was on the mend. It wasn't even the humiliation that came with the assault and the detention, the damage to my pickup, and everything else. The detail that stung the most was the district attorney's handling of the case and the unsettling suspicion that there was going to be no fair hearing for me at the hands of Judge Sandringham. The stipulation that I hire a lawyer from the county in which my case was to be heard also had me worried. I didn't know enough about the law to challenge it. It was a gut reaction that this was somehow unfair, that I should be able to hire the lawyer of my choice.

After my assault and false arrest, for which no actual documentation existed, I felt helpless and decided to call the number the attorney had given me. After explaining what went down on the night in question and the charges I had received in the mail, Bell explained to me, "This happens all the time." He said he knew how to deal with "these clowns." He told me to bring the original envelope with the charges in it to the preliminary hearing, where we would meet for the first time.

CHAPTER SIX

Forty-two days after the assault and false arrest, I went with my wife to the preliminary hearing in Lackland as scheduled, with considerable trepidation but nonetheless ready to answer the five charges.

I would have to face the men I was thinking of now as my three abductors, Officers Robert Frist, Blaine Hoover, and Thomas Penning.

Once we arrived and entered the small Lackland courthouse, we met attorney Marlin Bell.

Bell was a tall, slim fellow with a mustache, dressed in Western garb and wearing cowboy boots. This was not exactly what you'd expect of an attorney. Clearly, Counselor Bell was greatly at ease in his surroundings. After the formal introduction, Bell gave me his card, then asked for the envelope with the charges. As soon as I handed it to him, he stated, "I have to hold onto it for your case." It would be the last time I ever saw the envelope. I wish now that I had made a copy of the charges for myself.

Bell told me not to worry, just to tell the judge what I knew and that he would take care of the rest. Bell told Dawn and me that he knew how to deal with "these clowns," then he told us to sit.

Each one of "these clowns" arrived in that same courtroom ready to lie, ready to mislead the judge. Perhaps he was already in their pockets. I had no way to know how things worked there. How could I have? The only thing I could think of to do was to challenge the accusations as best I knew how. I asked that any empty beer containers allegedly found in my truck actually be produced for forensic fingerprint testing. No surprise, though, all three of the officers denied that they could produce such evidence; they stated that the empty beer containers, supposedly found in my vehicle, had all been destroyed.

Two of the charges were dismissed during this first trial, though, despite strenuous protests from the assistant district attorney. It would be one of the many issues I would have to revisit over and over again, in fact: exactly what I was charged with and how those charges were managed, which were dropped, and when. During this first trial, though, the paperwork showed that two charges were dropped and the other three were maintained. At first, Judge Sandringham was prepared to drop all of the charges. After all, it didn't take much to spot something very wrong with the prosecution's case, and I continued to assert my innocence. I can only wonder what went through Sandringham's head as he heard the so-called evidence against me, and the officers' version of events as contrasted with my own account. He dropped the charge of reckless driving, and the other for resisting arrest after I produced medical papers that corroborated my claims.

When I took the stand to defend myself, I spoke with absolute and unreserved conviction. I had the events as clear as day in my head, including each humiliating minute I was held against my will by police officers who were charged to protect and defend.

A court order was handed to me stating that I had to contact the Oliver Township Police Department within five days to be fingerprinted and photographed, before my next personal appointment in court before yet another judge, Robert Early, in Horseboro court. I had just argued my case to Judge Sandringham about what these police officers had done to me in the fire house basement; I had told him that Frist took instant photos of me and was passing them around, and had already fingerprinted me. Why was there a need to do all that again? When I pointed that out to the court, Judge Sandringham looked at Officer Frist, then me, and then he stated to ignore the order. It seemed to me that this court order had been drawn up before we even showed up for the hearing. I felt caught up in mindless red tape.

CERTIFICATION OF BAIL AND DISCHARGE	OTN E 186485-5		DJ NO: 04-3-01		DATE OF CHARGE(S)
			CC NO: CR-0000054-93		3/09/93
			NEXT COURT ACTION	Date / Time / Location	

COMMONWEALTH VS (Defendant Name and Address)
WAIKSNIS, JOSEPH CHARLES

COURT OF COMMON PLEAS
‗▉▉ ▉▉▉, ▉▉▉▉ PA.
MAY 10, 1993 @ 10:30 A.M.

☒ ROR (no surety) ☐ Nominal Bail ☐ % Cash Bail ☐ Straight
☒ BAIL (total amount set if any) $ 1,000.00

SECURITY OR SURETY (IF ANY)
☐ Cash in full amount of bail ☐ Surety Co ☐ Realty ☐ Gov't
☐ Money furnished by ☒ Defendant ☐ 3rd Party Bearer Bond

☒ Conditions of Release (aside from appearing at court when required). (attach addendum if necessary)
Defendant cannot leave the county without prior permission from:
*HE IS TO CONTACT THE ▉▉▉▉▉ TOWNSHIP POLICE DEPT
*WITHIN 5 DAYS TO BE FINGERPRINTED AND PHOTOGRAPHED

[handwritten] They Photographed ME 4 times that Night

☐ *[handwritten] They FingerPrinted AND Photographed me that same Night.*

CHARGE(S)
75 §3731 §§A1* DRIVING UNDER THE INFLUENCE OF ALCOHOL
18 §5104 §§ RESIST ARREST/OTHER LAW ENFORCE

TO: ☐ Detention Center ☐ Other
• Refund of cash bail will be made within 20 days after final disposition. (PA.R.Cr.P. 4016(b))
• Refund of all other types of bail will be made promptly after 20 days following final disposition (PA.R.Cr.P. 4015(a))
• Bring Cash Bail Receipt to Clerk of Court

I hereby certify that sufficient bail has been entered by: (Name and Address of Surety)
WAIKSNIS, JOSEPH CHARLES

JUDGE OR ISSUING AUTHORITY	DATE
▉▉▉▉▉ ▉▉▉▉▉	4/20/93

APPEARANCE OR BAIL BOND
This bond is valid for the entire proceedings and until full and final disposition of the case including final disposition of any petition for writ of certiorari or appeal timely filed in the Supreme Court of the United States.

DISCHARGE THE ABOVE NAMED DEFENDANT FROM CUSTODY IF DETAINED FOR NO OTHER CAUSE THAN THE ABOVE STATED
Given under my hand and the Official Seal of this Court
this _____ day of _____ 19___

_____ (SEAL)
(Clerk of Court or Issuing Authority)

WE, THE UNDERSIGNED, defendant and surety, our successors, heirs and assigns, are jointly and severally bound to pay the Commonwealth of Pennsylvania the sum of $ 1,000.00
The CONDITIONS of this bond are that the defendant will:
(1) Appear before the issuing authority and in the courts of the county of ▉▉▉ at all times as his presence may be required, ordered or directed until full and final disposition of the case, to plead, to answer and defend as ordered the aforesaid charge or charges.
(2) Submit himself to all orders and processes of the issuing authority or court.
(3) The DEFENDANT and SURETY must give written notice to the issuing authority, clerk of courts, the district attorney and court bail agency within 48 hours of any change of address.
(4) Comply with any specific requirement of release imposed by the issuing authority or court, such as a satisfactory participation in a designated program.
(5) Neither do, or cause to be done, nor permit to be done on his or her behalf any act proscribed by Crimes Code section 4952 (relating to intimidation of witnesses or victims) or section 4953 (relating to retaliation against witnesses or victims) (18 PA. C. S. 4952, 4953).
(6) Obey such other conditions as the court or court bail agency, with leave of issuing authority or court, may impose.

If defendant performs the conditions as set forth herein, then this bond is to be void, otherwise the same shall remain in full force and this bond in the full sum thereof shall be forfeited and a warrant for the defendant's arrest or remanding him to custody may be issued.
And further, in accordance with law, we do hereby empower any attorney of any court of record within the Commonwealth of Pennsylvania or elsewhere to appear for us at any time, and with or without declarations filed, and whether or not the said obligation be in default, to confess judgment against us, and in favor of the Commonwealth of Pennsylvania for use of the aforesaid county and its assigns, as of any term or session of a court of record of the aforesaid county for the above sum and costs, with release of all errors, without stay of execution, and inquisition on and extention upon any levy or real estate is hereby waived, and condemnation agreed to, and the exemption of personal property from levy and sale on any execution hereon is also hereby expressly waived, and the benefit of exemption is claimed under and by virtue of any exemption law now in force or which may be passed hereafter.
And for so doing this shall be sufficient warrant. A copy of this bond and warrant being filed in said action, it shall not be necessary to file the original as a warrant of attorney, any law or rule of the court to the contrary, notwithstanding.

I ACKNOWLEDGE THAT I AM LEGALLY RESPONSIBLE FOR THE FULL AMOUNT OF THE BAIL. (The following is also applicable if % bail is used)

THIS BOND SIGNED ON _____ 19___

AT _____ PENNSYLVANIA
Signed and acknowledged before me this

_____ day of _____ 19___

_____ (SEAL)
(Signature of Defendant)

_____
(Signature of Surety, signed in all bail situations, except ROR)

_____
(Clerk of Court or Issuing Authority)

_____
(Address of Surety, Surety Company or Defendant)

Please see attached pages for additional information.

CERTIFICATION OF BAIL   COMMONWEALTH OF PENNSYLVANIA
AND DISCHARGE   VS
CR-0000054-93   WAIKSNIS, JOSEPH CHARLES

CHARGE   DESCRIPTION

75 §3733 §§A FLEEING OR ATTEMPTING TO ELUDE
75 §3736 §§A RECKLESS DRIVING
75 §3714 §§ CARELESS DRIVING

*3 Photographs me
4 times that night*

They Fingerprinted and Photographed me that same night

Odder things were to follow. Judge Sandringham's document from the case, for instance, states that bail of $1,000 was posted for me. This never happened. I never had to post bail, I never saw a bail bondsman, and no one else posted that money on my behalf, at least not anyone I knew of.

During the preliminary hearing, there was no record of the cops' accusations that I had refused to sign a blood alcohol test consent form. I never made any such refusal and could easily have passed such a test.

In any case, I was to be arraigned, per the orders from Judge Sandringham, twenty-one days after the preliminary hearing and some sixty-three days after the night in question.

After the hearing attorney Marlin Bell wanted us to meet him back at his office to talk it all over. Marlin Bell's office was across the street from the courthouse in Horseboro, so it was easy to find. However, we had to wait some forty minutes before he showed up.

Once he was there, I desperately wanted to know how I could be brought up on charges some two weeks after the incident happened. Mr. Bell said that was the way the system worked. He said, "Believe me, I know how to deal with these clowns. Now about my fee..."

It seemed to me that Marlin Bell was not interested in my story; he wanted money for the hearing, and he charged me five hundred dollars for that day. Dawn made a check out for five hundred and signed it. After that he told us to be at his office May 10th before the arraignment. He repeated to us several times that we should just go home and leave the rest to him. Mr. Bell's secretary made out a receipt for our money, and we left.

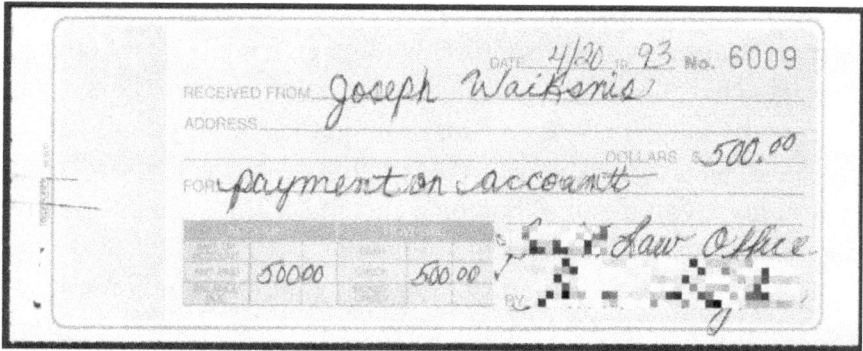

As directed, Dawn and I went to his office first before the arraignment; he had clearly stipulated that we were not to go to the courthouse first.

When we arrived, Bell was sitting behind his desk, leaning back in his chair, with his cowboy boot-clad feet resting on his desk. He recommended strongly that I plead guilty to the charges and leave Oliverville for a year. Apparently, I would lose my

Pennsylvania driving privilege for one year if I pled guilty. Yet going back to New York for a year, leaving behind our house, was hardly an attractive option or a viable solution under the circumstances, as I wished to start a married life with Dawn in the house that was rightfully mine. I refused to do as he said.

Let me add something the average person perhaps does not know about the U.S. justice system. I've alluded to it before. The judges, the lawyers, the police—everyone wants you to plead guilty, whether you committed the crime or not. Why? Because it saves them time, trouble, and money. It takes the risk out of things for everyone. You know in advance what your "punishment" will be if you agree to plead guilty. They'll bargain with you—plead guilty to this charge, and we'll drop another, or we will let you plead guilty to a lesser charge. This is called plea bargaining. They know in advance that if you plead guilty that they don't have to prove your guilt in front of a jury. Trials are long, expensive, and taxing. Court dockets are so full that they must move cases through as quickly as they can to comply with the Constitution.

For this reason, there is a tendency for police officers to "overcharge." Something that barely qualifies as a misdemeanor, or can barely be corroborated, will be charged as a crime so that they can bargain you down into pleading guilty to a lesser charge. They get their fines from you, a conviction of a lesser charge, and their court dockets cleared. You don't get justice if you didn't do anything, because you have to plead guilty—but you are relieved that at least you avoided having a serious crime such as a felony on your record and the risk of going to jail.

Many people plead guilty to crimes they did not commit rather than buck the system and risk being convicted by a jury of the higher crimes with which they are overcharged. Judges aren't necessarily pleased when U.S. citizens assert their rights to a fair trial. They may direct the jury in a certain way, and juries, impressed by judges, may do what the judge seems to be telling them to do. I've heard that judges also give the maximum sentence to "punish" you for clogging up the system by insisting on your right to a trial.

I, however, wanted and expected justice. I didn't think my ancestors had fought for the freedom of this country so that I or any other citizen would have to give up the right to a trial in order to get off a trumped-up charge.

Dawn noted the time and stated that we had better get over to the courthouse. At that comment, attorney Bell took his boots off his desk, leaned forward, and told me, "The DA already arraigned you." He pulled open one of his desk drawers and gently tossed to me, across the desk, a paper containing the three charges that I was going to be prosecuted on, signed by the district attorney. This paper listed only three of the original five charges: the DUI, the eluding, and the careless driving.

def copy 5/10

Information (1)

IN THE COURT OF COMMON PLEAS

OF

THE COUNTY OF ███

Criminal Action No. 163/93
OTN: E 186485-5
COMMONWEALTH OF PENNSYLVANIA

VS
JOSEPH CHARLES WAIKSNIS
The DISTRICT ATTORNEY of ███ County, by this Information,

charges that on (or about) March 9, 1993, in the said

County of ███ JOSEPH CHARLES WAIKSNIS did unlawfully operate or was in actual physical control of any vehicle upon a public highway within this Commonwealth while under the influence of alcohol to a degree which rendered him incapable of safe driving; to wit: defendant did operate a 1982 GMC truck bearing New York registration # PJ-4698 in ███ Township, ███ County, Pennsylvania, while under the influence of alcohol to a degree which rendered him incapable of safe driving; and

COUNT TWO: did unlawfully, as a driver of a motor vehicle, and willfully fail or refuse to bring his vehicle to a stop, or otherwise fleed or attempted to elude a pursuing police vehicle, when given visual or audible signal to bring the vehicle to a stop; to wit: defendant did fail to stop his vehicle when given both visual and audible signal to bring the vehicle to a stop by two police vehicles pursuing him; and

COUNT THREE: did unlawfully drive a vehicle in careless disregard for the safety of persons or property; to wit: defendant did operate a vehicle in careless disregard for the safety of persons or property by attempting to elude two pursuing police vehicles.

COUNT 1: 3731-a-1 of the Pennsylvania Vehicle Code
COUNT 2: 3733-a of the Pennsylvania Vehicle Code
COUNT 3: 3714 of the Pennsylvania Vehicle Code

Citation of Statute and Section
all of which is against the Act of Assembly and the peace and dignity of the Commonwealth of Pennsylvania.

Attorney for the Commonwealth

Bell informed my shocked wife and me that an appearance—at least, my personal appearance in court that morning—was unnecessary. I hardly knew what was going through Bell's head and I was beginning to question the inconsistencies in all the paperwork I was seeing and the advice I was receiving. However, I was glad not to have to go to court that day, given the stress that I was undergoing. The whole buildup of events had left me unable to sleep and struggling to focus during the day. Dawn and I had married so recently that the strain of my growing legal troubles was already forcing us to make compromises in what should have been one of the happiest periods of our lives, the honeymoon phase that so many couples treasure after marriage. We should have been working out the details of our new life together, but we were already feeling a sense of hopelessness, and there was an inevitability to everything that hit us, too.

A court date was set for a trial by jury once I refused to plead guilty to the charges. I was beginning to lose confidence in my attorney. Given his advice to me, that I plead guilty to a crime I had not committed, I questioned again the requirement that I hire someone from the Pennsylvania region where I was to be tried. Why not an outsider, and was it truly within the court's power to limit my choice for representation? And if it was not, in fact, a viable sanction by law, then, with an even greater sense of trepidation, I wondered what the judge and the district attorney were trying to prevent me from understanding. What were they trying to conceal? Did they have all the attorneys in that district in their pockets—was that why I was not allowed to bring in a more objective outsider?

A few incidents before the trial also seemed prophetic, signaling that things would not go well for me. Frist was spotted on my property by my neighbor, who called me to let me know he was parked in my driveway again. I looked out of the upstairs window and saw him walk over to my pickup truck, look around, and then walk to my wife's car, look in, and open the door. I saw him take mail out from the center console and put it in his pocket. Then he left. In fact, Dawn and I had established a private PO box in New

York State to be used exclusively by our families, because mail had gone missing before. Only family members knew of this box.

In addition, Dawn and I received two certified letters a month apart, sent to our private PO box. They were additional summonses to court, which we honored by showing up, before my trial by jury began. In both cases we waited at court for hours. Issued by Frist, the summonses charged us with having junked, abandoned vehicles on our property. Fortunately, they were dismissed by the court because Chief Frist did not bother to show up within the two-hour time period. However, we did pass him on the road home, and to our shock, he flipped us the bird.

During this interim period, we also heard a police walkie-talkie radio sound off, outside our downstairs bedroom window while we were reading at night. The next day we found two sets of footprints in the frozen grass outside the bedroom window. Dawn was also tailgated by `police, for no reason, which greatly upset her. I told her not to worry, that it was just to intimidate us because I had dared to assert my right to a trial by jury rather than just pleading guilty to things I did not do.

These additional examples of harassment kept my stress levels high, even before I had to go to court for my trial. In hindsight, it seems that they were warnings that I was not going to be left alone— the pressure was not going to let up. A letter even showed up stating that I should please be advised that the date set for my jury trial was July 20th at 9:00 a.m., and that if I failed to appear on that date at that time, a warrant might be issued for my arrest.

COURT HOUSE

OFFICE OF THE COURT ADMINISTRATOR
COUNTY
JUDICIAL DISTRICT
COMMONWEALTH OF PENNSYLVANIA

June 1, 1993

Joseph Waiksnis
Main St, P O Box
ville, PA

RE: Commonwealth v Joseph Waiksnis
163 CA 93

Dear Mr. Waiksnis:

Please be advised that July 20, 1993 at 9:00 A.M. has been set for a Jury Trial in the above captioned matter.

If you fail to appear on the date and time set forth above, the Court may issue a warrant for your arrest.

Respectfully,

Court Administrator

CLM/lmn

cc: Esq.
          Esq.
          Esq.
Probation
V/W Coord
Prothy
File

Chapter Seven

Dawn and I prepared ourselves to go to court once more. My case was to be heard by Judge Early, managing a panel of jurors. The courtroom itself seemed decidedly quiet.

I sat down next to my attorney on that first day and just listened to the low grumble of hushed voices about me. The courtroom was hardly filled; I can say that with confidence in my own memory from so long ago, but the air was no less heavy with an odd sense of anticipation. The grim expressions all around reminded me of the great and sickening importance of what I was about to experience.

Despite my innocence, I was terrified of the outcome that day. I wonder whether the innocent worry more than the guilty about such things. In my case, there was definitely reason to worry. The system was failing me already, and the more I was exposed to it, the more frightened I was by what I saw and understood.

On the first day of the trial, as the judge briefed the jury on their responsibilities, the great charade began. Contrary to standard practice in just about every other jury trial situation, my jurors were told that they were in fact not allowed to take notes.

The greatest injustice, though, was not in the instruction of the jury but in the blatant disregard for the trauma that I had experienced at the hands of the police. I considered that what had happened in the basement of the Oliverville fire house was nothing less than an assault—an assault that I could corroborate with witnesses, medical evidence, with reports and photographs detailing my injuries. Now they were referring to the scene of that assault as the Oliverville police station. As if treatment such as I had received would happen in a respectable police station.

Not only was the dank, empty basement passed off as a police station, it was passed off as the base for a police department—the so-called Oliverville police department—that did not actually exist. There was no such listing in the phone book, as I noted earlier. It was just an out of the way, dark, and underground place they used for their own purposes, where they were accountable to no one.

The four Polaroid pictures—pictures that were part of my nightmare—were passed off as part of the processing for my arrest, despite the reality that no arrest record existed. I had not been formally arrested, as I testified in detail during the trial.

The search and seizure of my vehicle, on the other hand, was another story altogether. That, according to the police officers who testified, was an impoundment, despite the total absence of any records detailing the reasons why or exactly how the impoundment was handled.

Of course, these specific details, these glaring issues with my trial, were hard to identify and track while the experience was going on. With the passing of time came distance, and with distance came perspective. After paying Marlin Bell, I was also able to obtain a complete trial transcript to help us with the filing of the appeal; this transcript showed the officers' testimonies and, perhaps most interestingly, the responses of Judge Early, who knew very well that there was no such Oliverville Police Department located in a fire house basement.

On the morning that Dawn and I arrived at the courthouse together for the trial, my heart was pounding so loudly I was sure everyone around me could hear it. The first portion of the trial was a conference in chambers between the judge, the district attorney, and my attorney. I could just imagine the three men in discussion. Apparently they determined that the judge would decide on the motor vehicle counts and the jury would decide on the drunk driving charge. My attorney made an effort to defend my right to a fair trial, but apparently did not object enough when the district attorney urged that the jury should hear all about the other charges anyway, even though they would not be deciding on them, and the judge went along with him. In fact, he insisted that he had to explain the other charges.

I felt the decks were being stacked even as Dawn and I waited to be called upon, even as I waited for the trial to formally proceed. Entering the courtroom, the judge and the two attorneys took their respective seats. Dawn and I were present; I sat in the defendant's chair, next to my lawyer. My wife was behind me, lending all of the support she could.

The judge introduced himself to the thirteen or so prospective jurors who were waiting to begin the selection process. Judge Early seemed to relish the opportunity to share information about his exalted position. He then introduced the two lawyers and me, the defendant, stating my name as if it were poison to his lips, as if my crimes were worse than any he had encountered. It was a criminal case, he insisted, detailing that I would be tried on three counts, the DUI to be decided by the jury. The other charges, the very mention of which seemed to tilt the scales even further against me, were, the judge said, "motor vehicle charges," which he would be deciding.

The trial would be short, he explained. It would probably be concluded in a day, he suggested, and asked that anyone unable to sit for that length of time excuse themselves now. My mind was racing, wondering how it could be such a short trial when there was so much at stake and so much in doubt.

The only evidence about my actions that night, apparently, was an unsigned DL26 form that Judge Early admitted into state's evidence. It became Exhibit One without any objections from my attorney. The police claimed I had refused to sign it, meaning that I had, in effect, pronounced myself guilty of drunk driving that night, giving up my rights to drive for one year. Would anyone sane do that?

The judge briefed the jury on their solemn responsibility to sit in judgment of me as one of their peers. It was quite a moving speech, of course, but there was little that could have comforted me about it. With every passing minute I felt my nerves pinching to an excruciating point. No matter what was said during that trial, despite the almost total lack of evidence against me, the only thing being the unsigned consent form for the blood alcohol test, I felt I was bound to be wrongfully convicted.

The first witness to testify was Officer Blaine Hoover, who was twenty-one years old at the time and, according to his statements that day, working for the police department for a little over a year. He had, in fact, only been a policeman for seven months. Somehow his training period got conflated with actual police work when the DA led him into saying he had been an officer for a little over a year. His training seemed minimal too, consistent with his age, I suppose. He had an associate's degree in Criminal Justice from a community college, and he was trained at the municipal police officer's academy before joining the force. He had recently graduated. He could hardly claim to be experienced in the particulars of the law or law enforcement. To participate in the kind of assault he and the other officers had perpetrated against me was either the act of a callous, reckless man—someone who had no regard for the law—or else it was the act of someone whose youth and inexperience allowed poor judgment to go unchecked.

That day on the stand, however, Officer Hoover gave plenty of reason to suspect that he was the former; callous, at least, and prepared to lie to conceal what he had done, to deflect blame or even avoid it entirely if he could.

He spoke about what he had observed as an officer. He emphasized the experience he had observing people under the influence, both in his personal and professional life. He described the signs of drunk driving as the DA wove his deceptive web of questioning to make me look particularly bad.

Hoover mentioned the speed of the vehicle, how excessive speed or unusual slowness can both point to a driver being intoxicated. Inconsistent signaling was the other characteristic, he noted. According to his experience, he said, when a driver is inconsistent about their turning, signaling left and then making a right, or weaving in and out of a given lane, they are almost always driving drunk. Erratic braking and turning, too, were red flags, with failure to recognize signs and signals along the road as another detail to watch out for.

In some twenty stops, however, Officer Hoover had only made eight to ten actual arrests for driving under the influence. This was according to his own estimation and best memory, too, at least casting some shadow of doubt on his ability to judge cases of drunk driving. He had a less than fifty percent success rate.

As the DA drew attention to the night in question, it became clear that my actions while driving were far from erratic or dangerous. Hoover was in uniform, and the vehicle he had been driving was, according to his testimony, a 1988 blue Chevrolet Caprice with an official seal on the side doors. Of course, I had seen him sitting there on the road, facing north. I had done all I could to pass by correctly, using my signal and not putting on alarming speed. They gave no indication that they wanted me to stop, and I didn't want to stop until I was inside the town limits anyway. Yet the only reason I could have refused to stop was put down to drunkenness by someone who had a fifty percent failure rate in detecting drunk drivers.

Describing his recollections of my behavior that night, Hoover said that I was traveling some 40 to 45 miles per hour in a 55 mile an hour zone. He also suggested that it was "unusual in that area" because the roadway is so flat and visibility was so good. He overlooked, apparently, that I was relatively new to the area and still somewhat unfamiliar with the local roads.

The more he described my driving, the more things became inconsistent and nonsensical. I had, apparently, crossed the center line twice over three quarters of a mile. Hoover even estimated how far I apparently crossed that center line—some three or four feet. This, he said, gave him probable cause to pull me over for drunk driving.

He recalled how he had turned on his lights and the wig-wags, a flashing beam of headlights on the high to low beams. He had also turned on his grill lights, two red and two blue, apparently, when he was some one hundred feet behind me. He insisted that the lights had no effect and that he had then turned on the sirens.

Hoover also testified that he had activated the emergency lights as

Penning radioed in their location. They did that, they claimed, because I refused to stop and was therefore threatening to the two officers.

Muddling through the events of that night, Hoover also stated that he had anticipated the "vehicle stop," calling that in, too, even though I apparently showed no signs of slowing down.

After Hoover had turned off the siren, seeing that I wasn't stopping, he recalled taking the microphone from Penning, who had been driving with him, and then he remembered that Chief Frist was also out on patrol that evening.

Frist, who worked for the Oliverville borough, was, conveniently, available to assist. As I continued on, Hoover described tracking me and relaying our location. Frist responded, apparently, that he would be on hand and that he would position himself. I was apparently now weaving in my pickup, although, even according to Hoover's testimony, I had not varied my speed at all. He could not lie convincingly or suggest that I had tried to escape at a breakneck speed.

Chief Frist was waiting for us around the corner, on the other side of the bridge. His lights, Hoover claimed, were on, including his spotlight, facing direct traffic. Again, I had apparently been oblivious to this. Hoover insisted that I had shifted "maybe one or two feet" into the southbound lane to drive around, still showing no signs of stopping as we then passed in front of the gas station.

"At that time," Hoover continued, "Chief Penning instructed Officer Hoover to pull around the vehicle and get in front of him."

I had slowed down anyway, since we were in a 35 mile per hour zone by that point. Even Hoover could not convincingly condemn me for breaking the speed limit and, although it was already on record as an indication of drunk driving, there was no credible way to suggest that I hadn't been observing the road signs all the while.

The next lie was simply about knowing me, about our relationship by that point and the reality that Officer Hoover and the other two almost certainly knew me and my truck. In fact, Hoover had to find a way to get around the problem that he had the opportunity to observe me clearly enough in the driver's seat. By his own admission, he could see into my pickup and he could see me. By Hoover's own testimony, I sat calmly in my vehicle, facing forward, my hands on the steering wheel during the stop. I was not resisting them in any way, so there was no reason for them to physically try to drag me out of the vehicle while I still had my seat belt on. His testimony, and the others', made me seem like an automaton who didn't notice them or obey them, when in fact, I had been frozen in fear and even praying that these officers, who knew me, knew my truck, and had stopped and bothered me before, would not become too harassing during the encounter. I was not given the benefit of any doubt; I was described as an unresponsive, resisting stranger whom the officers had to fear for their own safety. He claimed it was only later that he realized he had stopped me another time, only after he saw my name on my license. What was more, he claimed that he had asked me to take a blood alcohol test "along the way," which is so vague as to invite anyone listening to such testimony to think that the person was not being accurate.

He also said he had offered for me to take a blood alcohol content test during the stop on the road, which was not true.

"He was questioning why we were there at the fire station. I said it's because he refused to take a blood test. Had he consented to take a blood test, rather than taking him to the police station, I would have taken him directly to the hospital, to have a blood test taken."

When asked if I had refused to take a blood test "at the scene," Officer Hoover said, "Yes, he did. That's the reason he was taken to the police station rather than to the hospital." He also said I refused to take a blood test more than once, which was not at all true.

To make things worse, when Officer Hoover tried to explain the general procedure for blood alcohol tests, the DA interrupted him and would not let him explain standard procedure. Why not? Probably because it wasn't followed in my case, and he didn't want the jury to hear that. He claimed to have tried to give me a "field" test, when in fact, any testing they did took place in the fire hall.

Officer Hoover then claimed that he had asked me four or five times to take a blood alcohol test on the way to the fire hall, and that he had also informed me of the "implied consent" law in

Pennsylvania where I would have my license suspended for a year if I did not submit to such a test. As I've mentioned, I was never told such things at the time. He also said he smelled a strong scent of alcohol on my person, when in fact, another officer said it was moderate. To my mind, this could easily be explained by the fact that I did have some beer in the truck that I was transporting for Dawn, namely, one unopened bottle of Budweiser (the officer was truthful that it was unopened) and a couple of old empty beer cans that I had been throwing away as trash. Thankfully, he did tell the court that I had said I was not drinking that night and that, in fact, I don't drink. He claimed that the whole procedure, from start to finish, took about an hour, and I was safely in my home by 9:30. In fact, I wasn't taken home until somewhere between 10:30 and 11:00 p.m., making the ordeal's duration over two hours.

The DA repeatedly asked Office Hoover if, based on his "education, training, and experience" I was under the influence. Well, we have seen that his education, training, and experience were limited, and that he was wrong at least fifty percent of the time when he tried to single out and discern drunk driving. It made for a strong finishing testimony, though, when he said that yes, he had thought I was under the influence.

The story of my removal from the truck and then the blood test saga followed Officer Hoover's recollection of what Chief Frist had done. Frist, Hoover said, he had stopped behind me and was some ten to fifteen feet off my back bumper, blocking me in quite effectively and then I was removed from my vehicle by all three of the officers.

In the end, with all of the falsehoods told by the three officers, my case seemed to come down to an issue of credibility, as I am sure they wanted.

Although his manner of questioning seemed lackadaisical to me, and he did not counterpunch with the strength I had hoped he would, Marlin Bell was able to get Officer Hoover to admit that it was only a couple of minutes and less than two miles between the time he had his lights on (supposedly to signal me to stop) and the time I actually stopped. Bell also got him to admit that he couldn't tell whether the empty beer cans he found in my truck had been emptied recently or were somewhat old. He got him to establish that he could see my hands on the steering wheel and that I wasn't presenting any danger by making any fast moves with my hands. It also seemed to me that when he got the officer to admit that they had never discussed the possibility of a DUI among themselves before their attempts to pull me over, it made it sound like the cooked-up case it was. They had only thought of it after pulling me out of the vehicle and claiming to smell alcohol, and then using the empty beer cans as if they were proof.

I was hoping all that testimony drawn out by my attorney would help my case. It wasn't like I had fled from the police and it was also indeterminate whether the beer cans had recently been consumed or were empties from the past. I had kept my hands in plain sight and had offered no resistance, and they hadn't discussed a DUI prior to stopping me.

There was also some question about the decision to impound my vehicle, since I ended up so close to my own driveway. What was more, Office Hoover claimed that you couldn't do a DUI in less than thirty minutes, but he did not answer whether the time they had stated it had taken (106 minutes, which was not the truth) was excessive or not. Bell also got him to admit that, although the speed limit was 55 miles per hour in the area in question, there was no minimum speed limit, so I had not been breaking any speed laws by going the speed I was. The DA then objected and said Office Hoover couldn't venture a legal opinion, but he certainly could answer that my going ten miles below the speed limit wasn't in violation of any ordinances. Bell was also able to underscore the fact that Hoover had very little experience in actual patrolling—only six or seven months—and that he had, in fact, pulled me over before and given me some grief over the fact that my license had expired a few days after my birthday, even though I was new in town and my life was in transition at that time. (In fact, did they have some record of me that made them deliberately stop me just a few days after my birthday? Certainly, marketing people keep statistics on people's birthdays and make sure they send out the proper advertisements. Is it possible police do the same thing and make sure they stop someone right after their birthday in the hopes of catching them with an expired license?)

Then came Chief Robert Frist's testimony. He noted that I'd had an "intent" or "intense" look on my face when he stopped me. I was certainly tense.

He also admitted, "I opened, reached up and opened the door, and at the same time, pulled my weapon." He also said that the smell of beer was "moderate to strong," not as clearly strong as Office Hoover had claimed. He claimed within that time period to have holstered his weapon. Why did he have his weapon out in the first place? Is it common to pull a gun on citizens during a traffic stop?

He then claimed that he processed me through the Oliverville Police Department in the municipal building—which, of course, made it sound so official instead of admitting it was the basement of a fire hall where all due procedure was ignored.

"And so we went down to the Oliverville Police Department, which was in the municipal building," he lied. He then said he was not involved in the field sobriety test, which was not true. He had ordered it himself. He admitted, under oath, that the beer cans were amidst other trash, which strengthened my contention that they were simply part of the trash I was taking out of the old house to throw away. He also alleged that the photos Bell showed him of my vehicle after its impoundment, with the garbage bags all ripped apart, was not the vehicle he stopped. The officers trashed my vehicle during its impoundment. He also lied that the impoundment "was not my idea."

He also alleged to have been to my house several times, which was not true beyond snooping around our property and cars. He had only been there once officially when my mother called him to ask how to safely dispense with my grandfather's gun collection. He mixed it all up, claiming he had been called out on a disorderly person's matters regarding me and drinking when people were partying at my house. Then he said, "Complaints about him and from him, both." If it was several times, how many of them were either my or my mother's complaints, or how many of these alleged complaints were about me? It was just vague enough, and he cleverly linked it to drinking to make me look really bad in the eyes of the jury. It was ironic, because I hardly knew anyone in town. I was only friends with my immediate neighbors, who were very good people, and we hadn't had drinking parties together; they were a family with children.

He admitted he had arrested my grandfather, thus lending credence to my belief that, when he said to me, "I got your grandfather and now I'm going to get you," it was setting up an atmosphere of harassment and guilt by association.

When it came to the Miranda rights and giving me knowledge as to the nature of my "arrest," he said: "I had given him a form supplied by the Department of Transportation for the implied consent law under section 1547 of the Motor Vehicle Code, that tells him his rights, Miranda rights, and also his implied rights under the DUI law."

In addition to that, he lied that he was on my property because my truck was unregistered. He claimed he actually had little to do with the "arrest," admitted to taking the horrible photos of me, though, and said he took "a couple notes" rather than the list of personal questions he had interrogated me with, which had included asking me if I knew my house was haunted. He claimed he just hung around to help, because it was "my police department" and he needed to help them by letting them use his camera or his forms.

His inattention at the time was astonishing. He claimed he knew nothing about the Miranda rights – although he had just said he gave me a form with them on it – and that, as for the sobriety tests, "I didn't pay attention." In fact he was directing the whole thing.

In spite of the fact that Chief Frist himself admitted that "there was no resistance," and agreed with my attorney that it was "a rather peaceful cuffing," I had received in the mail a charge of resisting arrest. He also claimed he had nothing to do with how I had gotten home that night. He underplayed his highly active role in the whole thing.

When Officer Thomas Penning took the stand, he too glorified the basement of the fire hall by calling it the police department repeatedly. He also admitted that, although Chief Frist had said he agreed it was a "peaceful cuffing" with no resistance on my part, I was "in the cage behind" him and agreed with my attorney that I was handcuffed in the cage, like a common criminal or some sort of wild animal. He claimed I was asked several times to take a blood alcohol content and that he had given me the DL26 form, which was the Commonwealth's Exhibit Number One.

I wished that my attorney had objected to that form being introduced as evidence. He just went along and allowed it, as if he were joining the other side instead of defending me, as did the judge, who seemed to be rubber stamping the whole procedure.

Penning claimed it was his decision to impound my car, but that he didn't want to drive it in case of accident and that the search before the impoundment turned up nothing, including the missing micro-cassette recorder, which the police would clearly have an interest in confiscating. He corroborated my contention that I had a back injury that prevented me from performing the "tests" well. He did not recall truthfully where my truck keys were, and, most importantly, he said he had destroyed the evidence of the beer cans. "I believe they were destroyed," he initially said, and then admitted that he had destroyed them.

When looking at my photos of my messed-up truck after the impoundment search, he said that was exactly how the car had looked, full of litter, in contrast to Frist's testimony.

"Does this look like what was in there?"

"Yes. Pretty much," he said.

Why was his testimony so different from Chief Frist's? Was the jury taking note of this? I hoped they were noticing all the inconsistencies in the policemen's testimonies. What's more, he said he had smelled a "moderate" amount of beer on my breath.

He admitted I hadn't given them a rough time but that I had seemed to be "second guessing" them a lot. Bell tried to show that this might mean I had not understood what they were doing or why they had stopped me, but the policeman said he was sure I knew what they were doing and why. He admitted, "He was not aggressive, no." He also mentioned that I had been fine when I had walked between my car and the police vehicle and up my driveway on the way into my house when they finally let me go.

Because of all these inconsistencies and questions about the officers' testimony, I already had hope that the jury would see things my way. Now it was time for my witnesses to come to the stand.

CHAPTER EIGHT

My wife was the first of my witnesses. She testified that we had been together that day, first at work, then at her parents' house, and that I had drunk nothing but soda all day. She remembered me leaving her parents' house at around eight o'clock that night. Considering there were mostly unopened bottles of wine and beer in the very back of my truck when the officers conducted their illegal search, it hardly fits that I had had time to leave Dawn's parents' house and reach Oliverville by 8:27 p.m. if I also had stopped somewhere to consume enough alcohol to make me intoxicated.

According to Officer Hoover, I reeked of booze. He claimed to have leaned over me to undo my seat belt at one point, preparing to haul me out of my car. Yet, as Dawn explained on the stand, she was moving and had packed some of her belongings in cardboard boxes which were to go to Oliverville. Among the articles Dawn packed with her clothing were a bottle of beer and a bottle of wine, which explained why I had them at all.

Dawn went on to explain what we had been doing earlier that evening, mentioning our trip to get Chinese food in her Ford Escort because my pickup truck, far from being a reliable vehicle, had a tendency to break down. I rarely drove it in those days, and it was far more often seen sitting on my property in Oliverville or else parked close to Dawn's parents' house.

Expecting me to call her as soon as I had arrived home, Dawn had spent that fateful night wondering what had become of me. She called me the next day because it was her day off too, and we had plans to stop by the naval reserve office in New York.

When she came by, she remembered seeing me with a cloth to my head, bruised and decidedly shaken from the whole experience.

She said that I told her only I had been detained, because that was all I knew. I didn't know why I was detained or what I had allegedly done. The DA objected to the "hearsay" of Dawn's testimony on the point of what I had said I was cited for.

"It's self-serving," he insisted.

Dawn finished her testimony by explaining that it was the policy at her parents' house that if I did drink any alcoholic beverages, I would spend the night in the guest room rather than drive home. Dawn then stepped down from the stand with an encouraging smile to me.

Her father then stepped up and said that he had been home all day and, like any responsible father, had kept an eye on his daughter and anyone she happened to spend time with. Being retired, he was often home all day and certainly he knew well enough how Dawn and I tended to spend our days. He confirmed that we had first come to his home in the morning, right after finishing our work shifts. He mentioned also that I was helping Dawn move some things that day. He also insisted that Dawn and I had pretty much been within sight all the time we were at the house. We had been downstairs in the TV room, and in order to go upstairs for anything, we would have had to pass in front of him. It wasn't like we had been running up and down to guzzle beers between dinner and the time that I left to go home.

He reiterated how unlikely it was that I would have made it to the Oliverville area in twenty-seven minutes if I had stopped to have a drink or two along the way. Not unless I was "flying," he suggested.

It was heartening to have my wife and father-in-law testify on my behalf. The jury, judge, and DA could see that I had respectable people who loved and defended me. I took a deep breath, hoping against hope that the trial might go my way after all.

My star witness was my neighbor, Adda Gutierrez. A close neighbor of mine, Adda was among those in Oliverville who seemed aware of problems between residents and the police. On the night of my detention, she had been listening to her police scanner about the time that Officer Hoover and Chief Frist started to pursue me, just as I was coming into the Oliverville area.

Shortly after she took the stand, however, Adda was shut down. A sidebar was called in the trial and then Adda was removed and ordered not to return. Strangely, she wasn't formally dismissed. I could tell why she was forced out. The short testimony she gave clarified what she had specifically *not* heard over the radio. Despite their following me for a length of time, radioing each other, Adda was sure that there had been no mention of my vehicle swerving, crossing the center line, or otherwise showing erratic behavior, or that they were talking about a possible DUI. As well, they openly admitted that I wasn't speeding in their conversation.

This was enough to send the DA into a panic, and he talked to the officers to try to figure out what to do. He got around this problem—this clear evidence of the officers' lies—by insisting that the officers themselves had never admitted to radioing in about my erratic driving or swerving. If I was so obviously driving drunkenly, as Officer Hoover had claimed in his testimony, then how could the specifics of my erratic behavior not have been mentioned in the radio broadcasts between the officers? Adda heard the officers say my name. She also heard them say that I was not speeding. Nothing else was said on the radio broadcasts between the officers that night that actually confirmed that anything I was doing might warrant their attention in the first place. But the DA then speciously convinced the judge that Adda couldn't testify as to what the officers didn't say, even though she could testify to the exact timing of the broadcasts, including when immediately after the conversation I was dragged to the firehouse. At the time, I knew nothing of this since my own counsel refused to talk about it.

In the end, it took all of about ten minutes to crush Adda and her key testimony. She was silenced by the judge and her testimony rejected, thanks to the tenuous objections of the prosecutor, and in an opaque and unjust manner.

Later that day, Adda confided to my mother that she was afraid for her own family, having seen what happened in the courtroom that day. She was afraid, also, because of everything that she had seen and heard happening to me. Other members of Adda's family also came to me in the days and weeks following, telling me that they had never seen anyone "who received as much harassment" as I had at the hands of Frist and his cronies.

Frist firmly believed that Oliverville was his town, and he refused to let anyone challenge him or get in his way. If he did not like you, Adda's grandson had explained to me at one point, then he would make your life miserable. He would keep wearing you down until you wanted to leave, until you truly couldn't take any more.

Adda's grandsons were friends with the children of the only black family in Oliverville, and they attested to the underlying prejudice within the police, demonstrated, at the very least, by Robert Frist.

My mother then took the stand to relate some of the general concerns that had been brought to our attention about the Oliverville police. The whole time, though, she was battling with both the DA and my attorney to be able to express herself. Suddenly, the neatness, the exactness of witness testimony was a crucial issue. With the jury watching, listening to every interrupted, cut off statement, it must have been difficult for any impartial person not to feel that my mother was too emotional and not a credible witness. My attorney even had to provide an offer of proof to summarize what my mother was going to testify to, that she had advised me on several occasions to be wary and not to stop on poorly lit, empty roads, even if told to by the police. She tried to explain why I was so afraid of the police at that time.

The judge set the parameters tightly around my mother's testimony. He wouldn't allow her to relay that I had been assaulted or that I had had a loaded gun held to my head, striking these damaging facts from the record. He wouldn't allow that I was truly afraid and driving on to a more urban area, as they called it, simply to ensure my own safety.

My attorney explained that the charge against me, the one for fleeing or eluding arrest, was inaccurate on the basis that there are no specifications that you have to stop at exactly the spot an officer shows a clearly visible light or siren. A person was under no obligation to stop immediately if he or she perceived that it was in a danger zone, as the bridge and the poorly lit road were. What was more, I had not sped up or taken any sudden turns, he pointed out. I was clearly not trying to get away.

Yet the judge only allowed my attorney to ask my mother whether she had ever told me that I needed to be careful where I stopped. She was only allowed to answer yes or no.

"I will allow absolutely no hearsay. I will allow no opinion on her part," the judge bloviated.

As soon as my mother tried to explain what she had heard about the Oliverville police, of course, she was shut down in a second.

"Objection to what she may or may not have heard," the DA insisted, and the judge sustained it.

In the end, the only testimony on record from my mother was that she had spoken to me about the "incident" shortly after it happened and that she spoke to me often. She tried to explain what I had told her about the charges—that I actually didn't know whether I was going to be charged or even with what, since the whole experience seemed designed to intimidate me rather than involving any genuine mechanisms of the law.

"He really didn't expect any of those charges because he was released," she said. "What he said was that his truck was a mess, and that his micro recorder was missing. They had impounded his truck at the gas station in town," she added.

Without being allowed to go into much detail, my mother managed to get on the record that the gas station in question belonged to a relative of Officer Hoover, that in fact there was a definite conflict of interest with that particular station and no good reason for a vehicle to be impounded there by the police. Officer Hoover attempted to refute this later, claiming the station had been sold to someone outside of his family long ago.

Finally, it was my turn to testify and face off with the DA. At this point I had begun to question my own attorney's loyalty to me. His perfunctory defense left me unconvinced that he was working with anyone other than the judge and the district attorney.

I stepped up to the stand, though, decidedly nervous but determined to tell the truth. I had heard the officers speak against me, lashing out falsehoods about my behavior and theirs. My only hope was that the jury itself might be impartial and attending to the truth, not the most convenient lies.

CHAPTER NINE

When I stepped up to the stand, I felt all eyes upon me, burrowing into me as if I were already condemned. When I sat down in the witness seat, Officer Hoover re-entered the courtroom and sat one row back, right behind my wife, my mother, Adda, and Dawn's dad.

My attorney stepped forward and asked me to identify myself and speak of the events of that night.

In as steady a voice as I could muster, I stated my name and address. I then recalled my activities that day. I confirmed that, as my other witnesses had testified, that afternoon, after work, Dawn and I had packed up some of her belongings in anticipation of her moving in with me. We got Chinese food for dinner after putting several boxes in the back of the truck to go with me that evening down to the Oliverville house. I was getting tired, I remembered, and I decided to head home.

I remembered, too, that my truck had been acting up a bit that day while moving Dawn's belongings from her apartment in Sayer, and I was going through the best routes in my head, trying to figure out which was going to be the safest, the least likely to leave me in a problem situation if the truck stalled or broke down on the road.

I mentioned that I also had wanted to avoid the police because of the rumors going around town and also because of the sense I had from my grandfather that they had mistreated him about his house, throwing their weight around at every opportunity. I said that on several occasions Chief Frist had made a point of following me and pulling me over, always for a routine check and the chance to warn or perhaps threaten me he that was watching me.

On the night in question, though, I had been more worried about my truck. I had decided to take a back route with more houses around and thus plenty of places for me to go and get help if my truck broke down.

Trying to keep my cool on the stand, I recalled how I had seen the first police vehicle driven by Officer Hoover, parked, and with its headlights facing north. I recounted that I had done everything correctly, putting my turn signal on to pass the police car to try and avoid them, keeping my head down, as it were. I knew they noticed me as I passed, though, and as I headed towards Oliverville, I saw that, about half a mile to a mile out of town, the officers started tailgating me. They sped up to follow me, putting their high white roof lights on, just like a floodlight. Then they followed me for a while, making no specific effort to try to get me to stop. As I was turning to go over a bridge, though, they put their other lights on and the siren, trying to get me to stop before I drove onto the bridge.

I told the court how I had been pulled over about a month before and given a ticket. When the police started to pursue me the night in question, I double checked that everything on my vehicle was working properly: the turn signals, the brake lights. Everything was fine and I was also going under the speed limit. As I went over the bridge, I cut my speed down to 35 miles per hour, as the signs required, to avoid another ticket.

There was no reason for the officers to pursue me. There was no basis for stopping me at all. Knowing this had made me that much more concerned about what the officers were up to that night and I had wanted to protect myself.

I described how Officer Penning had put his hand on his gun to get me to put my hands up and keep them there. As soon as I told of how Frist swung open my door and held his gun to my head, trying to pull me out, and how terrifying that had been, the DA protested, saying something about how it wasn't Officer Frist's arrest; he was just helping. The facts were, he said, it was Officer Hoover's arrest. The judge then had my testimony stricken from the record. In the course of my testimony, these strikes happened three or four times.

I felt he and the DA were determined to keep anything unflattering about Officer Frist out of the record, so this important detail—that I'd had a gun held to my head—was expunged. I went on telling how the three officers together pulled me out of the truck, and how lying on the ground, I could see my truck started to roll and how Officer Penning had jumped in, putting the shifter in park.

I said I was dragged to the police car, with my head shoved down against the trunk, and that I was handcuffed and searched roughly, no matter how much I protested about how my back was aching due to my work injury.

I had to slow down as I described the details to the court because the stress of the incident, the trauma of it, was affecting me again. I was finding it hard to keep my voice steady as I remembered how afraid I was and how much pain I had been in.

It took all of the focus I could muster to recount it that day, even though I had relived and recounted it several times to Dawn, my mother, and anyone who cared to hear it.

I remember it being so bright in my rearview mirror at one point that I had to turn my head to the side to be able to see anything. Should I have taken this as a suggestion that the officers wanted me to stop, though? Not really. I had not crossed the center line. I was adamant about that. Nor was I speeding, weaving, or doing any of the things that Officer Hoover had said I was.

Yes, I explained in court that day, I had tried to make it to my own driveway, or to my neighbor's house at least, so that there would be people around me to be able to witness what was happening. I remembered all too well not only being pulled over and ticketed by Officer Hoover; Chief Frist also had pulled me over many times before. When I had asked why he was pulling me over, he said it was nothing but a routine check and that he wanted to verify my driver's license and registration again, the same as Hoover said.

I recalled how on those occasions I had taken out my license and handed it to Hoover. He had looked at it and commented that I was the one who was living at John's house. I said yes, I was. Unfortunately, my license had apparently expired on my birthday, two days before, so he ordered me to sign a form, accepting a ticket and a fine. He would cut me no slack.

"What was in the seat next to you?" my attorney asked.

"Nothing," I said. The trash bag on the floor. I didn't remember what had been in that trash bag. There was so much junk in the barn I was clearing out that it was almost impossible to tell.

In fact, when I moved into my grandfather's house, one of the first things I did was to buy some of those heavy duty black garbage bags and, with help from my neighbor's kids, I started to clean up the barn, attic, and basement of my grandfather's house, clearing out a lot of debris that included empty jars, bottles and lots of old steel beer cans. There were stacks of them in the barn and in the closet of the back porch.

My attorney asked then how the bags had ended up beneath the front seat, since establishing the reasonable explanation for any empty beer cans was an important part of my defense. I described, then, how Dawn and I had tossed the garbage bag into the front, so that we could throw it away more easily as soon as I got to the dumpster at work, and so that we could fit more of Dawn's stuff in the back.

The bag had been sealed, though, as I explained to my attorney. It had even had a tie-on concealing the contents and, perhaps more particularly, making the bag a container rather than something that the police should have been opening without a warrant.

I noted that the next day, when I got my truck back, it was clear that the bag had been ripped open and searched for anything at all that might be deemed incriminating. The only things they had found, apparently, were those empty beer cans—things that were, by definition, garbage.

I had taken a picture of the garbage bags, showing them ripped open and their contents spewed everywhere. I took it right after I picked the truck up from the gas station at the suggestion of a neighbor, who had also advised me to clean out the truck thoroughly in case there was something planted there.

My attorney offered the photographs to show the damage that had been done, but the DA interrupted to ask if the pictures were of the same vehicle. I said they were. Then he asked who had taken the pictures. I clarified that I had taken them.

"And where did you get them developed?"

"At the mall," I said, "at the one-hour photo."

"Did you take them in the morning the next day? Or when?"

Misunderstanding the question, I initially said, "Probably within a week, I would think. Actually, not even a week." I was referring to the time that the photographs were developed; I took the pictures the day I got the truck back.

"When was that?"

"In the morning, when I got the truck back."

The DA asked me to clarify that it was my truck. I identified the console in the middle and the bucket seat. He also asked where the truck had been situated when the pictures were taken.

"In my driveway," I explained.

I was not sure why he was asking me all these detailed questions, but I suppose it was to take away the impact of my narrative and those awful photos.

With my attorney picking up the questioning again, we came back to the issue of the ripped plastic bag. What would have been in the front of the vehicle? Because I was fixing up the Oliverville house a bit, I had tools for sure. I had mostly tools in the front and back of the pickup, behind the seats. Then my attorney asked about the beer cans, where they would have come from, and I gave the same answer I had offered at the preliminary hearing. I had been clearing out the barn at the Oliverville house and I had thrown everything, all the trash, into my truck, telling myself I would throw it all away when I had the chance. It was very possible that the empty beer cans could simply have been in those trash bags. An unopened forty-ounce bottle of Budweiser was in the back of the truck in the box that had the rest of Dawn's stuff.

"It wasn't something you intended to drink?" my attorney asked.

"No," I said, "It was in the back of the cab."

"Were you drinking anything?"

"Nothing whatsoever."

The line of questioning got hazy at that point.

"Not even a ginger ale?" My attorney asked. I wondered what on earth he was doing trying to make me look like I was being untruthful. He backtracked and apologized. "Did you drink any alcohol at all?"

"None whatsoever," I said again, and, when asked to explain what we had "consumed," I stated again that we had had Chinese food and ginger ale that evening.

With the drinking issue cleared up, though, the next thing we talked about was my recollection of the forms that were presented to me that night. It was a trickier subject, of course, but I said that I was a little bit concerned at first, questioning over and over in my mind what I had done to be in trouble.

"Why was I handcuffed?" I repeated that terrible question aloud that day in court, feeling something of the dread that I had felt that night as everything was unfolding before me. "Why was I detained?"

I remembered what I had been told in answer to those questions. I should have pulled over. Did that really warrant the way I was treated after that—like a dangerous criminal?

I recounted how Hoover was the one who put the paperwork before me, un-cuffing me and insisting that he needed my signature.

"I need you to sign here," he had said, adding then that the form would basically mean I was giving up my right to drive in Pennsylvania for one year. It would also, he said, give up my rights to an attorney.

"Was it ever clear to you that a blood sample was being requested?" my attorney asked.

"No," I said.

"Would you have given one?" he asked.

"A blood sample?" I said. "Yes. If I went to a hospital."

"Did they explain the procedure of giving blood for a blood test to you?"

"No. It was never mentioned."

Had I heard the officers say that they had asked me about signing the form some eight to ten times?

I had, I said, but I was afraid they were going to pull a fast one on me when they presented me with that paper. They didn't let me read it, and, after all, they had kept me hostage for some two hours, asking me questions the whole time, and making me do stupid things just to humiliate me, ignoring what I told them about my back and the fact that my work injury was causing me a lot of pain. This whole time, I had no idea it was a BAT form, assuming it even was.

"How long did they spend at the gas station after the interrogation was complete?"

"They spent approximately, I would say, ten to fifteen minutes. About ten."

I described how two of the officers had actually left the vehicle with me in it and had gone into the gas station, and how they finally had given me back my keys and dropped me off near my house.

I then talked about one of the key items that had been missing from my truck when I picked it up the next day—the micro cassette recorder that my friends had told me to get and keep in my car after the many routine stops, telling me to use the recorder the next time I was stopped and harassed by the police. I kept it in a small compartment in my truck, and it was there on the night I was arrested. The following morning, when I got my truck back, the cassette recorder was nowhere to be seen.

"Did any of the officers suggest that they suspected intoxication?"

No, I told the court. When I did the heel to toe test and the finger to nose test, standing on one foot for thirty seconds, the officers had given me no direct indication of what I was actually being investigated for. I felt I was suspected of being intoxicated at that point. It was not that difficult to figure that out. Frist had even said to the other officers, "Well, give him a sobriety test," not saying anything directly to me, though.

Had anyone suggested that I would be receiving a citation in the mail?

No. No citation or anything.

"You got up at what time in the morning that day?" my attorney asked.

"Approximately 5 a.m.," I explained, and he asked if I was tired.

The DA objected suddenly and insisted that we were straying off topic with this line of questioning. The point, though, according to Mr. Bell, was that I had been stopped after a long day. It was a question whether or not I had drifted off to sleep as I was driving home or had been driving a little erratically because I was tired. Was that the reason why I had been pulled over?

No, I said truthfully. I probably should have seized on this opportunity to create reasonable doubt in the minds of the jury and have said I was really tired. I was in the habit of telling the truth, though, not trying to manipulate juries. I explained that I had a room I could stay in at Dawn's parents' house. I would have stayed there if I had been too tired to drive home. I knew my own strength.

Bell then turned the questions to the Chinese food. He asked if there was anything in the food that night – spices, flavors, soy sauce, or anything else – that could have affected my behavior. Again, I answered truthfully. I said there had been nothing unusual; certainly there was no alcohol in the food or anything that might cause me to seem either drunk or tired. I probably missed another chance there to find an excuse for seeming drunk to the officers, but I told the truth.

I had always thought telling the truth was sufficient to keep a person out of trouble. I guess I was wrong about that.

CHAPTER TEN

The DA stepped up to the plate to begin his cross-examination. He started out with a handful of questions about my background and my education, as if these were somehow the most relevant details under the circumstances – how hypocritical of someone who objected that Bell's questions allegedly strayed off topic. How far had I gone in school? How old was I? At the time I was thirty years old, which my mother had testified to, and I had completed high school before entering technical school.

Apparently, this background was supposed to determine my knowledge of field sobriety tests.

"The test we have described," he began, "the one-legged stand, touching the nose, walking and turning around, heel to toe—didn't you know they were field sobriety tests?"

"I had heard of it, yes," I said. I knew what a field sobriety test was and I certainly had put two and two together. I had made that clear with my own lawyer, I think. More than that, I had stated repeatedly that, whether I knew about the tests or not, I was never actually told that I had been pulled over because I was suspected of being drunk, nor was I drunk at the time.

The DA did his best to make out that I was either lying or ignorant of the world as he went on to say, "Since you are thirty years old, and have a high school education, and some other training, and you live in the world, you know that sobriety tests deal with driving under the influence?"

Of course I did. I answered yes to that impertinent question, but it didn't change the situation. I hadn't been drunk that night, and no one had stated to me that I was pulled over on a suspected

DUI. Obviously, I put two and two together, as I had said in the testimony, but did that mean that I knew, or inevitably thought, that the officers were interested in me because of driving under the influence? No. I thought at the time they were just using it as an excuse to keep me there longer.

Was it my belief that the officers were having me take the sobriety tests only for the purpose of harassing me? Yes. If not, why had they not done the sobriety tests on the spot when I was pulled over? That was a glaring issue for me, but the DA jumped on me for putting out my suspicions.

"I'll ask the questions," he insisted, and the judge issued me another warning.

He picked up the questioning again to take me back over the testimony of Officer Hoover. I suppose the motive was to trip me up or something like that. Had I heard the testimony? Sure. I had been there throughout. The DA asked whether I remembered Frist's comments about their asking me to consent to the blood test. Did I remember anyone asking me?

No, I said again.

"Do you remember anybody, whether it be Mr. Hoover or Mr. Penning, asking you to consent to take a blood test?"

"None," I said.

"None?"

"None."

Then we turned to the exhibits. The form for the blood test was basically the only exhibit we had. Did I know what the form was, the one presented to me there?

It had been a while since I had seen the form and I hardly remembered what it actually looked like. The only context I had was that the form had been put in front of me and I had been asked to sign it. It hadn't been explained to me and I had been so terrified that night, I was looking at the officers, too. Did I recognize the form? No.

Did I remember the form being given to me? Yes. Was I given the opportunity to read the form? No. As soon as I refused to sign the form, which I did because they wouldn't let me read it, they took it away from me entirely. I didn't see it again.

The next question was about whether I had been given a Miranda warning appropriately, at any time, by the police.

Again, it was a "none whatsoever" response. I didn't remember any one of the officers Mirandizing me.

"Were the Miranda warnings given at the gas station?"

"No," I said, without hesitation.

"All right," he frowned. "How about at the police department? Were the Miranda warnings given to you then?"

"No," I said again.

"So, you couldn't see the form and they never gave you the Miranda warning, right?"

"True," I said.

"They just kept you there two hours?"

"Approximately."

"Two hours?" The echoing started again.

"Yes."

"Two hours? Did you ask to see the form then?"

"No."

"Did they ask you to sign the form?"

I frowned. "Yes."

"What did you say?"

"I asked them what it was. Officer Hoover said to me that the form made me surrender my rights to drive in Pennsylvania for one year and it also made me give up my right to an attorney."

The DA was distrustful. Not for the last time.

"So, he told you that this form gives up your rights to drive in Pennsylvania?"

"Yes."

"And gives up your right to an attorney?"

"Yes."

"But he wouldn't let you read the form?"

"No."

Whether he was unable to shake me or just tired of that line of questioning, I don't know, but he moved on to the next issue, which was the presence of the police car behind me and my awareness of it. I had been aware of it, of course, and that was an issue.

"You knew it was a police car, you knew they had their lights on, all sorts of lights. And you heard a siren. And it was behind you. Why didn't you stop?" "Harassment," I said.

"Harassment," he repeated. "Okay. Harassment from this police department?" as if he didn't know.

"The whole department," I said, resolute.

"Of what state? I mean, this state, some other state?"

"Oliverville."

"The Oliverville police department? Do you mean the township, under Chief Frist?"

I said yes.

"He had harassed you?"

He wanted to trick me, I suppose, asking me whether Penning had harassed me previously when he knew, from my previous statements, that it was Officer Hoover who had pulled me over in the past.

I backtracked and said no, Penning hadn't harassed me in the past. I knew who he was, though. I had met him once before, I said, and I recognized him in the car when the three officers stopped me that night.

"So, you're driving down the road, and the police car is chasing you, but you don't know who's in the police car, but you say, they're harassing me and I'm not stopping. Is that your position?" he asked.

"True," I nodded. There was no way around it. I couldn't explain how I had known that night that it was Hoover and his posse following me. It was instinct.

The DA then asked how many times I had been stopped and whether it was in fact Hoover who had stopped me. I said yes, and explained that it was one occasion on which I had been told it was a routine stop and that I had signed the form and sent it in, paying the fine for the two-day expired license.

All of this went on the record as the DA continued his line of questioning. Was it the first time I had met Officer Hoover? Certainly, it was the first time he had stopped me.

I said I had met Chief Penning of Olive Township before, but he had never stopped me when I was driving. I was out walking and jogging along River Road with one of the Gutierrez kids named Richard. A police car drove by, heading the same way, and disappeared over the hill. Not long after that it reappeared and pulled alongside us. There were two officers in the car. The officer in the driver's seat leaned forward to the passenger side and asked me who I was. I had identified myself, Richard next to me waved, and then the officer said, "I'm Officer Penning," and he mentioned that he recognized me as the person who lived at "John's old place," my grandfather's old house. Inside the police vehicle was the other officer. Chief Penning had turned to the officer in the passenger seating, stating to me, "By the way, this is the Chief of Police in Oliverville." I then held out my hand in the gesture of a handshake, but Chief Frist rudely refused, giving me a dirty look, saying these roads could be dangerous at night and I shouldn't be out wandering.

Richard warned me, "You don't want to be on his bad side," as the officers went on their way. I just brushed the incident off as their being curious about the new kid on the block.

Once Chief Frist learned my identity as the grandson of John, he knew where I lived. The harassment would soon begin. Frist would later show what I deemed at the time to be undue interest in me, especially given what my grandfather had said about the police in the area and their attitude towards him.

"He didn't stop you for a traffic violation at that time?" the DA asked, referring to the jogging incident, which greatly confused me.

The DA's agenda was clearly to undercut my belief that Oliverville Borough police were harassing me.

I had no way of knowing, I added, whether Chief Frist had been in the car when I was first stopped while jogging. That was the first time I met them, but it wasn't the last with Chief Frist. I repeated that on the night in question, I was afraid for my safety.

Cutting me off, the DA asked me about the officers' testimony: "You have heard all three officers say that they detected an odor, between moderate to strong, of alcohol on your person and in the cab of the vehicle. Was that a lie or a true statement?"

"When he pulled me over that night," I explained, "it was dishonest."

"Your goal was to drive to your house somewhere where you could get witnesses?"

"True," I said.

"Because of this harassment you had endured, you had a micro cassette tape recorder in your vehicle. If you ever got stopped again, you were going to tape it, is that right?"

I said only that I didn't have a chance to.

"You had a mile and a half before you stopped?" the DA smirked.

"At the time, he was just following me, and I thought maybe he was just following me and he would pull away and let me go."

I know I was in something of a panic while all this was going on. I could hardly think straight. Being on trial is truly being on trial—you feel anything you say could make things go against you.

"When did you think he might not pull away and let you go?" the DA asked. "When the lights went on or the sirens went on?"

"Basically, by the gas station," I said.

"Did you think they were going to let you go when you're going over the bridge, and over the river, with the lights and sirens going, they were going to let you go? Is that what you thought?"

I tried to explain that it was all before the sirens came on. They hadn't come on immediately or even for quite some time after they had started to follow me.

"Why didn't you pull out the tape recorder when the sirens and lights came on?" the DA asked.

"At the time I couldn't think," I said. "When I did stop, I didn't think they would drag me right out of the truck like they did."

I had to go back and contradict the testimony of the three officers at that point, detailing how I had, in fact, been hauled out of the truck very quickly. I wasn't asked to exit the vehicle as the officers had testified. Chief Frist had said twice that he had yelled in a loud voice, ordering me to get out of the truck, but this was a lie.

The officers pulled me out of the truck. They never told me to get out of the truck first.

The next issue was the direction I had traveled in. The DA asked me about what I had done that day, how I had helped Dawn to move some things and how the garbage bag was in the back of the pickup truck initially. I said I thought I had moved it to the front of the cab later to have more room to put Dawn's stuff. When I put the two boxes of her stuff in the back, I remember grabbing the bag and putting it in the front of the truck. I confirmed for the DA that I had known the location of the alcohol only vaguely; aside from the empty cans in the garbage bag, it had most likely been in one of the boxes that were packed up in Dawn's stuff.

The DA went out of his way to remind me that I had testified that Chief Penning had opened the door to my truck, pulling me out. I had to go over that again at the end of my testimony. I described how he had opened the door and started to pull me out and I told him that my shoulder harness was in place. When he couldn't get me out, he had reached over and then Officer Hoover and Frist and reached in and grabbed me.

I had to reiterate again, though, that it wasn't only Chief Penning who had pulled me out. It was all three. I described also how the truck began to roll because I hadn't put it in park.

"Who put it in park?"

"Officer Penning jumped in and put it in park," I said, although I was immediately undercut by the DA, who insisted that Officer Hoover had said that he had put it in park.

"Is he wrong?"

"Yes, he's wrong."

Then I had to recount going to the basement and the ordeal there. Contrary to Officer Hoover's words, I did comply almost immediately when I was told to stand on one foot. I recounted how I had told Officer Hoover, yet again, that I had a back injury that might well prevent me from completing the test effectively, especially since my back injury had just been aggravated.

Then we went over the form—my refusal to sign something that the officers said would force me to give up my right to drive in the state and my right to an attorney. We went over it all.

Next, they called Blaine Hoover to the stand.

After reiterating the alleged lack of connection between him and the gas station, the DA zeroed in on whether Officer Hoover had or hadn't informed me that I was being arrested on a DUI and whether he had or hadn't Mirandized me or shown me clearly the forms I needed to read and sign. Office Hoover claimed on the stand that he had done it all clearly and correctly and that I had known the charges because they were on the DL26 form he had given me. I had received no such form; nor had I ever been told during the whole process that I was actually being arrested, or on what charge. He claimed to have read the DL26 form to me and that it had stated that I was being arrested for drunk driving. This was all news to me. Mirandizing was done, he lied, and done properly. He also said I was taken to the police station in the Oliverville Borough, but then he did back down and say that it was not a police station but a fire hall. He also claimed that I had been given an opportunity to take a blood alcohol test at the scene of the stop, but that, because I refused, they took me down to the fire hall rather than to the hospital to get the blood test done.

Officer Hoover then said that in the "police station" they had read the form to me and that it said I had no right to consult an attorney before I made the decision to take a blood alcohol content test. He said that I had twisted that around to mean I was giving up my right to an attorney at any time, in order to rebel against signing the form. Of course, I had not understood that at the time; it was a rather fine distinction to be made under those frightening, poorly lit circumstances that night. He also said I had twisted other things around and misunderstood them. He said that because this was a civil case, not a criminal case, which had something to do with my not having the right to consult an attorney before taking a blood alcohol content test. Of course, in this court room, the judge had stated that it was a criminal case, but no one contradicted Officer Hoover when he said it was a civil, not a criminal, case.

"I explained to him," Officer Blaine Hoover said, "in there it states that you have no rights to consult with an attorney prior to making a decision as to whether or not you want to take a blood test. That is stated in that form. Then he, the defendant, tried to twist it around and said, 'You want me to sign this form to give up my right to talk to an attorney?' No, I tried to explain it again. Because this is a civil case and not a criminal case, and I tried to explain it, and he continued to turn it around." When asked whether I was being cooperative or uncooperative, he said, "Uncooperative," and when asked if he smelled alcohol on my breath, he said, "Yes, I did."

Then, when they asked my attorney whether he had any questions for Office Blaine Hoover, he said he didn't.

No questions? I was shocked. Why did my lawyer not cross-examine this man? He left his testimony standing as if it were the absolute truth of the whole matter. He did not question Hoover's own characterization of the case as a civil one, not a criminal one – why was I standing trial, then, in what the judge had said was a criminal case? He did not refute any of Officer Hoover's assertions. I was flabbergasted. What was I paying this man for if not a vigorous defense in court? After Bell shrugged off his opportunity to ask Officer Hoover any more questions, the DA said that the Commonwealth rested.

A. Yes.

Q. What would have then been the procedure, okay, take
    me to the hospital? What would that procedure have
    been?

A. Then we would have proceeded to transport to the
    hospital, directly. Rather than stop at the borough
    building.

Q. So you gave him some more chances at the Borough
    building to change his mind and...?

A. Correct. Before he lost his driver's license. And I
    read the form to him. As stated on there, I can read
    and write the English language. I did read it to him
    and did sit it down in front of him.

Q. Did he tend to twist the thing?

A. I explained to him, in there it states you have no
    rights to consult with an attorney prior to making a
    decision as to whether or not you want to take a blood
    test. That is stated in that form. And then he tried
    to twist it around and said, you want me to sign this
    form to give up my right to talk to an attorney? No.
    I tried to explain it again. Because this is a civil
    case and not a criminal case, and I tried to explain
    it, and he continued to turn it around.

Q. Was he being cooperative?

Note that in the third to the last line of the transcript, the speaker says "This is a civil case and not a criminal case." Why, then, was I treated like a criminal?

As the trial concluded, one of the male jurors was dismissed during deliberations, and he went directly to the court office to log a complaint. I wondered what had happened, and I found out that the dismissed juror intended to complain about both my defense attorney and the court itself. The juror was adamant that I had been set up to suffer the way I had. He complained that I had basically been targeted by the police and set up. Despite the complaints, though, and the extent to which they corroborated some of my own, there was never any investigation, never any consideration that the juror was right, that he might simply have been relaying the truth about the situation. Instead, he was dismissed.

Then came the closing arguments. My attorney spoke first. He explained to the jurors that I was an outsider from New York City, unfamiliar with the laws in this state. He went over what I did that day, from the time I was pulled over and arrested for driving under the influence to after I failed the field sobriety test. Nothing was mentioned about my back or being roughed up and taken to the fire house for interrogation; nothing was said about the four photos taken of me while I was handcuffed with my hands behind my back, standing facing the front of that cinder block wall in the basement. Bell said nothing about how I was processed and charged that night or about how I received those five charges in the mail two weeks later, with no idea that I was going to be charged with anything at all. He made it sound like my arrest was as normal as it can get. From my point of view, it was not a strong closing argument. It was bland and tried to appeal to a local, small town jury on the sole basis of my being an urban outsider. I could just imagine how persuasive that was.

Then came the DA with his closing arguments. He had the enviable task of simply agreeing with what my attorney had just said: that this was nothing more than a normal DUI case, that all three officers had done everything in a perfectly legal and procedural way, and that it was the duty of the jury to uphold the law in this great state and find the defendant guilty as charged.

The judge followed up with instructions to the jurors—fourteen pages worth. At the same time, juries are made up of ordinary citizens, and they usually can sense which way the wind is blowing. When the police, a judge, and a DA obviously think you are guilty, and the judge strikes things you said from the record and denies you your witnesses or makes your witnesses look bad and dismisses the one juror who thinks you are getting a raw deal— well, a jury knows what the law expects of them. Even if they have done their due diligence in weighing all the evidence, there is a subconscious wish to do the will of the authorities.

I was declared guilty.

CHAPTER ELEVEN

The DA threw up his arms, showing off his victory in court. The cops were shaking each other's hands in celebration. The jurors were excused.

As I stood in front of the bench with my attorney, the judge explained to me my rights about the different types of post-verdict motions I could file, mentioning that I had only ten days to file any such motion, starting that day. My attorney agreed to file any such motions immediately.

The judge then explained my rights to an appeal to the Superior Court if my post-verdict motions were denied. He also talked about sentencing. He mentioned that if I intended to retain counsel other than my current attorney, and I couldn't afford one, then in order to request court-appointed counsel free of charge, I would have to do that immediately too. He asked me if I had any questions. I certainly had plenty of questions, but mostly they were for Bell.

After the trial my mother, Dawn, and I went to Bell's office to meet with him. We were exhausted and confused. The rest of my witnesses went home. Once Mr. Bell showed up, we demanded answers to the many questions we had.

Mr. Bell assured us that it wasn't over yet; we still had the Superior Court on our side. I asked what taking this further was going to cost, and he replied that it would cost nothing; such appeals were already included in the $1,500 fee. My mother then demanded a copy of the trial transcript. Mr. Bell agreed that we could have a copy but told us it was going to cost an additional $200. My mother wrote out a check for the rest of the trial fee and the transcript fee, and as Mr. Bell was filling out the receipt for us, he said, "They're not going to get away with this; we have the Superior Court on our side." Tired and disgusted, we left for home.

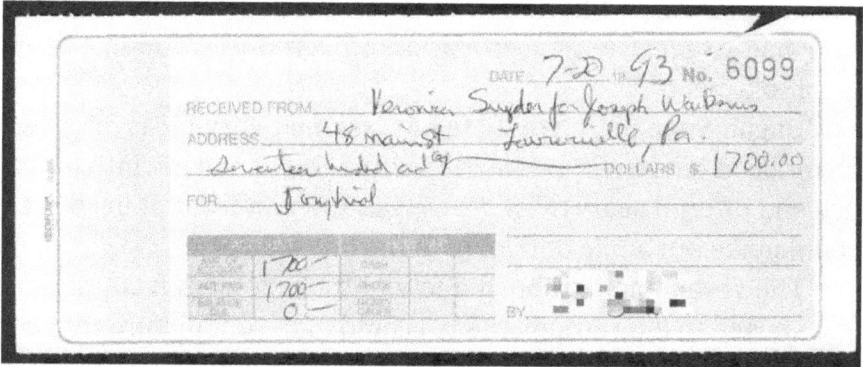

After the long drive home, we had to endure listening as the celebration of my defeat in court continued into the night. Around 8:30 p.m., Frist drove by the house several times in the borough police car, sounding his siren. I remember my mother telling us it was not safe for us to live here, and Dawn agreed. As Frist sped by, blasting his siren each time, my mother said she hoped he would get into an accident.

Her wish came true some months later when Frist was illegally speeding in town and ran into the back of a beer truck that had pulled out in front of him after a delivery. This totaled the borough's only police car. When I heard from my neighbor about this, I took my 35 mm camera to the back of the Oliverville gas station and took photos of the wrecked police cruiser and sent them to my mother.

"Justice," she said.

Following the guilty verdict, I faced the next stage of the sham trial—the pre-sentence investigation. Because I wasn't allowed to drive in Pennsylvania, my wife had to drive me back to the same courthouse where I had been put on trial. Never in my life had I ever had to meet with a probation officer, and we didn't know what to expect.

Dugan Spanner, a young fellow, seemed very pleasant as we introduced ourselves to him. He invited Dawn and me into his office and offered seats to us. As we sat down in front of his desk, I could make out a pile of folders to the one side of it.

The young man grabbed a few of those folders from the top and started to flip through them. I could make out pictures of people's faces paper-clipped to the inside of the folders. These pictures looked like mug shots of some sort. Spanner found the folder he was looking for, pertaining to me, and placed it on his desk. The difference between this folder and the others was that there were no pictures clipped to the inside of this folder. There were just a few papers in it, with handwriting on one. I looked at Dawn, making quick eye contact about what this might signify, but neither of us said a word.

Dugan asked me, "Do you have your driver's license on you?"

I did. I pulled out my New York State driver's license and handed it to him. He looked it over. He then picked up a paper out of the file and started comparing its contents with my license.

Then he stated, "I don't have the official police report just yet, but according to the DA's office, your address is 72 Market Street, Oliverville, Pennsylvania, and you were arrested by Officer Blaine Hoover for a DUI on March 9th in the borough of Oliverville, you had a jury trial, and were found guilty of count 1: Driving While Intoxicated on July 7th. Marlin Bell is your counsel. Is that correct?"

"No," I said. "I was never arrested for a DUI that night at all. I was being harassed by cops because of my grandfather's property. That night on the way home I was being tailgated by those cops. Ask my wife; they tailgated her too. I tried to make it to my driveway that night where I would have witnesses in my neighbors in case anything happened to me at the hands of the cops.

Before I could make it to my driveway, though, I was cut off by one of the cop cars, my door was swung open by the town cop, Robert Frist, who put his gun to my head, pressing it hard, and I thought I was going to be killed that night."

Spanner asked what happened next, and I explained how I was pulled out of my pickup and thrown to the ground, even though I was getting over a back injury and this caused me great pain. I was handcuffed, put in the back of one of the cop cars, and driven around the corner to the fire house.

Spanner looked at me in amazement. Then he turned and looked at a map of the county that was pinned on his wall, mentioning that he knew where Oliverville was. I went on with my story, explaining to him how the fire house was dark and locked for the night, and how Officer Blaine Hoover had unlocked the fire house door, and how I was pushed from behind by Officer Thomas Penning as we entered the building and walked in the dark following Blaine Hoover. I recalled that I almost had fallen down a flight of steps when we went down to the basement, which I had no idea was down there. When the lights went on, I could see that I was in the basement of the fire house, and I was told to stand and face a cinder block wall. I mentioned that I had no idea why I was down there.

I told the whole story in detail, concluding that they were harassing me because I refused to make a deal with the mayor in town to donate or sell my grandfather's property to the town for a discount price.

I could see that Spanner didn't know what to make of all this. I leaned forward, making him meet my eyes, and said, "There is no Oliverville Police Department; that's why you don't have a police report or any of those four Polaroid Instamatic pictures of me in that folder. This whole court case is nothing but a big cover up, because I have one hell of a lawsuit."

Spanner didn't say a word. He just sat, looking puzzled and surprised. Then he got up and excused himself, taking the folder and my driver's license with him, saying he would be right back.

He must have known I was upset and angry; he must have also known I was telling the truth because of the lack of vital documentation about my case. Dawn grabbed my hand, holding it tight.

I looked at her, saying, "Maybe this whole mess will be resolved. Maybe Dugan Spanner can do something for us."

Some time passed. We started to get fidgety; then finally Spanner came back, apologizing for the delay. He handed back my driver's license. Then he sat down and opened the folder he had left with, looking at a Xerox copy of my driver's license. He then started asking me personal questions, just like Frist did in the fire house basement. I didn't know what to make of it. I answered them, wondering where this was going. I noticed that he wasn't making eye contact with me; he was just staring at a piece of paper on which he made some notes.

Then suddenly he stated to me that this was a first offense DUI and carried with it a 48 hours jail sentence, but I was not to worry; nobody did any jail time, and most people just paid a fine.

"Looks like we're done here," he said.

I was stunned. Was that all?

He noted, "I will be sending a copy of this report to your lawyer. Thank you for coming."

At that point I knew Spanner was in the DA's pocket, and that there wasn't any justice in this county at all. If he could so cavalierly ignore the facts of that night, simply expecting me to pony up a fine or spend two days in jail for a trumped-up charge, then this was another dead end.

After the preparation of the pre-sentencing report, my attorney mailed me a copy, along with a letter to contact him as soon as I received the packet. Going over the report he had made, I could tell that Spanner must have been nervous after he heard my story; he made mistakes about what I had told him in the report. It was nothing major; he had written "30" over the "48" hours. When I did call my attorney and explained to him what I had found, he said, "Oh, not to worry, just a mistake, mail it back to me as soon as possible." I felt something was suspicious, so I kept it.

Notice how under the standard range of hours, someone wrote 30 on top of 48, probably Spanner

I had to appear in court again for sentencing. I wasn't simply taking the verdict as given, though. Even as I went through the motions of obeying the court orders, I had my attorney press my right to appeal.

Arriving at the courthouse with my wife and my father-in-law for sentencing, the three of us were stunned to learn that the sentence certainly was not 48 hours. The sentence was now 30 days in prison.

I tried to stay calm as I heard the 30-day sentence pronounced, but it took every ounce of my energy. After a few minutes, with Bell as a rather ineffectual backup, I spoke up to remind both the judge and the DA of my right to appeal, that an appeal was already pending, and I had strenuously protested the entire process, emphasizing the persecution from the very beginning.

Unfortunately, my pleas were overshadowed by those of the DA, who was adamant that the judge should absolutely not grant my appeal. In fact, Bell and I had to talk over the DA because he was so loudly insisting that I be sent directly to prison. Clearly, I was such a violent and serious threat to society that the most basic and fundamental rights of an American citizen could hardly be afforded me. Little did I know it was the first battle in a very long war.

The only thing that prevented the judge, I think, from giving in to the DA on this was the law itself and the reality that my right to appeal could not be overlooked or so poorly handled as to raise further suspicions about the way I was being treated by the system.

I had never suggested that I was at all in agreement with the court's decision to find me guilty, and it could hardly have been a surprise that I wanted to challenge the ruling. I had, for instance, tried to bring up issues such as possible jury tampering. I was also decidedly aware that my star defense witness, a woman who had heard the police radio communications on the night of my arrest, was not allowed to speak; her testimony was interrupted and cut short at what might well have been a critical juncture in the trial.

What if I had been able to corroborate my story? For example, what if a witness had seen Robert Frist holding his gun to my head, seen me being roughed up by him, handcuffed and taken to the fire house basement that was not at all a police department, but a storage area for Christmas ornaments with one desk and a cinder block wall?

I have no doubt that the jury would have believed me over the officers if there had even been one person corroborating what I had said about the way I was arrested and the way I was handled. I think even more important would have been the corroboration that I was not actually drunk at all when I was pulled over. That was hard to establish since all three officers had come forward and lied in court about my behavior when I was arrested. That and the reality that my attorney did not challenge the preposterous idea that I could have become completely drunk and disorderly by reputedly drinking the contents of the two beer cans.

Despite all this, the DA continued to demand my incarceration.

CHAPTER TWELVE

Despite whatever reservations the DA and judge had, an appeal was allowed and thus promptly filed. Nothing worked in my favor, though; I finally did get a copy of the motion from my attorney after the appeal was filed, but it was nothing like what we had spoken about. It was based on background information from my mother regarding occurrences prior to and since the incident of March 9, 1993, which the judge had disallowed at the trial as hearsay.

COMMONWEALTH OF PENNSYLVANIA : IN THE COURT OF COMMON PLEAS
vs. : OF ▮▮▮ COUNTY, PENNSYLVANIA
JOSEPH CHARLES WAIKSNIS : NO. 163, CRIMINAL ACTION, 1993

MOTION FOR ARREST OF JUDGMENT AND FOR NEW TRIAL

AND NOW, this 30th day of July, 1993, comes the Defendant, Joseph Charles Waiksnis, by and through his attorney, ▮▮▮ ▮ ▮ ▮ , and avers as follows:

1. Trial was held at the above term and number on July 30th, 1993.

2. A verdict of guilty was returned by a jury on one count of Driving Under the Influence.

3. Defendant believes and therefore avers the Court erred in denying Defendants motion to introduce background information by Defendants mother regarding occurrences prior to and since the incident of March 9th, 1993.

WHEREFORE, Defendant requests your Honorable Court to arrest judgment and find that the verdict, being against the weight of the evidence the Defendant shall be set free or, in the alternative, the Defendant shall be granted a new trial.

AND HE SHALL EVER PRAY,

_____, Esquire

Dated: 7-30-93

As we filed the appeal, my attorney made a point of telling us that he was happy to have us as a client because we paid our debt in full the same day of the trial, unlike many others.

Bell also made the point that the appeals process can take a decidedly long time, that it is not unusual for appeals to take sometimes upwards of a year or more to be concluded, but that was a good thing and that he would call me as soon as he got word of the Superior Court's ruling.

For the time being, though, I wanted to try to live a normal life with my wife. We were already beginning to realize that we probably wouldn't have a normal life; at least not for a long time, until the mess was behind us and everything was settled.

I was seeing a doctor at the time, trying to deal with the stress. I was also trying to cope with my relentless sense of injustice, and with the overhanging fear that I might still be sent to jail to serve out a sentence for something I had never done.

My mother tried writing to the DA again, as I had before, with no luck. This time she sent it certified mail, and we actually got a response. His letter said, in short, that no one but us had ever complained about the police in the area, and that we would have to go to the state District Attorney in Harrisburg if we wanted to pursue an investigation. He said he doubted if we would trust the results of an investigation carried out by him, especially if he found that nothing irregular had taken place. In essence, he passed the buck and wished us luck.

After that it was a waiting game. Hearing nothing the first year, I checked in with Bell for an update. He seemed annoyed when I did, assuring me that at this point it was looking real good for me and that I should sit tight. He told me that he would call me as soon as he heard something, and cut the conversation short. At this point I figured I would just wait it out, especially since Bell was assuring me that the appeal would be in my favor. The only thing I had to show that I even had an appeal filed was a docket number Bell had given me.

Then came another strange turn: with the deadline to file the briefs for the appeal fast approaching – only six days away – my mother received a telephone call from a person named James Potts. My mother was still in New York, but she kept up with every particular of my struggles in Pennsylvania. She was surprised to get the phone call, and when she said as much, he told her that he was working with my attorney and that he needed $2,000 from my mother to file the briefs for the appeal for me.

Bell had agreed to charge us a flat rate before the trial, stating the $1,500 included everything, including the appeal if we needed to file one, and we had paid an additional sum of $200 for a copy of my court trial transcript the same day we paid that rate after my trial, since it was important to have the transcript to make sure nothing was left out in the appeal, and we even made copies for my witnesses.

My mother was well aware that the appeal had already been paid for and filed. In response to this, Mr. Potts insisted that the "delay" of the appeal process was actually due to the fact that neither he nor my actual attorney could locate me.

At this point, of course, my mother knew that she was either being scammed by some con artist or I was being further threatened, through my mother this time, in order to prevent me from drawing further attention to my case. I hadn't moved. I was still in Pennsylvania fixing up the house with the help of my father-in-law, trying to make a life for my wife and me in the house that we legally owned, in spite of the police persecution and the overhanging threat of my conviction in court. There were also several Pennsylvania numbers, local dials for Marlin Bell, my house, and my work, at which I could quite easily be reached, and these numbers had never changed. There was no reason for anyone looking for me to call upon my mother in Long Island.

My mother asked James Potts to put his request for money in writing and commit to paper the nonsense he had spouted to her about his association with my attorney and the status of my appeal. Receiving a letter three days later stating, "Pursuant to our conversation it is incumbent upon you to contact my office before January 28th 1995, or your son's appeal will be lost. I suggest you contact your son and get back to me since you refuse to provide a valid telephone number for Joseph Waiksnis. Further, I do not believe that an appeal can properly be filed without the necessary time frame and funding."

He signed off by saying, "I am glad that you have taken so many efforts in attempting to contact various state agencies, but the enclosed Order is what must be considered. Please recognize time constraints and the need for a possible continuance before January 30th 1995. Therefore, I suggest that some movement be made to resolution of this matter. If you have any questions regarding this matter, please do not hesitate to contact my office. James Potts."

January 24, 1995

Ms. Veronica Synder

In Re: Appeal of Joseph Waiksnis

Dear Veronica,

　　Pursuant to our conversation it is incumbent upon you to contact my office before January 28, 1995, or your son's Appeal will be lost. I suggest you contact your son and get back to me since you refuse to provide a valid telephone number for Joseph Waiksnis. Further, I do not believe that an Appeal can properly be file with out the neccessary time frame and funding.

　　I am glad that you have taken so many efforts in attempting to contact various State Agencies but the enclosed Order is what I must be considered. Please recognize time constraints and the need for a possible continuance before Janusry 30, 1995. Therefore, I suggest that some movement be made to resolution of this matter. If you have any questions regarding this matter, please do not hesitate to contact my office.

　　Thank you for your time and cooperation to this matter.

Very Truly Yours,

, Esquire

JRS/lav
Enclosure**Order

My mother called and told me about the phone call and letter. I was shocked to hear this. I called Bell's office but nobody answered the phone. I finally got through the following day, speaking to Bell directly, questioning him as to who this person was, calling my mother and demanding money from her. "This had better be a sick joke," I told him, because I was in no mood for it.

Bell said he was sorry, but it was no joke; he'd had his assistant contact my mother because he couldn't get through to me; my phone was always busy. It must be a bad connection, he said. He also said he had filed the appeal, but now the Superior Court was demanding extra evidence as to what happened that March night when I got pulled over. He said he had been busy working on my case for the past week, getting ready to write up the briefs and that I should be aware that all of this cost money.

I didn't know what to make of it; I'm not a lawyer, so I guessed Bell was telling me the truth. When I asked him how much extra it was going to cost, he said $2,000, but he also said that the good news was that he could guarantee that once he sent in the briefs, I would win my appeal.

I agreed but mentioned that I would need some time to raise the money. Bell said that was fine; he would go ahead and file the briefs on a contingency basis. He said I could either drop off the money or mail it, as he knew my family was good for it. Then he said he would contact me as soon as he got a response from the Superior Court. He estimated that would be in about two months.

I explained to my mother why all this was happening, and that I had agreed to pay the extra money Bell needed to file the briefs, and that he was working on a contingency basis until I could. I assured her that Bell had guaranteed I would win the appeal, and that this was worth doing.

I had a barn full of antique stuff that John had collected over the years, and I figured I could sell some of that to raise the money. For example, there was a seven-foot-high safe that must have dated back to the turn of the century. Upstairs in the loft were long wooden tables full of old tools that were covered with heavy canvas army tarps. There was furniture too. The problem was it was in the middle of winter, so it was too cold for a yard sale. There were the two old cars and my grandfather's pride and joy: the Penn Yan boat he had restored. I remembered that there was a friend of my in-laws who was looking for a Penn Yan to buy and who had told me that if I ever decided to sell it, I should call him first, which I did. I sold it to him for a very reasonable price. It killed me to sell my grandfather's boat, being a boater myself on Long Island, but at least John's pride and joy found a good home with someone who would appreciate it and take good care of it.

The Penn Yan Boat

Once the money issue was out of the way, the next order of business was getting ready for my trip to visit Dawn, who was training at the Great Lakes Naval Hospital Corps School and was on full active duty by that point.

We kept in contact with each other mostly by writing. I still had to retrieve all of my private mail from our post office box in New York. Dawn was able to call me at times by use of a pre-paid phone card when she was granted permission.

I had rented a vehicle in New York twice, once in January and the other in February, and drove round trip some 1,500 miles to Illinois and stayed at the Waukegan Best Inn nearby. She was granted a four-day pass both times so we could spend some time together. I knew that Dawn was having a hard time. She was homesick and worried about me. Ever since she had left for the Great Lakes, I kept most of the bad news, like my appeal and money problems, to myself. I tried to see her as often as I could to cheer her up.

Naval Hospital Corps School Great Lakes, Illinois

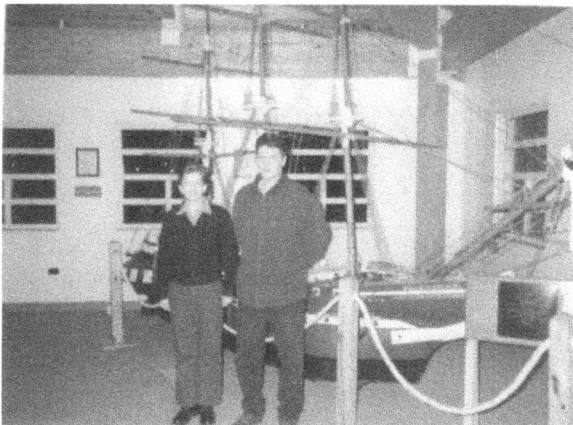

Visiting Dawn at the Naval Hospital Corps School, February 1995

It was now Wednesday, February 22, 1995. Little did I know that a mere six days later, I would leave, never to return to my grandfather's splendid home again. My father-in-law drove me back to Pennsylvania and on the way we made plans together for the next time he would come back over to help out. In the meantime, I had plenty of work inside the house I could manage myself.

My in-laws had given me a care package to bring home, and the ice box at the house was full. My father-in-law helped to bring in some of my belongings as I checked the answering machine. There were no important messages. I didn't tell my father-in-law about the extra money needed for my appeal; my in-laws had enough to worry about with their daughter joining the navy, so we parted with some optimism about all the forward-looking plans. After my father-in-law left, I called my mother to let her know that I was home safe and that there was no word about my appeal yet.

Not long after that Dawn surprised me with a phone call to make sure that I had gotten home safely. She also apologized for being sick and running a fever while I was there. I said not to worry and to get well. I was sorry as well; I wasn't in a good mood myself, worried as I was about my appeal and money problems. Dawn went on saying how much she missed and loved me and that she would make it up to me the next time we met. If all went well, I would be able to go back up to visit her at the end of the next month. We both promised each other things would get better before we signed off.

It was late in the evening by then, so I decided to start a fire in the fireplace and heat up a can of soup. Sitting in John's comfortable old chair in front of the warm fire, I fell asleep before long. I must have slept five or six hours before I woke up feeling cold. Putting some logs on the fire before heading into the kitchen, I noticed headlights in the front window. Someone was pulling into my driveway. Peeking out from behind the blinds, I could see it was the welcome committee—a police car. I could see the lights on top of the roof, but I couldn't make out who was driving. Then whoever it was backed out the driveway, driving away slowly while passing in front of the house.

I wondered what to make of it. Ever since Robert Frist had totaled the only borough police car in town, I hadn't seen him or Blaine Hoover, whom I was told had moved to Altoona. I would catch a glimpse of Thomas Penning driving by at times, but I couldn't recall seeing Frist at all. It seemed they were all lying low, leaving me alone. I thought maybe it was because I had lights on in the house and they knew I was back. Usually when I went away for a long period of time, I shut all the lights off in the house except for the back-porch light, which was on a timer. It was not hard to tell when the house was not occupied. Needless to say, I didn't sleep well that night, wondering about that car, my appeal, and what was in store for me.

I slept late the next day. It was now Thursday, February 23, 1995. Trying to forget about everything, I decided to finish hanging the new wallpaper in the living room; it was just one of the many projects I had going on.

Before renovations

The new wallpaper turned out nicely; Dawn and I were going to have a nice cozy home when the time came.

Stoking up the fireplace, I turned on my grandfather's old tube radio before taking a shower in the newly renovated downstairs half bathroom I had put in with the help of my father-in-law. Home was truly becoming homey.

After finishing one section of wallpaper, I decided to take a walk to the post office and stretch my legs. There were just bills and junk mail in the P.O. box. I headed back home, and as I was walking up the driveway, to my surprise I saw a police car parked in a small apartment complex nearby that housed folks who had lost their homes to the flood. The police car was parked at the corner of my property line, facing me with its headlights on. Sitting inside was Frist, staring straight at me. He then started flashing the high beams on and off, over and over, until I went inside the house.

He then pulled away and left. I wondered why they were watching me.

The only logical answer my mother and I could come up with when we talked about it over the phone was that it had something to do with my appeal. It had been almost two years since my appeal had been filed, and now the Superior Court needed extra documentation for my case. Bell had reiterated that it was a good thing they were being so thorough and that the ruling would be in my favor. That would give me a clear range to sue the cops, and they must have known it. She warned me to sit tight, telling me not to venture outside and stay off the streets until I could talk with my attorney. I agreed with her that I would call Bell tomorrow for an update. When I called the next day, an assistant told me he was out of the office for a week but would call me when he was back.

It should have been a peaceful time spent improving the house as I hoped to improve my future. I stayed inside, doing lots of constructive work. My father-in-law was coming back sometime the next week, so I figured I would wait to venture outside, picking up the mail with him.

I honestly thought things were looking up, even though I started getting more old-fashioned intimidation from Frist. He would drive by slowly again and again in a police car, looking at the house. I was praying that Superior Court would see things my way so I could finally put a stop to all of these civil rights violations being forced upon me and finally live in peace.

Dawn called February 25th to tell me she was feeling much better and that she had mailed me a letter with a list of things she needed me to do; one of them, she explained to me, was to get the number of the rectory at St. Mary's Church Southside of Elmira to set up an appointment so we could get our marriage blessed. She suggested that if we had the money and time, we could take a "mini" honeymoon before she started work at her new duty station. I guess my emotions got the best of me, because Dawn picked up that something was wrong, and I couldn't hide it. I told her what had been going on with the cops ever since I had come back from visiting her. Hopefully, I explained to her, whatever was going on, it was because things were being resolved in our favor, and the cops didn't like that. In the meantime, I assured her, "I'm staying indoors until I see your dad."

Dawn agreed and said she would call back in a couple of days, and that I should remember to pick up the mail the next time I was at her parents, so we could go over the list.

I wasn't feeling all that great at the time; I was having stomach pains again. Whether I had picked up some kind of an infection from Dawn when she was sick or it was psychosomatic because of all the legal troubles, I'll never know.

It was now Monday, February 27, 1995. Bell called, and I was thrilled at first, hoping to hear good news from him about a successful appeal. Instead, it was just the opposite. Bell was now warning me, saying that Frist, who physically had hurt me and had held a loaded gun to my head in 1993, was once again "AFTER YOUR FUCKING ASS."

Shocked, I yelled out, "Why? Why?"

Bell informed me that it was because I was to have reported to the county jail on February 20 at 8 a.m. to commence a 30-day incarceration.

"What the hell are you talking about?" I demanded to know. "What happened to my appeal?" Bell explained that it was lost; my appeal was overturned in favor of the lower court.

"When did this happen, and how come you're just calling me now?" I howled. My head was spinning from all of this.

Bell didn't answer my question, only warning me to keep a low profile. He advised me that he would make a last-ditch effort to straighten things out, but he also warned me not to let Frist catch me driving in Pennsylvania, because I still had a six-month suspension on my license.

His statement shocked me, because my original 12-month suspension in Pennsylvania had started in fall 1993. This great hardship mandated that Dawn and I live at her parents' home in Elmira, New York, since I was not allowed to drive in Pennsylvania. I thought the time had been served by now.

I was not even vaguely aware that I had been supposed to report to jail. Worse, Bell told me I was no longer his client, and that all this terrifying information was just a "courtesy call" on his part.

After discussing the situation with my mother, I packed up and left Pennsylvania, out of fear, mostly. While I was closing up the Oliverville house, the phone rang and it was Dawn, as promised. I tried to keep calm so as not to give things away, so she wouldn't worry about this new development. I told her that I was packing to visit my parents back on Long Island and that I figured it would be good to stay out of sight of the cops until this mess was over. I was planning on a trip soon anyway, so it made sense. Fortunately, Dawn didn't think anything of it, merely reminding me to pick up the mail in Horseheads on the way. She wished me a safe trip, good luck getting a loan we needed, and mentioned that she would call me at my parents' home in a couple of days.

What could I do, after all, in a place that was not safe? Living alone at my Oliverville house, as I then was, I could not risk further contact with barbarians like Frist—an abusive bully with a badge who had it in for me.

At four in the morning, February 28, 1995, I headed for the safety of New York, leaving behind what I had hoped would be a home for my children someday. My neighbors were behind me, though, and they too felt it was the safest thing for me. They had seen the harassment. They lived these fears themselves. I received a supportive note from a neighbor that shows the good terms we were on, and how much they were willing to help me in my harassment. What I didn't know was that this would be the very last time I would ever set foot in our home again. Now I was, in the clouded eyes of the state of Pennsylvania, a fugitive from justice.

March 3, 1994

Dear Joe,

Our Joe picked up your mail today — most of it was junk mail. These 2 items are important.

I don't know if anybody else knows where you are or if I should tell if I'm asked.

That's why I mailed this from N.Y.

Be good! Relax! See you!

Love,

Adda

Last photo taken of me in Pennsylvania just before leaving for the Great Lakes

I drove some two hundred miles, putting distance between me and Frist until I was back on Long Island safely in my parents' home. I strongly felt, as did my mother, that Bell had screwed me over, but what proof did I have?

I did receive a letter from Dawn sent to my parents' address, saying it wasn't right that I had to hide from the cops and to take care of myself. If she only knew about the phone call I received from my lawyer, I thought. I felt I had to keep it from her until she finished her navy training. I just didn't have the heart to tell her I had lost my appeal.

I never did make that third trip to see my wife in March, nor did we have our marriage blessed or a romantic mini honeymoon. I wouldn't see Dawn again until she graduated her navy training. When I did, I finally had the nerve to explain what really took place.

Joseph Waitonis
40 East Half Hollow Rd
Dex Hills, Long Island,
NY 11746

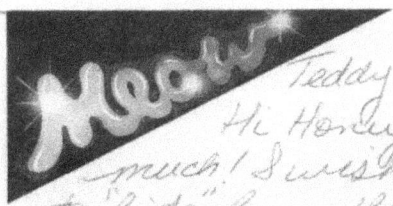

25 FEB 95

Teddy Bear,
Hi Honey! I love you so much! I wish you didn't have to "hide" from the cops. It's just not right! And I wish I was there with you to help you out. But I'm here & I just have to do my best to pass my tests & move on with my career.

Do you know what I miss the most about us? I miss cuddling up in front of a fire & watching the cats watch the flames. I also miss the ocean & playing in the waves with you. But soon we'll be playing in the waves again!

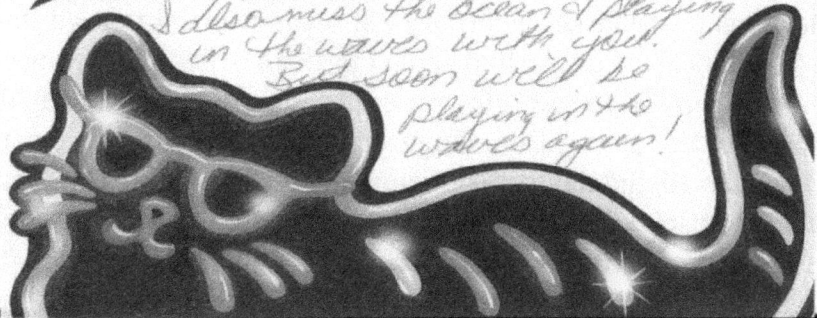

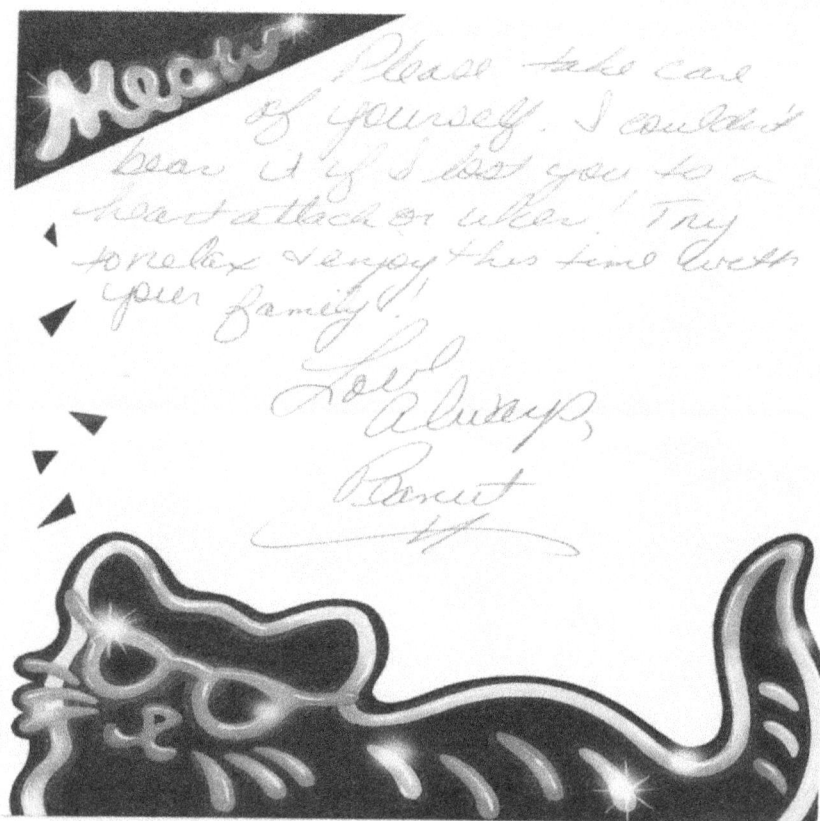

I received a big manila envelope from my neighbor Adda Gutierrez. Inside were two letters from Horseboro, one from Bell and the other from the probation department. The envelope from Bell was post-marked February 23. I was stunned to read Bell's letter: "Enclosed please find your copy of an Order instructing you to show up for your 30-day incarceration and copy of your dismissal of the appeal from Superior Court." The letter was dated February 20, the day I was to start my incarceration. One of the two Superior Court documents was demanding that the lower court and my attorney send in the past due briefs; it was dated December 19, 1994. The other Superior Court document stated that my appeal was discontinued from record and certification was being sent to trial court. It was dated February 7, 1995. It wasn't even a court ruling; my appeal was discontinued from record, but how?

February 20, 1995

Mr. Joseph Waiksnis

Dear Joe:

Enclosed please find your copy of an Order instructing you when to show for your 30 day incarceration and a copy of the dismissal of the Appeal from the Superior Court. If you have any questions, do not hesitate to contact my office at your earliest convenience.

Thank you for your time and cooperation in this matter.

Very Truly Yours,

k, Esquire

w/sgg
Enclosures

The last document was the order from the judge saying,

And now this 15 day of February, 1995 the court being informed that the defendant's appeal being withdrawn, it is hereby ordered adjudged and decreed that the defendant, Joseph Waiksnis, shall report to the County Jail on Monday, February 20 1995 at 8:00 a.m. to commence a thirty day incarceration pursuant to the court's sentencing order of September 27, 1993. Signed Judge Early.

This was the first time that I ever saw the judge's signature on a document, and it wasn't even a signature at all: it was signed in bold letters, a rubber stamp of sorts. I was also shocked that it claimed my appeal was "withdrawn."

COPY

COMMONWEALTH OF PENNSYLVANIA   : IN THE COURT OF COMMON PLEAS

           VS.   : OF ▬▬ ▬ COUNTY, PENNSYLVANIA

JOSEPH WAIKSNIS   : NO. 163 CRIMINAL ACTION 1993

O R D E R

AND NOW, this 15th day of February, 1995, the Court being informed that the defendant's appeal has been withdrawn, it is hereby ORDERED, ADJUDGED and DECREED that the defendant, Joseph Waiksnis, shall report to the ▬ ▬ County Jail on Monday, February 20, 1995, at 8:00 a.m. to commence a thirty day incarceration pursuant to the Court's sentencing order of September 27, 1993.

By The Court,

S/ ▬▬▬▬▬▬ ,P.J.
▬▬▬ ▬▬▬ ▬ .

cc: J. Waiksnis
     ▬ ▬ ▬., Esquire
     Prob
     DA
     Sheriff
     Warden

The second letter was from the probation department dated February 16. It was a money judgment in the amount of $1,587.

Approximately one year and four months after the appeal was actually filed, and after Bell had been paid to continue representing me in this phase of my case, he not only found a way to withdraw the appeal entirely without my consent, he also turned around and dropped me as a client, leaving me without counsel and, because the statute of limitations for most civil rights claims is two years from the date of the alleged violation, I was left with no legal recourse possible.

My mother and I sent numerous letters, with certified return receipts, to the Pennsylvania governor and attorney general to request a full investigation into corruption in their justice system, of which I could hardly have been the only victim. As I said, even my star witness spoke of fearing for the safety of herself and her children if she testified, even though she was prepared to testify about what she had heard on the police radio that night.

No sooner was my appeal withdrawn than Judge Early, who presided over my case, drew up a court order to commence a 30-day sentence. I was to go to jail.

Because I had just lost my attorney, though, and had not had sufficient time to acquire a new one, I didn't know this. Owing to the confusion, I was unadvised of this new decision. Since I was without counsel, I had no way to know how to handle the situation either.

My first appeal had been dismissed long ago, but I never even knew that until we came upon this notice among our many papers. Maybe all this time Bell had been filing various appeals and the options had finally run out, or maybe he was in the DA's pocket the whole time. I do not know. All I know is that, apparently, without realizing it, I had been living on borrowed time.

COMMONWEALTH OF PENNSYLVANIA : IN THE COURT OF COMMON PLEAS

vs. : OF TIOGA COUNTY, PENNSYLVANIA

JOSEPH WAIKENIS : NO. 163 CRIMINAL ACTION 1993

O R D E R

AND NOW, September 13, 1993, the Motion in Arrest
of Judgment and Motion for New Trial are dismissed.

The matter is scheduled for sentencing on
September 27, 1993 at 11:00 A.M.

By the Court,

HON. ███████ P. ██████, JR.

c.c.: District Attorney
███████, Esq.
Probation

Dawn have you seen this befor-

CHAPTER THIRTEEN

After I fled Pennsylvania in 1995, life was entirely different from what I had known. It would have been naïve to think my troubles were over. They weren't. But there were a new set of challenges, new circumstances to consider. A warrant out for my arrest in Pennsylvania meant trouble for my life outside of the state, at least until the issue was resolved.

I didn't want to be a fugitive from the law, but I was convinced of the need to find some kind of protection from the private vengeance of the men who had initially caused problems for me. Since it could easily take some time to resolve things, I had to find a way to survive in the meantime.

Sometime after I left Oliverville in 1995, my wife and her family rented a U-Haul truck to retrieve our belongings from our Oliverville home. Apparently two calls came in to our Oliverville home with messages left on the answering machine. We were both in the habit of keeping formal records of events by this time. Both the DA and Marlin Bell left messages, urging me to turn myself in.

On Monday at 2:37 p.m., Bell's message said:

> *"Joe, this is Marlin Bell. This is a courtesy call. I thought I'd made the last courtesy call, because I bought you some time because you didn't get your notice right away. If you go in there now, without further ado, you're probably not going to get on anybody's bad side, but you need to take care of this immediately. It is February 28th now; you've got to get in here, man, today. I've got to hear from you as soon as you hear this message, I don't know what else to say. I will do my*

best to keep things level but get in touch with me as soon as you get this message. Call me at my office or at the house."

Then on Tuesday at 9:19 a.m. there was this message:

"Joe, this is the District Attorney's office. I'm calling about the court order for you to turn yourself in to start your sentence. You're supposed to be in on February 20th at 8 a.m. If you fail to report by tomorrow morning, I'll ask the judge to issue a bench warrant. You will be looking at more time. If you have any questions, you can get a hold of me at (number)."

My legal problems were not going to go away, it was clear. My attorney screwed me over in how he handled my appeal, warning me that Robert Frist was after me and now telling me to turn myself in. The DA was threatening me with more jail time if I didn't show up to do time for a crime I had never committed. It was a weight upon me that I almost couldn't bear. Yet I was resolved to fight for my rights, and had already tearfully put my grandfather's home and Pennsylvania well behind me. I was not going there.

I believe that the entire original "arrest" was illegal. There are several reasons to believe this. One is that I was not properly processed in a *bona fide* police station. Pennsylvania law requires that a person be brought to a proper police station for questioning and for the processing of an arrest. In fact, when my grandfather was arrested by Chief Frist, this procedure was followed, and the charges against my grandfather were dropped as the nonsense they were. Is this why Chief Frist chose not to bring me to a proper police station for legal processing? Was he afraid the same thing would happen if he followed the letter of the law? Did he think if he harassed our family enough, over several generations, we would at last sell our house to the municipality? Was this some sort of grisly joke—" Okay, you won't let us have a proper municipal complex in your multi-purpose house, so we will show you just how painful it is to be taken to the municipal building we now have—the fire hall basement!" I don't know. It is up to the reader to judge.

Another reason was that events the police said occurred never happened. For instance, I was never told I needed bail to be set free that night and therefore I did not pay anything. Had they set bail, I would have been allowed a collect phone call to try and make bail. Although procedures on this may vary by locality, most American citizens accept that they have a right to make a phone call after having been arrested. I was not afforded this right, yet the police claimed they set bail and I paid.

The charges—five total before two were dismissed — showed up in the mail two weeks later, shocking me, as I was not apprised of any charges at all at the time of my detention. I was not read my Miranda rights. I'll go into all these irregularities in a little more detail. I am simply maintaining that my constitutional rights were violated, making what little evidence they cooked up against me inadmissible in court. The law states: *If a person's constitutional rights are violated in any way during an interrogation, then any evidence obtained during the interrogation is not permitted to be introduced in trial.* The law also states: *Individuals who are arrested by the police or security forces are said to have been unlawfully detained if the authorities arresting them did not follow proper procedures.*

The usual procedure for the DUI/DWI in Pennsylvania is that you are arrested, booked or processed, and put in a holding cell or the local jail to appear the next day in court. Mine must not have been considered a serious situation because I was released without need for bail.

I was not arraigned in person. The defendant is supposed to appear in court to plead guilty or not guilty. I was not given that courtesy.

They had no proof that I had been driving under the influence. They had assumed so because they could see some old beer cans in the garbage bags and because I did not want to take a Blood Alcohol Content test (BAC). I was considered guilty of a DUI because I did not want to take a test that would mean I automatically gave up my rights to drive in Pennsylvania for at least a full year. The law now states that your license will be suspended for a year for refusing to take a BAC test. For all the importance of stopping actual DUIs, the kind of draconian measures meant to force these kinds of tests represents a civil rights issue.

I was sentenced to thirty days in jail, in spite of the fact that it is rare to serve jail time on a first offense; if someone does serve time, it is 48 hours, but they can't assign you jail time if there is no BAC number to determine the length of time. A first-time offense in Pennsylvania usually carries probation for six months, a fine of $300, and mandatory highway safety classes.

Let me tell you how strict Pennsylvania law is on all this. Say you are driving home from a social event with friends, and you have had a little bit to drink and are sleepy. You responsibly pull over to take a nap before driving any further, so as to prevent endangering yourself or others. The police happen upon you resting in your car. If a police officer finds you and gets a whiff of alcohol, you are under arrest for drunk driving, and a jury may very well convict you even after knowing all the circumstances of your arrest.

Can you see how easy it is to run afoul of these laws? Now, I'm not much of a drinker, but Dawn, her parents, and I had a system in place where if I was just tired, I would stay over in their guest room so as not to risk a car accident. I wasn't even drinking. I believe in DUI laws and penalties. It's just that they can get to the point of absurdity when someone is trying to prevent an accident by resting in their vehicle so they can sleep off any effects of alcohol and that person undergoes the significant horrors of a DUI arrest and prosecution, and where their tests can be forced upon someone.

Sometimes it is just better to take what they give you, unfair as it may be, and work your way through it. I, however, wanted to stand up for my rights.

In fact, what happened to me might be legally defined as a kidnapping. Under federal and state law, kidnapping is commonly defined as the taking of a person from one place to another against his or her will, or the confining of a person to a controlled space under an unlawful purpose.

My apprehension was the talk of the town. No one had ever heard of the police taking and keeping a citizen in the fire house basement. I believe this is the main reason there was such a cover up. Had my attorney been more effective, he would have been able to uncover all this sleight of hand about the circumstances of my arrest. I think I would have had a strong case for a lawsuit against the three officers, and they themselves might have been facing jail time for the violation of a citizen's rights and malicious prosecution.

Let me go into "malicious prosecution" for a moment, in case the reader ever needs to know some facts about it. Malicious prosecution basically means that a person is a victim of police and prosecutor persecution. In a case of malicious prosecution, the police do not have "probable cause" to make an arrest, and this arrest and the prosecution that follows it are damaging.

We would like to believe that in our justice system arrests and charges are always justified. This is not always the case. If you are arrested and prosecuted for a theft, for example, and there is no evidence to support this arrest, you are a victim of malicious prosecution. Any time you are accused of and prosecuted for something you did not do, you are a victim of malicious prosecution. You can then sue the police for damages.

Winning such a suit means you have to get over a pretty high bar of proof, though. Your case has to have been dismissed with words from the judge like "malicious prosecution," "no probable cause," or "frivolous lawsuit."

You have to sue the proper parties, too. The person or persons you are suing must have had an active role in what happened. They also could not have had probable cause to arrest you or bring you to trial in the first place. Also, the defendant has to have pursued the case even though they knew it had no merit.

These requirements are a high bar, and I could not pass it without the aid of an effective attorney fighting hard for my rights in the courtroom. By the time my trial was over and a guilty verdict came in, I had no legal grounds to pursue a malicious prosecution lawsuit because I was down and out on the very first requirement: my case was not dismissed.

Legally, I may not be able to prove I was the victim of a malicious prosecution in a court of law. Morally, I know I was the victim of such, and things just escalated from there.

Fortunately for us, Dawn was working for the navy at this time and was able to support the two of us with her salary. In fact, we moved to a naval base in South Carolina after her training was completed at the Great Lakes. Dawn graduated April 28th 1995, and we both settled in our new home at the Naval Weapons Station at Charleston, South Carolina.

Department of the Navy
Naval Health Sciences Education and Training Command

Certificate of Graduation

Awarded To

Hospitalman Recruit Dawn M. WAIKSNIS

who has satisfactorily completed the prescribed
course of instruction for

Hospital Corpsman Basic
at the
Naval Hospital Corps School Great Lakes

28 April 1995
Date

CAPTAIN J. L. HIGGINS, MSC, USN
Commanding Officer

№ 33072

I was able to get a job on base doing maintenance work on the housing, while Dawn worked at the navy clinic. During our free time, we were writing letters and contacting people, trying to resolve the problems back in Pennsylvania. My mother was doing the same, as she had more time than we did, but she was taking it a step further. When she wrote a letter, she was sending it certified mail to make sure the recipient received it. In doing so, she ensured she would get a response back, even if it took several tries and cost a lot of money.

Eventually, she got one response that turned us all cold. It was from an attorney hired by Robert Frist. He acknowledged that my mother had written to the County District Attorney, the Pennsylvania Attorney General, the Governor, the County President Judge, and the Borough Council. He claimed that the accusations in her letter were both false and libelous and that she could incur criminal penalties if she continued to make them. The lawyer insisted that I had been dealt with professionally and that investigations had turned up nothing against my police persecutors. He reiterated that I had been arrested on such and such a date, found guilty at a trial by jury, and had then failed to appear for sentencing, and a warrant for my arrest had been issued. I was, he told my mother, a fugitive from justice, and if she had assisted me in any way, whether in New York or in Pennsylvania, she could be liable for criminal penalties herself.

Now officials in New York got involved. The police in her area were advised in 1996 by Pennsylvania authorities that I was wanted on charges of driving under the influence. If I was found, I was to be apprehended and extradited to Pennsylvania, as there was a bench warrant out there for my arrest.

My mother will never forget the first time the Suffolk County detectives on Long Island showed up at her door the summer of 1996, both ringing the bell and pounding on the front door. My mother was recuperating from an injury and my stepfather answered the door. She was in bed and heard yelling on the porch. Finally, after she limped to the foyer, my stepfather introduced her to the detectives as my mother. They started yelling that no matter where in the United States I was, I would be apprehended and taken back to Pennsylvania in chains. Their loudness seemed designed to embarrass; they were advised that I was not in New York. They asked where I was and were advised that I was in South Carolina. My mother later told me that they had no warrants to demonstrate the legal basis for their visit. The only thing given my parents were calling cards listing their names; in fact, there seemed to be no exact charges given them at all. After browbeating two elderly people, they left, stating that they would return, leaving their Suffolk County calling card.

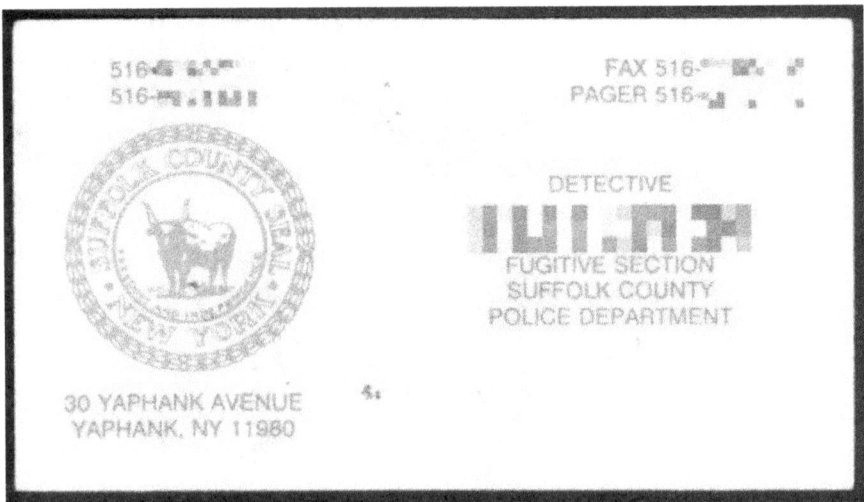

To this day, I have not been back to my house in Oliverville, although I continued to pay the property taxes and otherwise fund the maintenance of the house for several years. To return felt too painful. I actually relied on my neighbor, George Gutierrez, and his family, for the maintenance. My wife has been back to the house. When she was on leave, she went back periodically to check on the place. She even went to visit some of our neighbors, since we were both quite well liked in the town.

As 1996 ground on, Dawn gave birth to our son. I wondered at the time how I would ever be able to explain to him the kind of greed and hatred that animated the Oliverville officials, and how we came to lose our family home there. His birth was a motivation to me, on the other hand, a reason to keep fighting for my freedom so that I could care and provide for him. I didn't yet realize how long the battle would drag on; I figured he would have no memory of this nightmare. I became his full-time caregiver, quitting my job on base.

My son, Kelvin

CHAPTER FOURTEEN

After the police visited my mother, she immediately contacted the office of the Pennsylvania attorney general again, only to receive unhelpful responses without instruction on how she or I might seek to resolve some of the issues with my case.

She also contacted the U.S. Department of Justice, sending documentation, wanting answers as to why Pennsylvania was sending New York law enforcement to her home and wanting to know the exact charges against me.

Although things were beginning to seem truly hopeless, the Justice Department contacted FBI Special Agent Trevor Wirthin, whose office is located in Pennsylvania, not far from the county seat where the court and DA were located. Agent Wirthin wanted to investigate our claims, and he contacted my mother at her Long Island home. He seemed very polite to her at that time and informed her that he wanted my side of the story and that he needed to contact me. My mother gave him my South Carolina address and phone number. He contacted me in South Carolina, advising that he wanted to hear things the way I believed they had happened. He wanted our information on the police, the DA, and the judge involved in my case. He wanted to see everything we had collected over the years, to hear all the allegations so he could determine their validity.

Among other things we specifically asked Trevor Wirthin to investigate was the Oliverville Fire Department, which was passed off as a police department back in 1993 at my trial. We also requested that he investigate my appeal violation in 1995, plus the legal charges to warrant inter-state extradition by

Pennsylvania's DA. We asked Agent Wirthin to contact the Gutierrez family. They had witnessed Oliverville Police Chief Robert Frist trespassing on my property, even calling me on the phone to warn us he was outside our home and catching him taking mail from the console of Dawn's Ford Escort, from which he found our private New York P.O. box number and mailed summonses to it.

Agent Wirthin's interest in our case was a start, and my wife and I sent out a packet of information—everything we had—directly to him at a mailbox number in Pennsylvania. He advised us not to have it certified; he stressed heavily that we send all our originals directly to him to be turned over to the Justice Department, but we sent him only copies of originals to protect ourselves. Agent Wirthin spoke very courteously to me during the initial call.

Several days passed, and I put in a call to Agent Wirthin from South Carolina to check whether the documentation had reached him. He did a complete turn-around from our initial phone conversation and was extremely rude to me.

Agent Wirthin completely sided with law enforcement in the case. Perhaps his apparent interest in my side of the story was part of a ruse to try and draw me out of hiding, giving the authorities the chance to arrest and extradite me. He seemed to make up his mind pretty early on that I was guilty as charged. My mother also called him at his Pennsylvania office, and he sounded annoyed when my mother asked about the package we had sent to him, being decidedly rude to her and demanding to know why she was bothering him about this matter. He admitted, though, to having information from us unopened in front of him. He advised us that he would send it directly to the Justice Department in Washington, D.C. that day.

Some months later a letter from the Justice Department informed me that they did not find that my civil rights had been violated and that my case with them was closed. There was nothing more to be done following those avenues, and they must have convinced themselves that my corroborating evidence was permanently out of my hands.

The Pennsylvania photos of me had been sent to the New York police so that they could identify me and try to find me at my mother's home. They were abominations—two cut and pasted photos formulated from the original four Polaroid photographs taken of me the night of my detention. They were of poor quality and obviously doctored; the alterations were quite evident to the naked eye. The altered pictures showed me standing in front of a bright, white sign reading "Oliverville Police Dept." which was affixed to the dank basement wall in the fire house where, it appeared, they could do anything to me with impunity. One of the detectives who originally came to my parents' Long Island home in 1996 was the one who handed over the Pennsylvania papers to my mother at Suffolk County Police Headquarters. She immediately recognized him due to his stocky build and extreme height, and his full head of ghostly white hair. He handed her only the statement from PA listing a misdemeanor charge, stating, "The above subject is wanted by the DA's office in Horseboro, PA, on the charge of driving under the influence of liquor. The DA will extradite."

A field report stating that I was a fugitive from justice.

POLICE DEPARTMENT, COUNTY OF SUFFOLK, N.Y.
SUPPLEMENTARY REPORT

RE. WAIKSNIS Joseph
DOB 01/26/63

4/24/96 Received notice from PA. District Att.
That above subject is wanted on charges of.
Driving under the influence of liquor
if apprehended they will extradite.

No local warrants at this time

File is sent this date

4/30/96 Contacted DA Investigator
Det. He advised s-subjects poss. 6th address
ascertained through their DMV.
He also stated subjects brother Veronica Sweiden
lives in Babylon. He will try to acquire
photo's and forward them to us.
Det Phone #

5/3/96 Received Photos from

My mother demanded copies of the photos sent to them from PA. He asked her, "Do you really need them?" and received a big "Yes." This detective knew that they were doctored abominations, and he appeared to my mother to be too embarrassed to hand them over to her. He then went back into records and eventually, after much delay, returned to her with the pictures of me. My mother then telephoned him several days later about the tampered pictures. He replied, "That's the way we received them from Pennsylvania."

Copies sent to
Suffolk County NY
Police Headquarters
1996

White [illegible]
Police Dept.
sign added
behind body
of subject.

Joseph Charles Waiksnis
D.B. 01-26-63
03-29-93
I.D.# 9303395   DUI

Joseph Charles Waiksnis
D.B. 01-26-63
03-29-93
I.D.# 9303395   DUI

I thought the photographs corroborated my version of events, showing that I had, indeed, been taken to an unofficial police station and detained in the Oliverville fire house basement rather than an actual police station where I might have been formally processed and would have been afforded some protections of my rights.

The photographs themselves were confirmation for us of the questionable nature of the police activities in the Oliverville area of Pennsylvania, especially since they had been doctored. They could not be consistent with the standards for actual police photographs identifying offenders or those under arrest.

We later asked for help from a Pennsylvania senator to try to get some resolution of these issues. We asked this senator for help, explaining the problems that were ongoing, enclosing copies of documentation we had. In the end, after much contact, the senator advised us that he would send our letters and other documents to the FBI. The suggestion, of course, was that the FBI might actually undertake to investigate this time around, at the insistence of a senator. Indeed, this senator and his assistant were the only officials affiliated with Pennsylvania who actually did anything to try to assist us. Both men were proactive in trying to help, but it was still not enough.

The harassment of my family was about to become even more severe. More county fugitive detectives stopped by my parents' home, holding in hand those cut and pasted pictures of me, advising them that my name was in the National Crime Information Center (NCIC) computers and warning my parents that I had to come out of hiding.

The police in my mother's county had become increasingly involved in my case, trying to hunt me down and, failing that, to harass my parents. Fugitive detectives continued to show up at my parents' home, yet again without a warrant to explain their presence and authority. The detectives carried with them the altered, cut-up pictures of me that had been taken in the fire house basement.

"I see you have in your hand those tampered, cut-up pictures of my son," my mother challenged them. When they were told that I was not in New York, the two officers made further threats about the fate that awaited me if I did not give myself up. Then they left again, leaving my mother and stepfather once again with the unwelcome promise that they would return at some point in the future.

Chapter Fifteen

Realizing that it was possible for citizens to obtain copies of police records, and undergoing frequent threatening visits from the country police, my mother decided to try a new approach in 1997. She contacted the county police commissioner in her area of New York in order to stop the intimidation, harassment, and embarrassment she was undergoing as detectives continually showed up at her door and tried to intimidate her. It was also concerning to us both that the decidedly unprofessional, worn down photographs of me were being used. The cut-up photos were really a portrait of the kind of terror and corruption my family and I faced.

My mother contacted by letter and fax the police commissioner and described the behavior of the two detectives when they entered her property. She reiterated, of course, the particulars of my case that were troublesome, but more than anything, she stressed that I simply was not in New York and had not been since the warrant had been issued for my arrest, as she had told the officers when they first appeared at her home.

The response she received was quite surprising. The letter indicated that the police were no longer looking for me in New York, and they would no longer be contacting my parents. This, apparently, was because there was sufficient information to rule out my being in New York. My mother was also advised, once again, that she should contact the attorney general of Pennsylvania to address the complaints that both she and I maintained about the way that I had been handled on the night of my detention as it was no longer the responsibility of New York to try to apprehend me, since I was known to be living in South Carolina.

November 21, 1997

Ms. Veronica R. Snyder
█ █ █ █ █
█ █ █ New York 11746

Dear Ms. Snyder:

I am writing on behalf of Commissioner █ █ █ █ in response to your letter, dated November 6, 1997.

On May 1, 1996, the Suffolk County Police Department, Fugitive Section received correspondence from Chief County Detective █ █ of the _ █County, Pennsylvania, District Attorney's Office. Detective Davis requested our assistance in apprehending your son, Joseph Waiksnis, on a charge of DUI and provided photocopies of your son's photograph. Proper entries were made in NCIC (National Crime Information Center) which provides authorization for our detectives to arrest your son. Our detectives then spoke with you on two separate occasions and eventually ascertained from you that your son is now living in South Carolina. Since your son is wanted by authorities in Pennsylvania and is residing in South Carolina, the Suffolk County Police Department has no further role in this case.

In your letter, you allege that there were improprieties committed in Pennsylvania in regard to your son's arrest and prosecution. These matters fall within the purview of the State Attorney General's Office in Pennsylvania and you should address your concerns to that office. The Suffolk County Police Department has no authority to intervene in this matter.

If you require further assistance, please don't hesitate to contact me.

Sincerely,

Commanding Officer/Fugitive Section

JNF:mh

A Suffolk County Police letter to my mother

In 1998, the DA from Pennsylvania was in contact with a Detective Matthew Heraldo of the South Carolina Duck Creek Police Department, not far from where we lived on base. Eight pages of fabricated information meant to smear me were faxed to South Carolina from Pennsylvania, along with the altered photos of me for identification.

Unlike the 1996 incident in New York, when the District Attorney in Pennsylvania sent one and only charge to New York (driving under influence of liquor) to have me extradited, this time the District Attorney fabricated even more charges, trying desperately to get a hold of me. On a blank sheet of white paper that was made to look like a warrant, having nothing but a rubber stamp in bold letters, the note stated that the "charges" against me had escalated. He cited a failure to appear for a year and a half sentence that didn't exist, and on top of that added a charge of violation of probation. The original 1993 pre-sentence report shows I never had or was on probation; I had only to fulfill a standard 48-hour jail time.

There were new alterations to the photos. The cinderblocks behind me were colored in black. Now the South Carolina local police had an arrest warrant for me in their possession; the offense was listed as being a Fugitive from Justice.

South Carolina Warrant for my arrest

On August 4th 1998, just after lunch, a small army of police officers were dispatched and ordered to surround my home on the South Carolina naval base where my wife worked. In front of my son, the officers handcuffed me and forced me into the back of a police vehicle. My wife had to come home from work early to take care of our son, and she was screaming and crying. For weeks, even months afterwards, my wife would have to answer or else try to dodge questions about the incident from neighbors and the people she worked with: "Why was he arrested? What do they want with him?" The questions were incessant and humiliating beyond words; yet another form of torment for my family and me.

After the arrest I was taken straight to jail. I was denied bail and told that I would be kept at the jail to await extradition to Pennsylvania.

It had been five years since the initial incident, and I had become a fugitive from justice—a serious charge—because I had been unaware of the summons to appear to begin my sentence. I had not known my appeal was dropped, the appeal that could have spared me the ordeal of a jail sentence in the first place.

I was handcuffed, denied an attorney, and full of fear as I was held overnight in a cell with two other inmates. I felt sick from the stress of being held away from my family, worried about what they were about to go through. It was enough to give me the runs and make me feel painfully nauseous. I kept trying to tell the officers that I was set up. Fortunately, an attorney, William Morrow, got me released the next day. The downside, of course, was that my stepfather had to take out some $5,500 dollars from his retirement savings to pay Morrow's retainer.

Morrow explained in a lengthy discussion with Judge Sheila Meritt, who had signed my arrest warrant for South Carolina, that the original offense that had everyone in such a state about me was a first offense DUI. It was a misdemeanor, not a felony, and the standard sentence, according to the law, was 48 hours. The records produced by the Pennsylvania authorities confirmed the motion that a 30-day sentence or less was allowed for such an offense.

Our experience under Judge Sheila Meritt was the first time in more than five years that my family and I were treated justly and sanely. The judge ordered my release after reviewing the mountain of evidence that my family had collected, detailing every element of my case. She saw the reports on my sentencing and the details of the trial. Dawn told me that she could tell the judge was very upset when she saw our documents. Judge Meritt not only released me, she offered an apology on behalf of the court. She ruled that I did not have to put up bail, that I did not have to return to court, and she also insisted that there were to be no restrictions on this ruling. She also explained to me and to my wife that she was going to make up a personal reconnaissance bond for the arrest warrant information that needed to be input into the computer system. To offset the computer input, she told us, she was going to indicate a return court date of 9/9/99. It was not, she insisted, an actual return court date but simply a way around the red tape bureaucracy of the system.

Form Approved By
S. C. Attorney General
Section 17-15-40
March 7, 1990

Ticket or Warrant No. *F-425399*

BAIL PROCEEDING
FORM I

STATE OF SOUTH CAROLINA
COUNTY OF _____
State of South Carolina
vs.
_____
Name of Defendant

Offense Charged: _____

IN THE ( ) COURT OF GENERAL SESSIONS
( ) MAGISTRATE COURT
( ) MUNICIPAL COURT OF _____

ORDER SPECIFYING METHODS
AND CONDITIONS OF RELEASE

IT IS HEREBY ORDERED

I

That the above named defendant be released from custody on his own recognizance without surety on the condition that he will personally appear before the designated court at the place, date and time required to answer the charge made against him and do what shall be ordered by the court, and not depart the State without permission of the court and be of good behavior.

II

That the above named defendant be released from custody upon a recognizance without surety executed by him.

Appearance Recognizance Without Surety

On the _____ day of _____, 19__ personally appeared before the undersigned judge the defendant named above who acknowledged himself indebted to the State of South Carolina, in the sum of _____ dollars, to be levied on his real and personal property for the use of the State, if the defendant shall fail in performing the conditions of this Order.

III

That the defendant will notify the court promptly if he changes his address from the one contained in this Order and will comply with the following other conditions of release _____

_____
_____
_____

IV

That the defendant shall appear at (check one):

☐ the term of the court of general sessions beginning on [Date:]_____ at [Time:]___:___ o'clock, ___.M., at [Place:]_____ and remain there throughout that term of court. If no disposition is made during that term, the defendant shall appear and remain throughout each succeeding term of court until final disposition is made of his case, unless otherwise ordered by the court.

☑ the session of magistrate / municipal (circle one) court beginning on [Date:]_____ at [Time:]___:___ o'clock, ___.M., at [Place:]_____. If no final disposition is made during that session, the defendant shall appear at such other times and places as ordered by the court.

SCCA/310 (3/90)   FORM CONTINUES ON BACK

Following my release, it was back to the navy base, back to caring for my son, and deflecting questions about my arrest. It did feel wonderful to seemingly have most of the weight of my legal struggles lifted from my shoulders. I was convinced that this was the beginning of the end, with Meritt's opinion something I hoped to use against my persecutors in Pennsylvania. On the other hand, I knew the war was not won yet. My son, barely two years old, had grown up in a world already marred by the degree to which I had been living in fear. As his primary caregiver, I had worried constantly about what would happen if I were to be taken away, imprisoned in Pennsylvania, far away from the place that we called home by then, while my wife was working for the navy. Nothing had been secure, and that feeling of insecurity pervaded everything still.

Unfortunately, the embarrassment of my arrest was also something that did not dissipate. My neighbors and my wife's colleagues could not forget it, and nothing we said, no amount of explanation, would erase the image of me in handcuffs. My reputation, our image as a family, was forever marred.

Then, of course, there was the good old-fashioned wakeup call that awaited us. As I feared, we were not at the end of our struggles; far from it. In fact, once we had won the day in court, the situation escalated in a kind of domino effect into a disaster over the next several years. Icarus crashed into the sea. Every letter my wife and I sent out for help got no response. I tried to enlist the help of the media, but it was all the same response: nothing.

The DA from Pennsylvania contacted the South Carolina authorities again and further fabricated charges against me, suggesting that I had failed to appear for a criminal trial this time around. The South Carolina judge had said it was preposterous that I should be extradited based on a failure to appear on a misdemeanor charge, especially since I had lost my counsel and had not actually been aware of the initial summons to appear. That was even before the problem of my appeal was factored into the mix—an appeal that was pulled without my consent or knowledge, leaving me defenseless and expected to appear for a sentence that I had very much hoped to see overturned.

Having the docket number of my appeal and wondering why it was pulled, I called the Superior Court in Pennsylvania and spoke to a woman there, explaining that I was in the navy and asking her why my appeal was withdrawn. She explained that under normal circumstances, she couldn't give out such information, but she said she would look it up. Then she read the information to me over the phone, saying that the lower court never had sent in their briefs, and neither had my attorney. The Superior Court had contacted both the lower court and my attorney to immediately send in their briefs before the deadline for an appeal, but then my attorney had withdrawn my appeal. Once that happens, the lower charge sticks. I asked her if she could please send me a copy of that. I gave her my South Carolina address and, sure enough, when I got it, that's exactly what it said.

```
08/27/96          SUPERIOR COURT OF PENNSYLVANIA
1521                    OFFICIAL DOCKET

                     DOCKET # 00709HBG93

FULL CAPTION
  999E  COMMONWEALTH OF PENNSYLVANIA
              V
  001T  JOSEPH WAIKSNIS

COUNSEL                                   TITLE    FOR   MAIL

    33850                                 001T     Y



    29069                                 999E     Y



CONSOLIDATED DOCKET NUMBER

BACKGROUND DATA
    TRIAL COURT RECORDS
         CATEGORY:              CR
         COURT NAME:            CRIMINAL
         COUNTY:
         JUDICIAL DISTRICT:     04
         CASE TYPE/CHARGE:      DRIV.UNDER INFLUENCE
         TRIAL COURT CHARGES:
         JUDGE(S):
         DISPOSITION TYPE:      ORDER ENTERED
         DISPOSITION DATE:      09/27/93
         APPEAL FILE DATE:      10/26/93
         DISPOSITION ENTERED:
         TRIAL CRT DOCKET NO.:  163 CRIMINAL 1993
         OFFENSE TRACKING NO.:  E1864855

STATUS INFORMATION

DOCKET ENTRIES                                 FOR
    10/29/93  NOTICE OF APPEAL                  001T
    10/29/93  DOCKETING STATEMENT EXITED        001T
    12/01/93  DOCKETING STATEMENT RECEIVED      001T
              11/12/93  DOCKETING STATEMENT DUE
    12/19/94  APPELLANT'S BRF DUE/NO TR CT RECORD
    01/13/95  LOWER COURT RECORD RECEIVED
              12/05/93  LOWER COURT RECORD DUE
              RECORD IN 1 PART, 2 TRANSCRIPTS & 1 EXHIBIT
              (SMALL ENVELOPE)
    02/01/95  PRAECIPE FOR DISCONTINUANCE       001T
```

A letter about my appeal

In any case, the South Carolina embarrassment pushed the DA to be resourceful and start misusing the law to his advantage once again. By saying that I had failed to appear for a criminal trial, he set the tone for my treatment, even by the South Carolina authorities, as harsh and unforgiving. A criminal trial, a criminal charge, was an entirely different matter.

The South Carolina Attorney General's Office received a letter from the Pennsylvania governor, which was particularly ominous in nature. It identified me as a "fugitive from justice," set to be extradited and dealt with in Pennsylvania "according to the law."

Among the many issues this document raised for me and my family was the lack of an extradition hearing to coincide with it. The document was put into effect almost six months before an actual extradition hearing that questioned Pennsylvania's authority to transport me across state lines. There was no opportunity for a judge to review the request and weigh it against the overall validity and strength of any case against me.

The Pennsylvania authorities were on an interstate roll, applying any and all pressure they could to threaten me and make my life extremely complicated.

For instance, a letter was sent to my parents' home addressed to me from the Department of Transportation in Harrisburg, Pennsylvania, from the Bureau of Driver Licensing. According to the letter, as a result of my conviction on reckless driving, my driving privilege was being suspended for a period of six months.

The same letter also ordered me to surrender my Pennsylvania driver's license, which I did not even have. I had always maintained a New York State driver's license because that had, for the most part, been my state of residence.

Besides all that, the reckless driving charge had been dropped at the preliminary hearing for my case by Judge William Sandringham at his court back in 1993. I had no idea that the charge had been reinstated and that I had been convicted of it.

```
COMMONWEALTH OF PENNSYLVANIA
DEPARTMENT OF TRANSPORTATION
Bureau of Driver Licensing
Harrisburg, PA  17123
NOVEMBER 13, 1998

JOSEPH C WAIKSNIS                    9831061160118l0 001
                                     11/06/1998
                                     24166764
```

Dear Motorist:

As a result of your conviction on 04/20/1998 of violating Section 3736 of the Vehicle Code, RECKLESS DRIVING on
03/09/1993, your driving privilege is being SUSPENDED for a
period of 6 MONTH(S) as mandated by Section 1532B of the
Vehicle Code.

In order to comply with this sanction, complete the enclosed
DL-16LC Form(Acknowledgment of Suspension/ Revocation/ Dis-
qualification) or a letter acknowledging the sanction of
your driving privilege.

Credit will not begin until the DL-16LC Form is received by
this Bureau.

WHEN THE DEPARTMENT RECEIVES YOUR FORM, WE WILL SEND YOU A
RECEIPT. IF YOU DO NOT RECEIVE THIS RECEIPT WITHIN 15 DAYS,
CONTACT THE DEPARTMENT IMMEDIATELY. OTHERWISE, YOU WILL NOT
BE GIVEN CREDIT TOWARD SERVING THIS SANCTION.

The effective date of suspension is 11/13/1998, 12:01 a.m.

The above mentioned sanction is in addition to any previously issued sanction(s).

You will be notified of any outstanding restoration requirements approximately 30 days before the eligibility date
of the restoration of your driving privilege. You must
follow those instructions very carefully in order to have
your driving privilege restored.

The dizzying merry-go-round began again, though I did have one bittersweet victory; not long after my arrest in South Carolina, I had received a phone call from Pennsylvania one morning. It was my neighbor, Richard, who had always been sympathetic to me. He told me Robert Frist was on my property with other people, and that he was removing my grandfather's antique cars from the barn and loading them onto a flatbed truck. A car pulled up in front of my driveway, and a person got out and yelled at the people who were removing the items out of the barn that I didn't own the house, that my wife owned it. That's because in 1993, after I was held captive in the fire house basement, knowing the police would do anything to get my grandfather's property, I had hired an attorney in another county and put the deed of the house in Dawn's name; I'm guessing nobody had picked up on it until now. Yet someone was standing up for my rights, even when I wasn't there.

It wasn't hard for me to figure out whom was behind the raid on my grandfather's property and my home state definitely played a role in it. Two weeks prior; I received a 65,000 dollar money judgment in the mail from New York. Examining the document, we noticed it looked just like the documents that came out of Pennsylvania, forged. This illegal, fabricated money judgment was about what the house was worth at the time, so I figured they used that judgment amount to make it look legal when they tried to confiscate the property. But it failed; this created a new problem for me over the years because the judgment didn't go away, simply opening a new front in my personal war.

ORDERED that judgment be entered in favor of the Suffolk County Department of Social Services at P.O. Box 15630, Hauppauge, NY 11788-5630, against JOSEPH MAIENNIS in the amount of $65250.00 together with costs and disbursements in the amount of $10.00, for a total sum of $65260.00. (interest will accrue at the prevailing rate of interest on judgments as provided in the Civil Practice Law and Rules).

Dated: **NOV 17 1998**

ENTER

[signature]

PETER _____, ESQ.
Hearing Examiner

ENTERED

[signature] M. O_____.

CLERK OF FAMILY COURT
DATE: **NOV 17 1998**
BY: _____

DISTRIBUTION:
PETA: _____ M. _____
ATTY:
RESP: JOSEPH MAIENNIS
ATTY:

SUPPORT COLLECTION UNIT

Judgment for 65,000 dollars

CHAPTER SIXTEEN

It had been almost four months since I had been arrested at our home in South Carolina, and the mounting legal difficulties were swirling all around me. I had heard nothing from the court or my attorney, though, so I hoped that the problems had died down a bit after all the hysteria.

One morning, on a day that had started without incident, I heard a knock at the door. It was the delivery of a certified letter addressed to me. It was from the governor's office of South Carolina, at the request of Governor Malden. It noted that a hearing into the "above captioned matter," Pennsylvania V. Joseph Waiksnis (Extradition), had been scheduled in Room 149 of the Attorney General's Office, Friday, December 4, 1998 at 9:30 a.m. I was told that I was, of course, expected to attend.

My heart started racing again. I picked up the phone and called Morrow, and he said he had received the same letter from the governor's office. He told me, "You'd better go."

I couldn't believe what I was hearing. I went back and forth with Morrow, questioning him about the matter.

I told him, "You know why this DA is coming after me; he's afraid he's going to be investigated for covering up what those cops did to me. You have copies of my paper work. Call the governor's office and explain to them what you told the judge. How hard is that?"

Morrow could hear how upset I was by the tone of my voice. I said further that I was going to be contacting the Attorney General's Office in Washington, D.C. Morrow said, "I'll see what I can do."

I felt confident after we hung up, knowing that this was not Pennsylvania, and I seemed to have a better shot at justice here. My attorney was paid well to represent me and do a good job. My stepfather had paid a total of roughly $30,000 from his retirement fund to allow me to go on fighting; I hoped this would be the end of it.

I heard nothing from the governor's office or from my attorney. The holidays came and went without incident. It was now 1999.

That spring, while talking with my mother on the phone, I noticed she didn't sound well. She sounded congested, so I asked her if she was feeling all right. She said she felt like she was coming down with something, she was so tired and worn out from all the stress the DA in Pennsylvania was putting us through and all the red tape and run-around she was getting as she tried to open up an investigation.

"Nothing seems to be working in our favor," she concluded.

Feeling bad at hearing my mother sound like this, I tried to bring her spirits up by saying, "This is the United States of America. I do have rights, and our South Carolina attorney is trying to defend them. Remember the ruling of the judge here in South Carolina; she even apologized to me for my trouble and sent me off a free man. Don't worry. It's just a matter of time before someone gets involved and helps us out. Dawn and I have written letters to put an end to this madness. It can't last forever."

To give her something to look forward to, I mentioned that Dawn was due for some leave, and then the three of us—Dawn, myself, and our son—would fly to New York for a wonderful family visit. I encouraged her to feel better and to look forward to good times together.

So much of our lives had been taken up by the struggle to demonstrate my innocence and the fight to keep me out of prison for a crime I didn't commit. I was looking forward to the New York trip. As a family we very much needed a break and some relief from this situation that was always hanging over our heads. This was about to happen—or so I thought.

As far as I knew, there were no restrictions on my travel, and there were no other court appearances that I was required to make. Judge Sheila Meritt in South Carolina had told me I was a free man, one who had been treated unfairly by the court system. I thought that about summed it up, and that my legal troubles were drawing to a close.

In the following days, while sifting through the daily mail, I came upon a letter addressed to me from the State of South Carolina, Office of the Attorney General. It wasn't certified this time, so I figured it must not be that important. I thought it was just a letter saying that the matter was closed.

I opened the letter and was horrified once again; it was the same type of letter I had received last year, another extradition hearing due to an attempt to get me back into Pennsylvania. A new hearing had been scheduled for Thursday, April 8, 1999 at 10:30 a.m., in a different room this time, but with the same expectation: "Mr. Waiksnis is, of course, expected to attend."

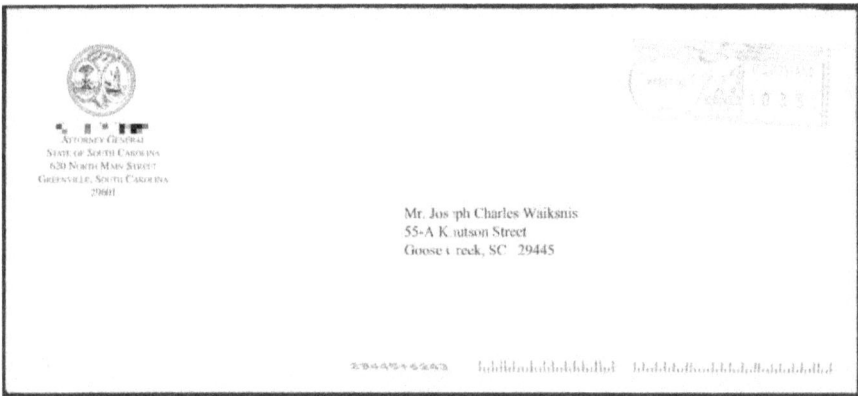

ATTORNEY GENERAL
STATE OF SOUTH CAROLINA
620 NORTH MAIN STREET
GREENVILLE, SOUTH CAROLINA
29601

Mr. Joseph Charles Waiksnis
55-A Knutson Street
Goose Creek, SC 29445

ATTORNEY GENERAL

March 24, 1999

North Charleston, SC 29406-6096

Re: Pennsylvania v. Joseph Charles Waiksnis a/k/a Joseph Waiksnis a/k/a Joseph Waikenis
     Extradition

Dear Mr. ▮:

This will confirm that a hearing has been scheduled in the above matter for Thursday, April 8, 1999, at 10:30 a.m., Room 516, Rembert C. Dennis Building, 1000 Assembly Street, Columbia, SC. Mr. Waiksnis is, of course, expected to attend.

Upon arrival, please go to Room 501 and have the receptionist notify me that you are here.

If you have any questions, please call me at (803) 734-3710.

Sincerely,

Legal Assistant

/rho

cc: Mr. Joseph Charles Waiksnis
     Mr. ▮
     Detective ▮

What the hell is going on here, I wondered. Why doesn't Morrow take care of these things? Why is this so contradictory to what a South Carolina judge had ruled? Why did I have to keep going through this? I called Morrow once again, but this time he was out of town, and his receptionist didn't know when he would be back. I left a message for him to get back to me as soon as possible.

I tried to stay calm. I didn't want my family to be any more upset than they already were. I broke the news to Dawn gently after she came home. She started to cry. I reassured her that it was all just a big mistake; I was sure my attorney would straighten it out; it was probably just an oversight. I asked her not to say anything to my mother, as she was in bad enough shape as it was. Since my attorney was out of town, I had Dawn write a letter on my behalf, and we faxed it to Morrow's office from our apartment.

The following morning there were several knocks on the door. I refused to open it for anyone, keeping quiet in the bedroom with my son. Later on, I heard the phone ring, and our fax machine stated to print out a fax. It was from William Morrow. He said he had received Dawn's fax, and he was responding to explain why I had received another letter from the South Carolina Attorney General's Office. He said I needed to understand that this was an extradition hearing, not a court hearing. It was an administrative hearing held by the South Carolina Attorney General's Office to determine three things: number one, whether this was me, whether I was convicted, and whether I was under the jurisdiction of South Carolina. After the hearing, he told me, the South Carolina Attorney General would make a recommendation to our governor as to whether to extradite me to Pennsylvania or not.

Morrow's letter continued, saying that I was not notified of a hearing date before this because the Attorney General's Office, knowing that Morrow was my attorney here in South Carolina, had tried to set up a hearing with me probably two dozen times, but I had been unavailable.

He went on to say that it was too bad my answering machine wasn't working, and he was sorry, but he had had to send a strange man to our home. He also said that he had been unable to reach me by telephone and that I had not kept in in touch with him as most of his clients normally did.

The second fax page went on to say that he had been in touch with my former attorney in Pennsylvania, and that he needed to go over things with me before the hearing, but again, if I couldn't come, I couldn't come. He said that earlier in the letter too.

Then Morrow went on to say that if we lost the administrative hearing in Columbia, I would be arrested and put in jail in South Carolina, and South Carolina would then notify the Pennsylvania authorities and I would be placed in chains and taken back to PA. There would be no bond hearing. Then he asked me to tell him, please, what I wanted him to do.

I couldn't believe what Morrow was saying in his fax. He was making it sound like it was all my fault. To my knowledge, there was nothing wrong with our answering machine, and, in fact, I had been trying to reach him at his office only to be told that he was unavailable and out of town. That was why I had sent the fax in the first place – to try to get in contact with him. At that point I felt as if something was up with all of this. I didn't trust anything Morrow was telling us anymore. I felt like I was being set up again.

The only reason I could think of as to why my attorney and South Carolina were setting me up was because I was trying to open up an investigation. The arrest in South Carolina had been illegal, and South Carolina was going to follow in Pennsylvania's footsteps and try to cover it up. I remembered Morrow saying to me after I was released from jail that we could have one hell of a lawsuit if we wanted to. That was the only sane reason I could come up with for these new events: my rights had been violated and no one wanted anyone to know.

From all I was learning about extraditions, they hardly applied to a misdemeanor DUI charge. I would have had to commit a felony of some sort, like a robbery or murder. You hear about such things on the news; extraditions are dramatic events for serious crimes. No governor extradites a person for a misdemeanor. It's unheard of.

After talking to Dawn about it, she agreed that it would be best for me to lie low, out of sight, making believe I was out of town on a fishing trip or whatever. We decided we would only communicate with the outside world via letters and faxes. This way we would have a record of what my attorney and the South Carolina Attorney General's Office were trying to do to me and catch them in the act.

My plan went into full swing. I lay low, and Dawn did all the communication through letters and faxes to Morrow's office, telling him there was nothing wrong with our answering machine, and asking all kinds of questions about this hearing. The responses we got back from him were always the same. He was now leaving messages on our answering machine: "I need to talk to Joe."

On April 5th, I received a letter in the mail from Morrow. "Dear Joseph and Dawn, writing letters and sending them by fax is not appropriate. I need to talk to Joe. Joe is out on bond, which may mean additional criminal charges could be brought if he fails to appear."

He went on to say that if I did not go to the hearing on Thursday, he was confident it would be lost. At the same time, he said, he had serious concerns as to whether it could be won even with me there.

Thinking about what I had just read, it sounded to me like no matter what I did, I was not going to win and I would be extradited back to Pennsylvania. The letter went on to say: "What will happen next? Unless I hear from Joe, person to person, I have no choice but to deduct the time I've spent thus far and refund the balance of the funds."

Dawn and I had no idea I was out on bond. How could I be on bond when Judge Meritt had set me free, saying she was sorry?

Once again, I dictated to Dawn another letter to Morrow, asking him about his letter and the extradition hearing he so desperately wanted me to go to. Then we faxed it to him.

It didn't take long to get a response. The following day our fax machine hummed with the reception of several pages from Morrow. He explained that the reason for the hearing was because I was sentenced in Pennsylvania to one and a half years in prison. He said that was what the sentencing report from the District Attorney's Office said. Under federal extradition guidelines, this would fall within the rules.

This was the first time I had seen any sentencing document. Yet sure enough, among the seven pages of bullshit, it read: "The defendant is committed to the County Jail for a minimum period of thirty days, a maximum period of eighteen months."

```
 1  read as follows.  And now, September 27, 1993, the
 2  defendant Joseph Waiksnis, having been convicted at
 3  jury trial on July 7, 1993, is sentenced as follows:
 4  Count 1, the defendant is committed to the Tioga County
 5  Jail for a minimum period of thirty days, a maximum
 6  period of eighteen months.  A fine in the amount of
 7  $750.00 and costs of prosecution are hereby imposed.
 8  The defendant shall pay a supervision fee of $35.00 per
 9  month and pay an administrative fee of $20.00 per month
10  for each month that he is under the supervision of the
11  Tioga County Probation Department.  The defendant's
12  driving license and privileges are hereby suspended for
13  a period of one year.  The defendant shall be subject
14  to the provisions of Act 122 regarding drug and alcohol
15  abuse and pay any fees related thereto.  And the
16  defendant shall be subject to such special conditions
17  of probation regarding drug and alcohol abuse that the
18  probation office may impose.
19          Now, Mr. Waiksnis, you've heard the sentence
20  the court has just imposed.  We had a jury trial, you
21  were found guilty, and your post-verdict motions have
22  already been denied.  You would have the right now to
23  file a written motion to modify this sentence just
24  imposed if you do so in writing within ten days from
25  today.  If you fail to file such a motion or if you
```

When I got to the last page, the only real signature was that of court stenographer, Arianna Tupper. There was no real signature of Judge Early but another rubber stamp in bold letters.

```
 1

 2

 3        I hereby certify that the proceedings and evidence

 4   are contained fully and accurately in the notes taken

 5   by me on the hearing of the above entitled cause and

 6   that this copy is a correct transcript of the same.

 7

 8

 9        _____

10                  Court Stenographer

11

12

13

14

15        The foregoing record of the proceedings upon the

16   hearing in the  above entitled cause is hereby approved

17   and directed to be filed.

18

19

20        S/ R_____, Jr.
          _____

21        Hon. _____, Jr.

22        President Judge

23

24

25
```

Can't these people see this is not a legal document? I wondered.

To make matters worse Dawn and I started to argue over this; she was yelling and crying, "Haven't these people done enough damage to this family? When is it going to stop?" Holding her in my arms, I was at a loss for words.

I had no choice but to call home and explain to my mother what was going on in South Carolina. The news back home wasn't good either; my mother was getting over a cold and now my grandmother had become ill as well. Mother was having a hard time running back and forth to her apartment to take care of Grandma, and she needed some help.

"Why don't you tell your attorney you have to fly back to New York to help out your 85-year-old grandmother? I bet that would give him something to think about," my mother said.

I thought that might be a good thing. While I was there, I could take a train to New York and try to hook up with one of the big media networks, explaining my story while showing them the documents.

"That sounds like a plan," my mother said. I told her I would talk to Dawn about it and get back to her.

When I spoke to Dawn about going back to New York and what I was going to do while there, she got scared. She was still crying, "What about the baby? He has well baby appointments coming up; he can't miss them."

I told her to talk to her superiors and explain that her husband had a family emergency and had to fly back to New York immediately.

"I'll make copies of the ticket for you to show them," I said. "This way you can stay home with the baby and take him to his appointments."

Holding my wife in my arms, I felt sure this whole mess would be straightened out before I came home. It simply couldn't go on forever.

Back in New York, my mother got involved with this so-called extradition hearing in Columbia, calling and writing letters to my attorney and the South Carolina Attorney General's office. She explained to them that the DA in Pennsylvania was covering up civil rights violations caused by the local police where we used to live.

"Can't you see the DA is falsifying documents by forging the judge's signature with a rubber stamp in bold letters? He's trying to get hold of my son before he can open up an investigation."

My mother's letter must have scared Morrow, because he bailed out by turning over my extradition hearing case to another attorney in Columbia without even consulting with me.

In an April 12, 1999 fax to me, Morrow said he had gone to Columbia to meet with Attorney Richard Borkowich. He said, as he had said before, that Attorney Borkovich was the only attorney in the state who could do me some good because he used to be the number two man in the South Carolina Attorney General's office.

Morrow went on to say that he had reviewed my file with Borkowich and had given him all the insight he had about my case. He wrote, "Richard tells me that there is a chance he can help you, but only if you show up in Columbia with him. Richard also told me to tell you two things. 1. If you do not show up at the hearing, there is no need to hold it. The judge will simply find against you and send the paperwork to the governor's office for extradition. 2. You need to call or fax Richard Borkowich."

Before I had time to think, the phone rang and our fax machine started to print. It was another letter from the Attorney General's Office in Columbia addressed to me and Richard Borkowich, confirming that an extradition hearing had been scheduled in the above matter for Thursday, April 15, 1999. Borkowich was now my attorney, whether I liked it or not.

Again, I was being set up. So often I had been promised that if I just showed up, an attorney would get the charges dismissed, get them reduced, get them taken care of. My mother felt the same suspicions. I finally just booked a flight to New York. Dawn drove me to the Charleston International Airport with our baby. During the whole drive, Dawn had tears in her eyes. I had my arm backwards, holding my son's little hand while he was sitting in his car seat. I couldn't believe it was coming down to this. I had a strong feeling the outcome in Columbia was not going to be good.

As soon as I landed at JFK, I called Dawn to make sure she and the baby had made it back safely and assured her that I would call back that night. My mother picked me up from the airport. In one way she was happy, because she was having a hard time taking care of everybody back home. On the other hand, we were all apprehensive about this South Carolina extradition hearing and what the results of that would be. As we headed back to Long Island, I went over everything that was happening down in South Carolina.

"Who's this new attorney, Borkowich?" my mother asked.

"I really have no idea," I answered. "I guess Morrow jumped ship after reading your letter. I know either way the outcome in Columbia is not going to be good unless I can get somebody like the media involved. That's one of the things I'm going to do while I'm back. I'm taking copies of the documents on a train to New York to meet with some big media networks to get them to investigate my story."

"What does the navy have to say about this?" my mother wanted to know.

I said that the folks Dawn worked with in the Navy Department couldn't believe it either and had said it sounded like a personal war between the DA and me.

At the time, my grandmother was staying at my mother's house because of her condition. It was good to see her, and she was happy as well. Later that night I spoke to Dawn. All was quiet until the following day when Dawn received a fax. It was just a fax cover sheet to me from Richard Borkowich with some phone numbers on it, hinting for me to call him.

It was now April 20th, and as far as I knew the extradition hearing had been held without my presence. My mother then wrote a letter to Morrow demanding to know what the outcome of the hearing was and about the retainer fee that was owed us. She faxed this letter to his office.

The following day Morrow responded back with a fax, stating:

"In response to your April 20th letter asking 'WHAT IS THE OUTCOME?' enclosed is the letter and warrant I just received.

"In response to your question 'CAN JOSEPH AND DAWN AND KELVIN LIVE IN SOUTH CAROLINA?' The answer is Dawn and Kelvin can; if Joseph comes into South Carolina, he will be arrested and held for a representative from Pennsylvania to pick him up.

"As for the next two paragraphs, I have nothing to respond to.

"As for answers and copies of documentation, these have been provided.

"As for 'PUSH FOR MEGA MEDIA ATTENTION,' nothing, it seems, has worked in Joseph's favor thus far. Good luck."

Enclosed was a copy of a letter to Detective Matthew Heraldo from the governor's office dated April 16th:

"Dear Detective Heraldo:

"An extradition hearing regarding the above captioned matter was conducted by the South Carolina Attorney General's Office. As a result of that hearing the recommendation was made, and Governor Malden has concurred, to honor the extradition request of the State of Pennsylvania for the return of Joseph Charles Waiksnis.

"Accordingly, enclosed are the original and one copy of Governor Malden's rendition warrant and the agents' commission from the State of Pennsylvania which authorizes you to deliver the subject to the agent(s) named therein. Please notify the District Attorney when the subject is available for release. Thank you for your continued cooperation and assistance.

"Sincerely,

"Extradition Assistance."

I recognized the name of the detective; he was the one who had arrested me and driven me to jail, only to pick me up the following day to be released.

The next page was from the Commonwealth of Pennsylvania Governor's Office, saying: "KNOW YE, That I have authorized and empowered and by these Presents do authorized and empower TRANSCOR AMERICA, INC. to take and receive from the proper authorities of the State of South Carolina, JOSEPH CHARLES WAIKSNIS aka JOSEPH WAIKSNIS, a fugitive from justice, and convey him to the Commonwealth of Pennsylvania, there to be dealt with according to Law. Given under my hand and the Great Seal of the State, at the City of Harrisburg, this 19th day of October in the year of our Lord one thousand nine hundred and ninety-eight. Thomas Rogers, Governor of Pennsylvania."

Commonwealth of Pennsylvania

GOVERNOR'S OFFICE

THE GOVERNOR OF THE COMMONWEALTH OF PENNSYLVANIA

TO ALL TO WHOM THESE PRESENTS SHALL COME:

KNOW YE, That I have authorized and empowered and by these Presents do authorize and empower

TRANSCOR AMERICA, INC.,

to take and receive from the proper authorities of the State of South Carolina,

JOSEPH CHARLES WAIKSNIS aka JOSEPH WAIKSNIS, JOSEPH WAIKENIS,

a fugitive from justice and convey him to the Commonwealth of Pennsylvania, there to be dealt with according to Law.

GIVEN under my hand and the Great Seal of the State, at the City of Harrisburg, this __19th__ day of __october__ in the year of our Lord one thousand nine hundred and ninety-eight.

_____
Governor of Pennsylvania

By the Governor:

_____
Deputy Secretary of the Commonwealth

I couldn't believe what I was reading. Examining the document, it did have a real signature on it, unlike the rubber-stamp-in-bold-letters documents I had from Judge Early. It also had a big black state seal with serrated edges, but I couldn't make out any markings on it at all; it was solid black. I had never seen a governor's warrant until now, and it looked terrifyingly real to me.

The next and last page were from the Executive Department, State of South Carolina, saying: "The Governor of the State of South Carolina, Jim Malden, To Any Sheriff or Other Officer of the State of South Carolina to Whom these Present Shall Come, GREETINGS.

"WHEREAS, a requisition has been received from His Excellency the Governor the State of Pennsylvania for the rendition of JOSEPH CHARLES WAIKSNIS, aka JOSEPH WAIKSNIS who stands convicted of or charged with the crime(s) of Driving Under the Influence of Alcohol or Controlled Substance, Failure to Appear, Violation of Probation, and Failure to Report to County Prison for Commencement of Sentence in said state and who had Fled therefrom and taken refuge in the State of South Carolina.

"NOW THEREFORE, I, JIM MALDEN, Governor of the State of South Carolina, do hereby command that the said fugitive be delivered to Transcor America, Inc.

"IN WITNESS WHEREOF, I have hereunto signed my hand, and caused the seal of the Executive Department to be affixed, at Columba, this 16th day of April in the year of our Lord One Thousand Nine Hundred and Ninety-Nine and in the Two Hundred Twenty-Second year of American Independence, Jim Malden, Governor of South Carolina."

Examining the South Carolina document, it all looked real to me. There was Jim Malden's signature signed in script. The only thing was, unlike the solid black seal of Pennsylvania that stuck right out, there was no seal. The space on the document where it should have been was blank on the document, all white. The only thing I could think was that this seal was not a sticker like the Pennsylvania one but one that was pressed into the page itself.

Executive Department

State of South Carolina

The Governor of the State of South Carolina

To Any Sheriff or Other Officer of the State of South Carolina to Whom these Presents Shall Come, GREETINGS

WHEREAS, a requisition has been received from His Excellency the Governor of the State of Pennsylvania for the rendition of Joseph Charles Walkonis aka Joseph Walkonis aka Joseph Walkonis who stands convicted of or charged with the crime(s) of Driving Under the Influence of Alcohol or Controlled Substance, Failure to Appear, Violation of Probation, and Failure to Report to Tioga County Prison for Commencement of Sentence in said state, and who had fled therefrom and taken refuge in the State of South Carolina.

NOW THEREFORE, I, ⋮⋮⋮ ⋮⋮⋮⋮⋮ Governor of the State of South Carolina, do hereby command that the said fugitive be delivered to Transcor America, Inc. who is authorized to receive and carry Joseph Charles Walkonis aka Joseph Walkonis aka Joseph Walkonis to the State of Pennsylvania for trial, in accordance with the laws in such case made and provided.

IN WITNESS WHEREOF, I have hereunto signed my hand, and caused the seal of the Executive Department to be affixed, at Columbia, this 16th day of April, in the year of our Lord One Thousand Nine Hundred and Ninety-Nine and in the Two Hundred Twenty-Second year of our American Independence.

_____
Governor of South Carolina

_____
By the Governor's Chief Legal Counsel

Thinking about what I had just read, I realized it had to be true. I was extradited out of South Carolina. That meant I was stuck in New York; I couldn't go back home to my wife and child.

I had to sit down, feeling the cold sweat run down my face. I was feeling dizzy and confused. First, I was run out of my grandfather's home in Pennsylvania; now I couldn't go back to my family in South Carolina.

My mother didn't waste any time contacting Morrow, sending faxes and demanding answers. It took several days for him to get a response back to us. This is what Morrow had to say in his one and only response addressed to my mother:

"Dear Mrs. Snyder:

"You really have a misconception about 'the system.' Nobody convinced Governor Malden to do anything.

"Bureaucracy runs itself. Some clerk in the Pennsylvania governor's office got the paperwork from some bureaucrat in the Pennsylvania Attorney General's Office and sent it to his person of like station in life in the South Carolina Governor's office. That person filled out a form, stamped Governor Malden's signature to it and sent it to the appropriate police department. The officer arrested Joseph, Dawn called me, I got in touch with a judge, she set a bond hearing; Joseph got out of jail, the 'warrant' was held in abeyance because Joseph did not sign a waiver to be extradited; South Carolina law dictates that the governor's designee (in this case an assistant attorney general who handles these types of paperwork problems) held a 'hearing' that Joseph did not show up for; he sent his 'recommendation' to the clerk in Governor Malden's office, who got a pre-signed form off the shelf and filled in Joseph's name and sent it to the police department to pick Joseph up.

"Very truly yours, William Morrow."

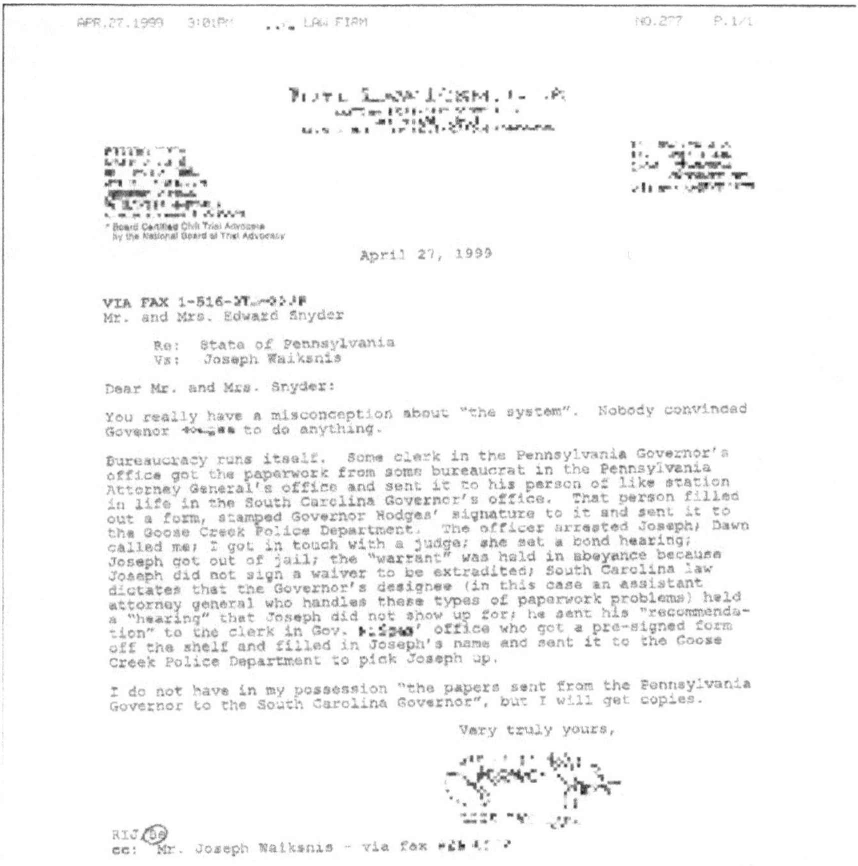
APR.27.1999 3:01PM [illegible] LAW FIRM NO.277 P.1/1

[illegible]

* Board Certified Civil Trial Advocate
by the National Board of Trial Advocacy

April 27, 1999

VIA FAX 1-516-[illegible]
Mr. and Mrs. Edward Snyder

Re: State of Pennsylvania
Vs: Joseph Waiksnis

Dear Mr. and Mrs. Snyder:

You really have a misconception about "the system". Nobody convinced Govenor [illegible] to do anything.

Bureaucracy runs itself. Some clerk in the Pennsylvania Governor's office got the paperwork from some bureaucrat in the Pennsylvania Attorney General's office and sent it to his person of like station in life in the South Carolina Governor's office. That person filled out a form, stamped Governor Hodges' signature to it and sent it to the Goose Creek Police Department. The officer arrested Joseph; Dawn called me; I got in touch with a judge; she set a bond hearing; Joseph got out of jail; the "warrant" was held in abeyance because Joseph did not sign a waiver to be extradited; South Carolina law dictates that the Governor's designee (in this case an assistant attorney general who handles these types of paperwork problems) held a "hearing" that Joseph did not show up for; he sent his "recommendation" to the clerk in Gov. [illegible]' office who got a pre-signed form off the shelf and filled in Joseph's name and sent it to the Goose Creek Police Department to pick Joseph up.

I do not have in my possession "the papers sent from the Pennsylvania Governor to the South Carolina Governor", but I will get copies.

Very truly yours,

[illegible]

RIJ/bs
cc: Mr. Joseph Waiksnis - via fax [illegible]

It seems the presiding judge had little choice but to grant the extradition request. The South Carolina authorities were embarrassed and apparently exhausted insofar as they had stood up to the might of Pennsylvania and won a small victory for me. When the second round commenced, South Carolina decided to go down for the count. The governor himself agreed to honor the extradition request, extraditing me to Pennsylvania and authorizing whatever means necessary to achieve this end.

Even though I was the full-time caregiver to my son, even though my wife was serving in the navy in South Carolina and our lives were there, I could not reenter the state, because I would be arrested and sent back to Pennsylvania in chains.

With my son at our naval base apartment

Thus, what was supposed to be a family visit designed to help my mother quickly turned into yet another nightmare for my family and me. Suddenly, I could not go home. It was as simple as that. I was denied the freedom to live with my wife and son in our home. My only choice, it seemed, was to remain in New York, in my parents' home, until some legal remedy could be arrived at.

CHAPTER SEVENTEEN

On the night of May 20th 1999, a few minutes after 11 p.m., the phone rang. I had just settled down to watch the night time news, having become accustomed to late nights as a parent and homemaker husband. When I answered the phone, though, I was stunned to hear my wife on the other end, crying and screaming in a state of absolute panic.

South Carolinian FBI agents and police had gone to the naval base where my wife worked and lived. In the middle of the night, while she and my son, alone in the house, were fast asleep, the FBI and police demanded that the Base Security unlock our front door. The request was granted, and a storm of officers entered our home, terrorizing my wife, who had been asleep in bed. These men ransacked our upstairs apartment without my wife's permission, threatening her and flashing a stark light in her face.

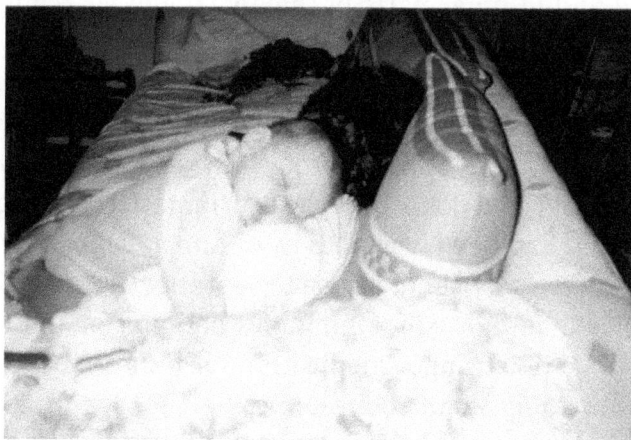

**Dawn and baby peacefully asleep
in our naval base apartment**

Groggy from sleep and the antidepressant medication she was taking, largely as a result of the stress brought on by my continued legal struggles, Dawn was terrified as these men went through all of our belongings in spite of her insisting that I wasn't there.

There had been a build-up to the invasion of our home. These are the messages, word for word, left on our answering machine prior to the incident.

Thursday 10:49 p.m.

Web Base security. Give me a call at 437-7290

Thursday 10:56 p.m.

Dawn, we need you to pick up the phone. This is Detective Heraldo from the police department. We are outside. I need you to go ahead and come out and have Charles come out also. If you do not come out, we will be coming in, and you will be charged and also the child will be going to DSS. You need to be coming out right now. Pick up the phone, Dawn. We know you're in there; we can hear you.

Thursday 11:12 p.m.

Charles, pick up the phone.

On the phone, even in her state of panic, Dawn was very groggy from sleep and depression pills, crying to me that there were several men in our bedroom and that they had frightened her and made threats to her regarding my whereabouts. There were people in the hall and in other parts of the apartment searching for me, even going up into the attic space. Dawn advised them I was not in South Carolina, and told them to contact my attorney, Mr. Morrow, whereupon she was informed, "He don't have a lawyer!"

After threats and searching, they left, but it was not the end of the damage they had done. Dawn was traumatized. Because of the attention that had been drawn to us on the naval base where she worked, Dawn also lost her security clearance. Apparently, my legal troubles made her something of a liability for the navy. She also had to go on stronger medication for depression, due to the trauma of that night raid of our home.

It truly was a raid, as we confirmed later by talking to our neighbors. Our downstairs neighbors, Ben and Jessica Berenger, told me that they had heard noises outside and, when they turned on the outside light, they were startled by the armed men surrounding the residence. More alarming still was the fact that they were carrying automatic weapons and wearing vests marked FBI. It was apparently a joint effort between the local police department and the FBI to accommodate Pennsylvania and capture me, an alleged fugitive from justice, who, at least officially, was never actually arrested that night long ago in Oliverville.

Our neighbors had also spotted surveillance trucks parked across the street from our house every day for a week prior to the raid. Since they must have seen the comings and goings from the house, realizing that I most probably wasn't there, it begs the question why they would conduct such a raid at all. Another question I have asked myself over and over, posing it to a few officials, too, is how on earth the FBI got roped into such a fiasco.

The facts of the matter did not really matter in any case. We knew that, as did my family back in New York. We had also been split up by this last attack and were reeling from that. Dawn, losing her security clearance at work, had also lost me at home. Our son had lost his full-time caregiver parent, and was also suddenly denied the support therapies that he had been receiving while on the base and under my care.

Anyone with an exceptional child knows how demanding it can be, how much time it requires. I was not only my son's primary caregiver but the one who could facilitate his therapies, taking him to appointments and evaluations while my wife was working. Without me at home, it became impossible to get Kelvin the support he needed. It wasn't long before Dawn felt she had no choice but to fly with our son to New York so that I could care for him, or, in the meantime, he could stay with my parents or hers.

No matter how busy
I may be

I'm always thinking
loving thoughts of you.

Please do
whatever it takes
to get home soon.
We miss you;
need you here
Love,
Dawn;
Kelvin

My family needed me at home

As if things were not bad enough, Kelvin also lost his Medicaid coverage and benefits because of the disruption. Although he could regain them if we applied to pick them up in New York, the disruption was another problem to add to the list. To this day, though, Kelvin is in my custody while Dawn continued to pursue her naval career. Perhaps the most wrenching problem we experienced as a family was this forced separation; first my removal from the home, and then my son's. I wonder still what would have happened to us, if we would've been able to stay together as a family, if we had not been so forcibly ripped apart by these events.

**Our last Christmas together as a normal family on base.
In spite of her smile, my wife was undergoing
a lot of stress and strain**

Money was also a tremendous concern for me. Because of the severity of the situation we now faced, things were worse still than anything we had experienced yet. We seemed to learn over and over that you can always sink lower.

Having settled as much as I could back into my parents' home, my first order of business was to identify a competent and honest attorney to take on my case back in Pennsylvania and now also in South Carolina.

After much back and forth discussion, I met with representatives of the law firm of Rosen and Weatherall, based in Philadelphia. We obtained their information from the Philadelphia bar association, having advised the bar just what kind of attorneys I needed and the kind of law firm necessary to handle my case.

Meeting face to face with my new attorneys was a challenge because I was not able to enter the state of Pennsylvania without risking arrest. The meeting was scheduled to take place in a conference room at a hotel in New Jersey and resulted in Rosen and Weatherall formally agreeing to represent me. A crucial part of what I needed, though, was protection from the system; protection of my rights in a system that was so decidedly corrupt. Investigating the DA's charges and the sentencing was also an important step. It was going to be necessary to examine the validity of various documents.

Laying out our needs, we also discussed that there was information to obtain from the Department of Transportation in Harrisburg to determine just who had issued me a Pennsylvania driver's license and when, since I had never applied for one. There was also the conviction for reckless driving with the mandatory suspension of this fictional Pennsylvania license that I never had applied for, not to mention the fact that the reckless driving charge was dropped years ago.

To manage this sizeable amount of work, Rosen and Weatherall requested and were paid $1,000 in cash and some $19,000 produced as a bank check and made out to them. Thanks to my stepfather's retirement fund, I could at least come by this sort of money, but it was not easy, certainly not after nearly seven years of this battle. At the very least, we could not go on without the money actually buying us results.

To get things started, my new attorneys indicated that they planned to visit county officials in Pennsylvania by a certain date. The date came and went, however, and there was no visit.

No sooner had the ink dried on our contract with Rosen and Weatherall, however, than the fugitive detectives were at my parents' doors again, knocking on the front door after ten o'clock at night and demanding to "check in" with me. They were, after all, required, they said, to do a "once a year checkup" on the status of my case. My stepfather explained I was not home, since I was upstate visiting my wife's family. In any case, the detective presented no warrant or subpoena for my parents to inspect. He asked about the particulars of my representation, whether I had obtained a Pennsylvania attorney yet. It was a puzzling question with even more suspicious timing.

Alfred Rosen telephoned my parents, speaking to me, my mother, and my stepfather, all of us on separate telephones. He explained that, in fact, he had not gone to Pennsylvania but instead had talked on the phone with the DA, with whom he said he had a great rapport.

He also told me, per his conversation with the DA, that I had been resentenced, extending my sentence from 30 days to eighteen months while I was living in South Carolina. He also kept insisting that I should accompany him and turn myself in to the DA, as if that would magically resolve the situation. I would be put on work release, he insisted, and allowed to serve out my sentence, which could even be converted back to 30 days.

Rosen insisted that he could go to Pennsylvania the following week and suggested that it would be the perfect opportunity for me to accompany him per the plan he had outlined, setting events into motion that would, he said, result in a final end to my struggles. I found out later from the DA's chief detective that there had been a deal made between Rosen and the DA that insured no such safety and hope of freedom for me. Indeed, the deal Rosen negotiated was for his benefit only, and involved turning me over to the DA the moment I was in Pennsylvania. After paying Rosen and Weatherall some $20,000, we were advised in writing, shortly after the telephone conversation in which I was advised to return to Pennsylvania, that it would cost another $5,000 to get my eighteen-month sentence converted back to 30 days.

Law Offices

Philadelphia, Pa 19107-3603

November 24, 1999

Joseph Waiksnis
Mr. & Mrs. Edward Snyder
40 E. Half Hollow Road
Dix Hills, NY   11746

Re: Joseph C. Waiksnis

Dear Mr. Waiksnis & Snyder Family:

   Pursuant to your communication received November 18, which would have been responded to sooner but for the fact that I was in a serious motor vehicle accident, I hasten to reply.

   Immediately after our meeting, I carefully analyzed and reviewed all of the materials which you supplied, as did Mr. ▪▪▪.   We did this independently so that we could discuss the matter in multiple, alternative ways.   We found no reasonable basis within the testimony showing any actions which were out of the ordinary. Although they may not have been what occurred in another trial, with other judges and other witnesses, nothing that we saw had any merit in which a Federal habeas corpus action might be grounded.

   Subsequently, as you know, I made numerous phone calls and began to develop an amicable working relationship with the ▪▪▪ County District Attorney and the District Attorney detectives, in order to smooth the process in alleviating this unfortunate situation.   I had culled out time to make a trip and, in accordance with that, wanted to have communication with my clients regarding the availability of Joseph Waiksnis for purposes of carrying out his surrender without any additional prison time attaching.   This was the result of discussions with the powers that be in ▪▪▪ County and a

verification that the judge was amenable to not increasing the
sentence up to the potentials of 18 months but only the 30 days that
were originally imposed by the mandatory laws of Pennsylvania.

Additionally, I made inquiry with respect to the potentials of
work release, and that information was communicated to you as well.
Your response, of course, was negative, and you indicated that you
were now afraid the county jail would be a dangerous place for
service of the 30 days, although work release would mean merely
sleeping in the jail and remaining there for the 16 hours other than
the work time.

I made contact once again with the District Attorney and the
investigators, advising them of your concerns, and found that the
transfer to another institution for only a 30-day period would not be
possible.   I thereafter tried reaching you by fax and mailed
communication and finally, after at least 6 weeks, have received a
response in the form of your letter.

I have additionally made inquiry and, contrary to your beliefs,
the fugitive warrants are, in my opinion, lawful and have been signed
by the appropriate parties.   If you had re-contacted me and were
still absolutely convinced that there was some unlawful action, I had
intended to quickly go to Harrisburg and see the Attorney General's
Office, to formally notate the existence of the warrants.   However,
you did not contact me.   I have thus been unable to move further in
the direction of closing this matter, and it appears to me that I
can't help you unless you communicate with me and follow my
suggestions that you have retained me to provide.

At this point, it is my opinion that once Joseph is apprehended
he will be stiffly sentenced, and may well be looking at 18 months.

I await your advice.   I will return the balance of the fee upon
your direction, and advise the authorities I am no longer involved.

If you wish me to attempt to resurrect a 30-day incarceration, the fee will be an additional $5000, and I will return the balance of $10,000.

I still believe that a cause may lie against the authorities, and could advise you if that is a feasible direct after Joseph has completed the sentence.

Please advise me

CJF:net

I was informed it would cost an extra $5,000 to get my eighteen-month sentence converted back to 30 days.

The longer things were drawn out by this law firm, the less we trusted them. In the end, we could not help but feel convinced of their betrayal. They had sold us out in every sense. We suspect that they were paid off with greater concessions, crossing all manner of ethical lines.

Nothing got resolved. One day in 1999, my mother and step-father were out visiting my grandmother when county police officers crossed the 250-foot yard on my parents' property, knocking on the door and ringing the bell incessantly.

I was alone with my son that night and flatly refused to answer the door. I knew so much better by that point. I sat with my son and ignored the sounds, knowing that the men on the other side of the door could not present any court warrant or subpoena to me that might justify their behavior or give any credence to their actions at all—their fourth visit to the house.

At approximately 10:00 p.m., my mother and stepfather returned home and saw an unmarked vehicle parked in front of the house. They could see figures going through their curbside paper trash. So obvious was this invasion of their privacy that my parents rolled down their van window and asked what they were doing. Putting a flashlight in my parents' faces, almost blinding them with the glare as if it was the perfect show of authority, a detective flashed his ID badge, which identified him as the executive officer of the county fugitive section. He wasn't in the least timid. He not only looked through the paper trash, he looked through my parents' van with his flashlight, glaring through the windows.

The fugitive section was looking for Joseph Waiksnis, he said, and my mother explained that they couldn't take me to Pennsylvania because I was the full-time caregiver to my son.

"I don't care if you have one or fifteen grandchildren," Brown glared. "We are going to get your son."

Suddenly, a county police vehicle bumped the rear of my parents' van, blocking the driveway so there was no escape. Several uniformed police officers suddenly appeared, moving out from our home to the front where my parents' van was blocked. One of the officers ran from our residence to the front driveway, informing the head detective that there was movement detected within the house and my mother screamed out, "What do you want to do—shoot my son in the back?"

The detectives finally allowed my parents to move down their driveway toward their home. Then my parents got out of the van.

The chaos was manic, terrifying, as my mother cried out again, "Why do you keep coming here? Where are the warrants and what are the charges?"

My mother began to lose her temper, growing ever more fearful and disgusted by the behavior of the small army then surrounding her home.

"Go ahead and arrest me!" my mother was yelling, determined not to be intimidated by the array of detectives and officers. Another of the detectives found himself having to intervene, as my mother began to shout louder. He tried to calm the situation, insisting that they were all there because the Pennsylvania county district attorney "keeps bugging and bugging us to pick up your son." It was the only answer given but it was intended to suffice, to explain these numerous trespasses onto private property.

Before they left, the detectives also told my stepfather and my mother that I should "not leave the property." They insisted they would be back on Friday to collect me.

Although this follow-up meeting did not happen, my mother sent a fax to the county police commissioner, complaining formally about the trespassing and the overall handling of my case. She sent a copy of the fax by certified mail too, hoping that one way or another, the complaint would register.

CHAPTER EIGHTEEN

Despite the enormity of the fee we had paid Rosen and Weatherall, not a single investigative report was provided to us. The firm ignored all of our written letters and faxes requesting such information. We contacted Cameron Steward, who owned two private detective agencies, one in New Jersey and one in Pennsylvania. Steward was advised of our mistrust of the firm, Rosen and Weatherall. We filled him in on the details of my case, too, forwarding a good portion of the documentation.

After reviewing our case, Steward informed us that he could effectively obtain the information we wanted along with also investigating the degree to which Rosen and Weatherall had actually investigated the case on our behalf. It would take approximately two weeks, though, and require some $10,000 down for them to begin.

To reassure us after the negative experiences we had had recently, Steward forwarded me newspaper clippings of his casework to promote his services and close the deal. To do a good job, he insisted, the down payment was very necessary along with a signed contract, both of which we ultimately agreed to and went along with.

My stepfather had come up with the money, the $10,000 deposit, from his retirement savings to help me, and Steward said he would go to Pennsylvania to continue his investigations.

As soon as the deposit check cleared, we asked about the specific charges and asked about the validity of the documents that we had been presented with. We had also asked Steward to establish the charges from the attorney general's office in Harrisburg.

Of course, none of this happened. Instead, we received a letter from Steward with feeble excuses as to why he was keeping our deposit without actually producing any investigative results to justify the charges. Steward even got my first name wrong in his letters to me, the ones claiming I had not cooperated with him.

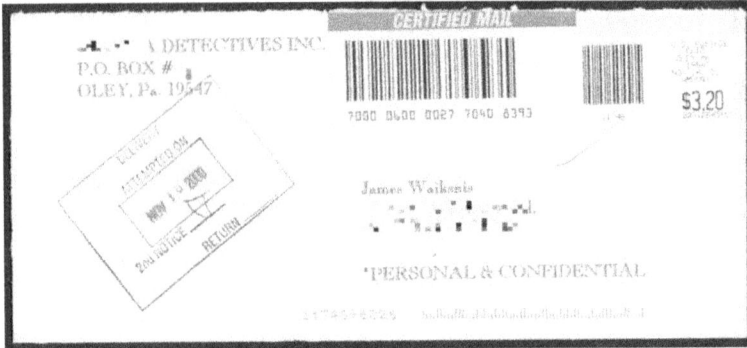

**Both the envelope and the letter
were addressed to the wrong first name.**

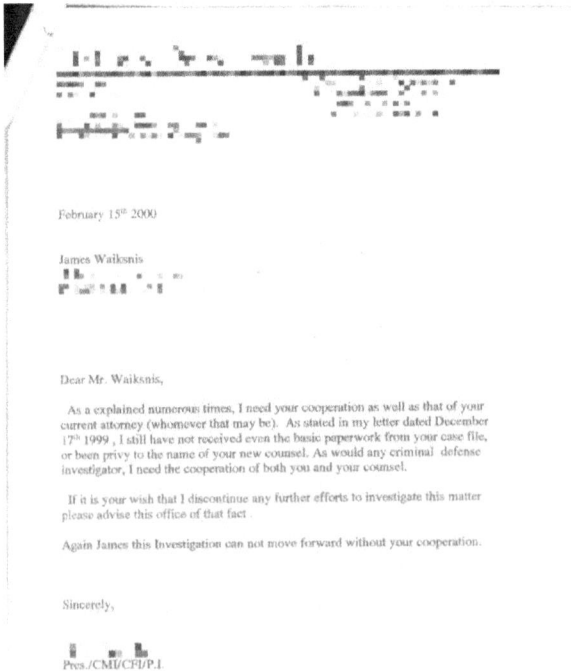

February 15th 2000

James Waiksnis

Dear Mr. Waiksnis,

As a explained numerous times, I need your cooperation as well as that of your current attorney (whomever that may be). As stated in my letter dated December 17th 1999 , I still have not received even the basic paperwork from your case file, or been privy to the name of your new counsel. As would any criminal defense investigator, I need the cooperation of both you and your counsel.

If it is your wish that I discontinue any further efforts to investigate this matter please advise this office of that fact .

Again James this Investigation can not move forward without your cooperation.

Sincerely,

Pres./CMI/CFI/P.I.

Short some $30,000, I contacted a new detective agency to try and get some perspective on everything. The Acme Detective Agency was advertised in the Philadelphia telephone directory, and we spoke to one of their investigators, Jim. We gave him specifics about my case and paid him by credit card to get things started.

His fee paid, a detective at the Acme Detective Agency contacted the Pennsylvania attorney general's office in Harrisburg and was told that, yes, there was a warrant out for Joseph Waiksnis. When the detective asked about the nature of the charges, though, he was told that they were "confidential." Jim insisted that it was actually public information under the Freedom of Information Act. He was told in no uncertain terms, though, that the information about the warrant and the charges that led to it were confidential and under lock and key.

In 27 years of dealing with investigations and warrants, Jim insisted, it was an absolute first. "They are hiding something mighty big!" Jim said. Rosen, Weatherall and Steward, for $30,000 between them, had not been able to come up even with this much insight into the case. It was quite clear to me that Rosen and Weatherall had been more focused on involving themselves in deals with Pennsylvania officials to get me to turn myself in. Of course, the system is based on people making deals—that's why it is called making a plea "bargain." Maybe they thought they were doing the best they could for me, given the system, but I felt that, at the very least, these people were robbing my stepfather of his hard-earned retirement money with their unsatisfactory results.

```
- - - - - - - - - - - - - - - - - - - - - - - - - - - - - - - -
| NATIONAL OUTSTANDING WARRANT SEARCH |
- - - - - - - - - - - - - - - - - - - - - - - - - - - - - - - -
name submitted:    JOSEPH C WAIKSNIS

dob submitted:     01/26/63

ss# submitted:     ▯ ▯ ▯▯ ▯▯

Sex: M   Race: W

SEARCHED FOR ALL WARRANTS CURRENTLY OUTSTANDING NATIONWIDE

note:              **         0 POSSIBLE RECORD(S) FOUND         **

** END OF REPORT **
```

**Jim faxed us his findings from the Internet,
showing zero outstanding warrants.**

Since nothing was working by hiring lawyers and private detectives, I decided to try my idea of contacting the media in New York. How could I lose? My story was one of a kind.

I remembered that our local Long Island newspaper had a featured columnist named Edmund Depson who was known for his wit and ability to capture people and their stories. I decided to try him first since the newspaper company he worked for was a short distance away.

I contacted Depson and was told to drop off copies of the documents along with my story in brief so that he could review it, which I did. It was just a matter of days before Depson called my parents' home. He wanted to meet with me that same day. Waiting for him in the atrium, I heard my name being called and when I looked up it was Depson, walking at a fast pace towards me, holding papers in his hand.

"My God," he said, "you were never arrested and you were put on trial. Now this district attorney wants to extradite you?"

It was hard, certainly, to absorb the truth, but there it was. We both sat in the atrium. Depson was asking many questions, and he was stunned by my answers as he wrote them down. I finally felt confident something good was going to happen.

After an hour of questions and showing him additional documentation, Depson agreed he would write my story. He said he was going to get to the bottom of this and make some important phone calls, starting with the authorities of Pennsylvania. This, of course, is standard journalistic practice. He had to get both sides of the story.

I left there in high spirits and couldn't wait to call Dawn about the good news. Finally, I was going to get the truth out and expose the guilty parties who had been destroying my life.

As I told Dawn the good news, I said, "It's just a matter of time before this whole mess is finally over and I can come back home."

Over the next week I spoke with Depson by phone, answering his questions. He even told me, "In all of my years of journalism, I never came across a story like yours." He was hard at work writing it, but there was a problem. The DA in Pennsylvania was never available. For his story to have journalistic integrity, Depson had to get his side of the story. Every time he called his office, the DA was always away on vacation or somewhere else.

"I'm feeling this DA is trying to avoid me altogether," Depson said. "That's okay, though, because I'm going to call the Attorney General's office in Harrisburg and ask about this governor's warrant. It doesn't look official to me. What I did find, though, is that, like you said, there is no Oliverville Police Department listed at the fire house or even in the town itself. What sold me were those two different cut-up police pictures of you with the Oliverville Police Department, with the sign added in behind you. Examining them, I could see the cut marks around you in one and the other colored in to hide the cut marks. It is truly outrageous what is being done to you and your family, and I promise I will get to the bottom of it."

My hopes were high until I received a subsequent phone call from Depson, who sounded very upset and wanted to meet me right away in person. We met again in the atrium. He was holding papers in his hand, saying in a nervous voice that he had bad news.

"I called the Attorney General's office in Harrisburg to obtain the charges behind that warrant and was told, 'Yes, there is a warrant for Joseph Waiksnis.' When I asked what you were being charged with to have you extradited out of New York, I was told, 'You don't want to get involved.' Stunned at hearing this, I explained again who I was, that I was investigating his story. I was getting frustrated with the person, and then he hung up on me. Later that day I got a call from my superiors, telling me to shelve your story because of the seriousness of your situation."

"Why, why?" I cried out, unable to contain myself.

"Calm down," Depson told me. "I'll explain to you why I have to put a hold on your story. Believe me, in all of my years doing journalism, Joseph, this is a first for me. First of all, my hands are tied right now, but maybe later I can get back into it. It's not something that a relatively small local newspaper can manage."

I knew Depson was lying to me, trying to make it sound better than it really was. Somebody higher up must have gotten a phone call from Pennsylvania or New York telling the paper to squash my story.

There was little he could do, he said. In the end, he suggested that I contact all of the national media organizations like CBS and NBC in New York City, asserting that one of them would take on my story and expose the people behind this extradition.

I could see how truly upsetting this was for Depson. He warned me of the seriousness of my situation, describing the inevitable outcome of an investigation, if it were ever managed. The inevitable outcome of the truth's exposure could be, as Edmund put it in his last message to me in early 2000: "Many people will lose their jobs and some will be going to jail."

I did not waste any time. I gathered up a list of all the major outlets in New York City and started contacting them by fax and mail with a brief story of my extradition, but to no avail. Weeks went by with my never hearing a word and wondering why.

My hopes of bringing my case before the media, into the court of public opinion, were seriously diminished. Not only that, but the tremendous pressure put upon me by the Pennsylvania and New York fugitive detectives was wearing me down psychologically. In fact, the pressure was so devastating that I ended up having a total emotional breakdown at my parents' home. That day, my mother had no choice but to call 911, for my hands were bloody and bruised from hitting the family room wall. About fourteen police officers responded to the call, seeing me at my very lowest, my heart breaking, and my eyes streaming with tears. I poured my heart out to everyone who showed up as I was taken into the police car and to the hospital for medical attention and mental observation.

So began a new form of persecution—persecution from my own body and mind. I had already endured so much; I wonder why depression affected me so absolutely at that point. All I know is that it did, and cooped up in the hospital, surrounded by doctors and social workers, I found myself struggling to get a handle on myself even as I told my story again and again.

I found out later that my mother and stepfather were quite regularly contacted by the hospital staff that attended me after my breakdown. The reason, of course, was that these staff members, these people listening to my problems, needed to verify whether I was actually telling the truth. Was I telling the truth or was I losing my grip on reality?

The doctors must have been truly surprised to hear that every word I spoke was the truth. The final diagnosis, though, was depression, and the cause easy enough to figure out. I think the most disturbing detail for the hospital workers was that the Pennsylvania state officials had done absolutely nothing to help me and done nothing to put a stop to the DA. The inconsistencies in my case were enough to prove the DA was out of line.

Even while I was at the hospital, the persecution did not abate. There were two uniformed officers guarding me. Over time, in fact, we got to talking about my case and the charges against me, and how my case had been handled. Of course, I tried to convey all I could about the illegality of my persecution. I tried to convince the men guarding me of the fact that they were doing the bidding of criminals, not true agents of the law. These officers didn't necessarily accept everything I said, but they did speak openly of the strange pictures of me that had been sent from Pennsylvania. They even told me that there were no specific charges in the NCIC computers relating to my case. I was listed as a fugitive from justice, they said, but, where charges were normally detailed, on my file there was simply a note that said to direct inquirers to the Pennsylvania county DA. No police officer in the country, then, could actually know what I was charged with. I could have been a murderer, a rapist, or a common thief; there was simply no way for officers to know.

The more I thought about the NCIC entry the more concerned I became. It compounded my depression, of course, that the true purpose of this rather cryptic, deceptive input was to encourage law enforcement agents to consider me seriously dangerous. I could have ended up dead, surely, since law officials would inevitably approach me with maximum caution. They simply could not know that I was only charged with a single misdemeanor DUI charge.

Even more profound, though, was the response both the officers and the hospital got when they contacted the fugitive section of the county. Apparently, upon hearing of my whereabouts, they said only that they were no longer looking for me. It was quite obvious, too, that they wanted to distance themselves. Certainly, they would have had to answer to someone if my depression had led to suicide.

I was released from the hospital to the care of my mother, and set on the road to recovery, having at least received some therapy for my condition, along with the benefit of some recognition of how difficult my situation was.

It was now 2000, a new millennium, and almost seven years after the fire house and police melee. Life went back to somewhat normal in my parents' house. The police now knew where I was, of course, but now it seemed they were lying low. I didn't dare go out, knowing that something could happen. I was constantly looking out the front window, especially when my one of my parents was leaving the property, watching to see if anything suspicious was taking place. Standing watch soon paid off when I saw a person wearing a hoodie running from the front of our newest neighbor's house to one of the pine trees near the street, watching my mother driving off. Seeing the person walking back to the house, I recognized him as the homeowner who lived next door. I truly didn't know what to make of it. I sat and waited for my mother, who returned without incident, so I brushed it off.

Soon, though, in early January of 2000, at approximately five o'clock, they once again trespassed. The doorbell rang at my parents' house, and at the door was yet another county detective. No uniformed officers were observed, but there stood Detective Anthony Scazzero, who told my stepfather that he was now in charge of my case.

He had just recently been promoted to detective, and he was preening quite a bit about his new status. My stepfather said through the storm door that I was not home and demanded to see a warrant, and there was none. He left his card like the others; he then left one page of a two-page document—an arrest warrant supposedly signed by the Judge William Sandringham in Lackland tucked in the channel of the storm door.

Scazzero then wanted to see me in person and talk to me about this new warrant. My stepdad told him I wasn't home and that I was living in Canada. I was quietly listening in the dining room, peeking out the window from behind the shades. I saw only this one detective and nobody else.

Scazzero returned to his unmarked police vehicle. From the windows we saw him back out of our driveway and drive right up the driveway of our newest neighbor, Mr. Balbo, leaving his car lights on while he went to the Balbos' home for a chat. Then he returned to his car and drove off. Since it was winter and the trees and foliage were bare, we had a fairly clear view of what was going on.

My mother was embarrassed that the police felt free to talk to our neighbor about my whereabouts, but by this time I was pretty sure that Balbo was in with the cops. In fact, my mother had in the past noticed what she thought were unmarked police cars hanging around the dead-end street. She had also, sometimes, while driving up to Balbo's house, seen a hooded figure, like I did, running. This person also emerged from Balbo's property and consulted briefly with people in one of the cars.

My mother was suspicious of this too. Why were the police visiting only the one neighbor and not the others? It didn't make any sense to us. Was it because the police knew Balbo personally, or was it because they knew he was keeping commercial dump trucks and running an illegal roofing business in his backyard? Were they pressuring him to spy on us or else? The questions piled up. We knew very little of him, or his family, only that they were newlyweds when they moved in. The best we could tell was that he wasn't with law enforcement, or so we thought.

The police were keeping the pressure on me; they had alerted the neighborhood to my presence. Since most of the neighbors were unaware of what had really happened in Pennsylvania, they were ready to believe that a major criminal lived under my parents' roof.

We had lived at this address since 1972, moving here from Brooklyn. Growing up here, going to school, over the years we got to know most of the neighbors around us. My mother decided to go over in person to the neighbors she knew and ask if they had been visited by the county detectives. They all said no, asking what was with all the commotion with the police cars in our driveway at times. She tried to explain to them what had been going on with the district attorney in Pennsylvania and the police here, that we were trying to get a judge, a DA, and some cops investigated for what they had done to me in Pennsylvania and South Carolina.

My credibility and my parents' standing in our Long Island neighborhood was being undermined, marred by the behaviors of these local county police, as well as by the behavior of the Long Island detectives, specifically Scazzero, and this was taking a toll on the family.

The aggression continued well into the new millennium. At about 9.30 a.m. one morning, Detective Scazzero orchestrated a scheme to try and gain access to my parents' home. He telephoned my parents' and spoke to my stepfather first. Scazzero asked if I was there. My stepfather told him, quite simply, that he should speak to my mother.

Handing over the phone to my mother, my stepfather must have flinched to be threatened yet again. To my mother, though, Detective Scazzero said that he had forgotten to hand over a second page of the Pennsylvania arrest warrant signed by the county judge. He also told my mother that he wanted to stop by our home to present this second page to her in person and "to discuss the details" of the warrant and what it meant. He would be passing through the area shortly, he added, trying to ignore what my mother had said about leaving a copy of the missing page in the curbside mailbox some 250 feet from our front door. Detective Scazzero insisted that he had to hand deliver the document in person to my mother to explain the contents.

It was intuition on the part of my mother that caused her to become decidedly suspicious as this conversation went on. She figured that Detective Scazzero was looking to push his way through the front door somehow, still without any New York court warrant or subpoena, and without any documentation at all that we could trust.

It was truly a cat and mouse game. I started leaving the property with my mother for my son's doctor appointments and other activities. I was always on the lookout, seeing who was parked out front, since I knew my neighbors' cars parked on the dead-end street we lived on, and nobody really parked on the main street either, since our neighborhood didn't have curbs for parking. Every house had its own driveway. If the police were waiting to pounce on me, I definitely would have seen them coming while making quick trips to the store, always keeping alert and returning home more quickly than we had planned, just to be safe.

Scazzero showed up at my parents' home again the following month, demonstrating in his manner that the hunt for me was once again becoming more aggressive.

The day before my son's birthday, we decided to take a chance and take my son to the train store at the mall so he could pick out his birthday gift. As usual, we took all precautions before we left the driveway. I was looking down and up the street, seeing nothing out of the ordinary, only seeing our one neighbor wearing a hoodie, standing on his doorstep smoking a cigarette. Remembering what I saw before, I tried to put it in the back of my mind, trying not to think the worst, as we left to shop for my son's birthday gift on what I thought would be a happy day for all of us.

It was around dinnertime, about 5:00 p.m., as we were returning home from this shopping trip that, as we drove down the driveway to the house, activating the garage doors, we were followed by an unmarked car.

The car followed us down the driveway, and just as the garage door was slowly closing, we saw that Detective Scazzero was forcing the garage door back up to gain access. With him were a couple of other detectives, who helped him with the door, entering our garage.

Approaching my mother's van, which we had duly locked to protect ourselves, Detective Scazzero flashed his badge and yelled through the glass windows, demanding that we open the doors. He tried to force the van doors open, shouting for us to come out. He threatened us if we did not.

"If you don't open the doors," he said, "we'll smash the glass in."

He called for backup and brought a small army of police vehicles and officers to our driveway. Yet again, my mother was threatened with arrest for simply asking questions, for asking on what charge we were being arrested, and even on what basis they were entering our property. Where were the warrants?

After threatening to smash the windows and then threatening to arrest my mother, the detective lied to us both by saying that he had a warrant and that it was on the seat of his car, his unmarked vehicle. If I surrendered, he would show me the papers, he said.

"Show me the papers!" my mother stepped in and stared him down.

While she was still inside the van, my mother was threatened with arrest. Not only that, but Detective Scazzero threatened to take my son to social services. Our suspicion, at that point, was that Detective Scazzero had been bribed and we certainly deemed him determined enough, as he threw around such threats of harming the three of us, especially the threat of smashing the windows of the car with my toddler son sitting in the back in his car seat.

With such threats against my son, I did the only thing I could do. I allowed myself to be arrested to protect my family. I was put in handcuffs and escorted to the back of Detective Scazzero's vehicle. Still, I was never shown an arrest warrant and there was certainly no warrant on any seat in his car.

CHAPTER NINETEEN

Following my arrest, Scazzero's next order of business was to attempt to convince me that I should return to Pennsylvania. I said, "No way." Scazzero started to drive, and we ended up at the second county police precinct that was nearby. I was taken inside the building and handcuffed to a table. Detective Scazzero sat on the opposite side and tried again to talk me into going back to Pennsylvania voluntarily, stating to me, "You can do 30 days standing on your head; it's no big deal."

It seemed like he was begging me to go back, his hand weak. Detective Scazzero stopped talking when a big, white-haired detective appeared at the doorway in a beige suit, pointing at me and saying, "That's him, that's him," smiling like it was some kind of a joke. Eavesdropping on their conversation, I then recognized who he was. He was Gary Miller, one of the original detectives who showed up at my parents' house in 1996. Detective Scazzero was waving his hand to keep Miller quiet after hearing him say, "I see your spy finally paid off."

It was certainly an odd thing to say. Could those police visits to our neighbor Balbo have something to do with it? As they say, do the math.

I noted that suddenly my sentence was 30 days, not eighteen months. Suddenly there was an advantage to voluntarily returning. Suddenly it could be deemed voluntary to return to a place while under arrest.

I was held overnight at the second precinct.

Before I knew it, it was my son's fourth birthday, and I could not be with him. In the early morning I was taken to Central Islip court for arraignment in room D11, represented by a Legal Aid attorney, Dino Cabrini. This was the same court that handed down the sham judgements starting in 1998 that were used to try and seize my grandfather's house.

Refusing to voluntarily return to Pennsylvania, refusing to sign any waiver, I was denied bail because of misleading statements from the county district attorney's office, which, apparently, was cooperating fully with the Pennsylvania DA. My attorney advised me that there were two men out in the hallway waiting to take me back there.

As I sat in the jail, I wondered who these men were. I saw one of them peek around the corner, looking at me. He was wearing a suit. I believe he was the DA from Pennsylvania.

At the jail in Riverhead I was once again on suicide watch because of my depression. My mental health, again, was very poor. I was devastated to have missed my son's birthday and extremely worried about his welfare. For any child to experience such change is devastating. For my son to lose me a second time this way, with men dragging me away in handcuffs—I did not want to imagine what it must have done to him.

By the next day, though, my mother and stepfather were looking to get me a qualified criminal attorney, one we could rely on after all the money we had paid so far only to be disappointed. Feeling as though she had made this phone call a thousand times before, my mother contacted the office of a Mr. Bassist and explained the situation to his secretary. The next day, she had an appointment to meet his assistant, who received an account of my story and much of the supporting documentation. She would, the assistant said, turn everything over to Attorney Bassist so that he could make a decision about the case.

However, we soon heard back from Mr. Bassist's assistant, who telephoned my mother and left a message on the machine, that Mr. Bassist was unwilling to take the case. He had spoken to the DA and had been told without qualification that "no matter what" I was going back to Pennsylvania. Legally or illegally, I was going to be extradited. No federally mandated interstate extradition guidelines would stand in the way, either, as I found out all too soon at my bail hearing.

Sometime in the morning—I could hardly keep track of time by that point—I was taken from the suicide ward into court. The Legal Aid attorney once again stepped forward to represent me and, although my family had paid so much to hire attorneys for me in the past, with Dino Cabrini, it was perhaps the first time that there was even a halfway impartial attorney supporting our case. Not only that, but the judge was quick to take my side, too. Based on the documentation presented to the court, it was clear to him that my sentence had only been for 30 days.

"This kid did his 30 days between South Carolina and New York," the judge insisted. In fact, he was even ready to dismiss the case, having strong words with the District Attorney. He only gave way when the DA insisted that I was facing an additional two years. I listened, stunned to hear that the sentence had increased yet again. It had gone from 48 hours to 30 days, from 30 days to eighteen months, and now to two whole years, even after everything that I had already suffered and all the time that had already gone by.

To bluff his way through the hearing, the DA insisted that the additional charges were coming down from Pennsylvania. With input apparently from said DA, the New York county DA even insisted that there was justification for the so-called extradition: failure to appear, violation of probation, and failure to report to the Pennsylvania county jail for commencement. Again, I sat there reeling. Failure to appear where, when? What violation of probation? I was never on probation, to the best of my knowledge.

We had no idea about the additional charges. Everything in the case was hushed up.

In the end, though, even though the DA's office was ready to argue that additional charges were pending from Pennsylvania and that I should be incarcerated and denied bail, the judge granted me bail for $1,500. Dino Cabrini explained to my mother he couldn't believe the bail was only $1,500. That amount was unheard of, since normally bail for a fugitive from justice would be so high that people put their homes up as collateral.

Yet again, my stepfather had to take out money from his retirement fund to help me. I was released that night from the jail after spending a whole week there. It was a small break in the agony we had experienced over so many years.

    The following day, my mother and I stepped up again too, calling yet another law office. This time we made sure we were going to hire a well-publicized law firm on Long Island. We had one in mind: one Albert Fisher, who had taken on an attempted murder case that was a love affair between a young teenage girl and an older married man, old enough to be her father. It was all over the tabloids and later became a movie.

We called the law firm and spoke with one of Fisher's assistants, a young attorney named Michael Schultz, who stated, after speaking to Albert Fisher, that they would accept my case. They would help me to fight the extradition hearing to Pennsylvania. As the dust began to settle again, with my stepfather once again footing the bill, we set up a meeting with our new law firm.

At the meeting Schultz called Pennsylvania. He spoke to my former attorney, Marlin Bell, and asked him what the charges and the sentence were, all the while looking over our documentation. My mother and I could hear Bell over the phone. He was saying that he had nothing to do with the whole situation. Schultz asked again what the charge and sentence were. Bell was upset, and you could hear him going through paperwork before he finally said, "DUI and pre-sentence report 48 hours, but Mr. Waiksnis got 30 days. I have a copy of it right here," Bell said. Then he repeated, "I have nothing to do with this extradition; you need to call the DA." Schultz told Mr. Bell to calm down and to please fax him that pre-sentence report, and he gave Mr. Bell the fax number. Then he hung up.

Schultz laughed, smiling, saying, "He's full of shit!" Not long after the phone conversation, a fax did come in; it was seven pages of what I thought was the original pre-sentence report from the probation officer, Dugan Spanner. Schultz read it over and pointed out that it said 30 days, clear as day. My copy said 48 hours, and when I compared the two, it looked like someone had tried to alter it by writing "30 days" over the "48 hours." Schultz compared the two documents and pointed out the dates of both reports were the same, 8/25/93, but that the signatures were different. They were the same name, but the signatures were not even close. How could that be? Trying to get to the bottom of it, Schultz called the probation office in Horseboro, Pennsylvania and asked to speak to Officer Dugan Spanner. Finding out that Officer Spanner had left the department years ago to become a state trooper in Pennsylvania, Schultz was amazed. He said the document saying "30 days" was nothing but pure forgery. People could go to jail for this, he said. I was wondering just who forged Dugan Spanner's signature. Was it Marlin Bell? But then he had said he had nothing to do with it and that we needed to call the DA, whom I felt was the master mind behind all of this. Because Schultz was so sharp, I really thought this time around, I had a law firm that was going to protect me and my family.

We paid out some $2,500 dollars, and we talked over all of the details of my case, speaking frankly about everything I had experienced over the years. In no uncertain terms, we were told, "No governor would sign extradition warrants for a misdemeanor and only thirty days." I was also told that there should be an extradition hearing in Albany, to which Schultz, my new lawyer, would go. We asked him to get us copies of the arrest report because I really didn't have anything to show I was arrested at my parents' home. He agreed to get me copies of the police report and whatever else he could find. Before we left, I asked Schultz if it was possible to get my case out to the media.

He said, "Don't worry. Mr. Fisher is well known and knows how to get everybody's attention."

We hoped and prayed that this promise would actually be fulfilled.

My mother had unsuccessfully continued to contact the county police commissioner to complain about the constant harassment, trespassing, and mishandling by the fugitive detectives, but she was advised that she was not able to as "He's a very busy man." However, several days before my bail hearing, a law officer personally telephoned my mother, but she felt he was "fishing for info" from her. When my mother mentioned the bail hearing, this officer sounded dumbfounded, stating, "Your son is going back to Pennsylvania." He claimed that the governor was signing an extradition warrant as they spoke.

How could an extradition warrant be signed when there had been no hearing? I had, after all, flatly refused to leave New York State and voluntarily return to Pennsylvania.

Valentine's Day was my first New York appearance at the first district court. I had to return to Room D11. I met my attorney Michael Schultz, and he told us that the DA had 90 days to prove their case. After that, the case had to be dismissed. Handing me copies of the police arrest report we asked for, Michael Schultz stated to us that everything looked in order.

Interestingly, this time around the judge was just confused and determined to delay the hearing to the following month because he was lacking paperwork on me. He asked the DA what I was wanted for; the DA stated that I was on bail and that he was waiting for additional paperwork from Pennsylvania. Standing next to my attorney, I would have thought he was going to jump in and make a case out of it all for me, but Michael Schultz simply stood there and took it all in. The judge had my case adjourned until the next month.

Once home I finally had something in hand to show for my arrest. Examining the paper work, I looked at this one particular document which I presumed was the police arrest report that had in bold letters on top: "District Court of The County of Suffolk, New York, docket number 2000SU-4542." Reading through it, I noticed the arresting officer was not Detective Anthony Scazzero but a Detective Tom Vannon. Further on, I saw that this report was filled out at police headquarters in Yaphank. I wondered how that could be when I was taken and spent the night at the second precinct. I distinctly remembered that Detective Anthony Scazzero was sitting on the opposite side of the table filling out paperwork. I even had my copy of prisoner's property receipt and teletype messages from that very same day sent by Detective Anthony Scazzero to the DA in Pennsylvania. Confused about who arrested me, I made it a point to ask Schultz about it, since he was the one who had gotten me the documents. He merely said, "It's police protocol. Everything is in order."

The following month a U.S. Coast Guard friend was in town, and he took a ride with us for my second appearance at the district court. I went accompanied by my mother. The courtroom was full of people, just like before. Another judge presided over the hearing but he was really no better than the first. He was confused, too, about the case and didn't seem ready to do anything about it. He determined that we should appear again the following month. He ordered a continuance, apparently allowing himself more time to review things.

CHAPTER TWENTY

It was another month to wait, but I was feeling quite confident that my case might actually be dismissed. My attorney had assured me that a dismissal was actually very likely, at least for the Pennsylvania charges. He insisted that all we had to do was make this last appearance and everything would be alright. For what was supposed to be our last appearance, I decided to take my son and planned, after court, to buy him his favorite pizza and then take him to visit his cousins for a playdate.

Joseph Waiksnis

Arriving at Room D11 for the final time, I positioned myself with my son on the last row. It was particularly quiet that morning, too; quieter that morning than any of the other appearances.

It wasn't long before I realized that it wasn't just quiet. It was downright empty, and that was unusual. The arraignment room on the first floor was almost always full of people and noise. This morning, though, there were not even the defendants and their lawyers. No friends and family were about. There wasn't even any sign of a judge or court clerk. My attorney Michael Schultz was there, of course, standing next to the district attorney and several other men, presumably working with him. It was downright eerie.

All of a sudden, out of nowhere, I was jumped by a group of detectives. I was handcuffed in front of my son, who tried desperately, in a fit of hysterics, to get to my wrists and free me from the grip of the detectives, men who thought nothing of terrifying him.

The most sickening detail, though, was the total absence of judges. There was no judge for me to cry to, no one to intervene and stop the sudden and violent apprehension. I screamed out to my attorney, asking him why this was happening. All he would say was that they had gotten a governor's warrant. I was crying and screaming for answers, in a fit of hysterics myself, asking how an extradition warrant could be served when there was no hearing, no opportunity for me to explain my position and beg for assistance? I was then taken to a soundproof room adjacent to the court where no one could hear me. At that time, I had no idea where they took my son.

Through the window Albert Fisher appeared. I was seeing him for the first time that day. He frowned, shrugging his shoulders and pretending that he had no idea about the warrant or about the scheme that had apparently been set up to ambush me in the courtroom.

I kept yelling, "Why? Why?" I was shouting at the top of my lungs but all he could say was that they had a governor's warrant, and that was that.

I kept yelling out, "How can that be?" but from my own attorney I heard that I was helpless.

"No matter what, you are going to Pennsylvania," he said as he kept on shrugging, over and over, as I repeated my question. I have no doubt he feigned complete surprise that morning. There was nothing honest or transparent about that morning at all. It was a conspiracy, plain and simple, with my own attorney signing off on the whole thing. Instead of representing me, Albert Fisher turned to me and glared.

"Why did you bring your son?" he asked, as if I was supposed to know about this ambuscade.

All those lawyers that I had hired and paid for their services! With over $30,000 shelled out to try and fight the charges against me, I had no one to represent me as I was finally kidnapped from New York and taken back to Pennsylvania against my will.

The best response I got to this setup was surprise. The attorneys were all allegedly surprised, my New York attorneys in particular, because there was no extradition hearing notice, and I had never signed a waiver of my federal rights. I had made sure that an adult accompanied me to every single one of my hearings in New York, except that last one. The reason for the adult companions was simply to minimize the dishonesty and the manipulation by the courts and the attorneys working with me. The reason I brought my son to that last hearing was that Schultz had told me that my case could be dismissed outright. I had believed it.

I was holding on to the hope of reason, to the hope that threats and accusations were not going to hold up. Everyone, including the lawyers, had said, to my mother and to me, that no matter what, I was going back to Pennsylvania. My fate, apparently, was sealed.

The governor had indeed signed the warrant to have me extradited. This was, of course, while we were dutifully making appearances at court, expecting to be given a date for an extradition hearing. The governor's warrant authorized Pennsylvania officials to take me out of the custody of the New York authorities and transport me to Pennsylvania. At least that is what the document claimed.

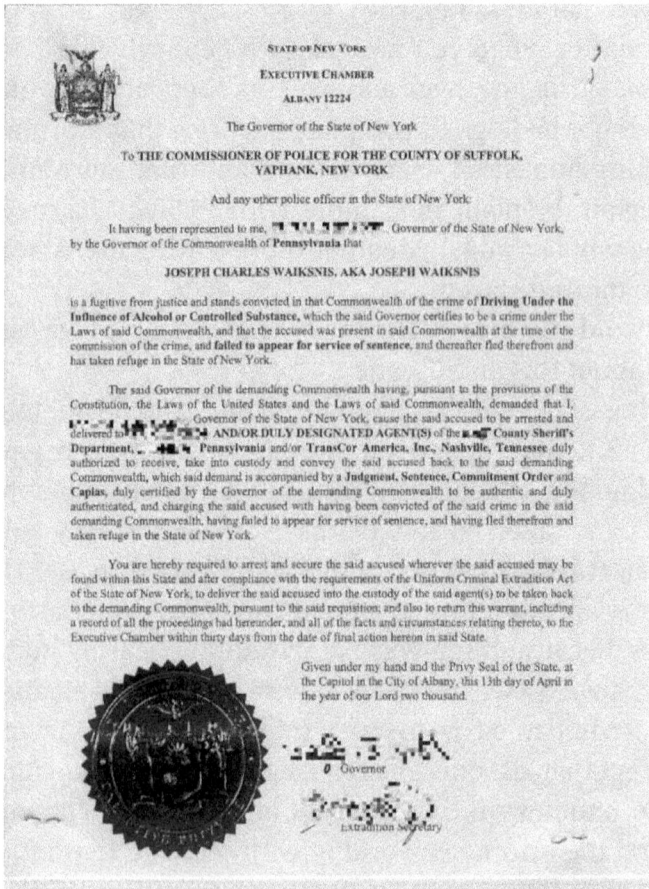

RETURN ON WARRANT

STATE OF NEW YORK

COUNTY OF
CITY OF
I,
the officer entrusted with the execution of the within warrant, do hereby make the following return thereto:
On the ___ day of ___ 19__
I received the within warrant by ___
and on the day of ___ 19__
I arrested the fugitive — named therein by my subordinate officer.

Thereafter said fugitive informed by my direction of rights under the Uniform Criminal Extradition Act of the State of New York and the following proceedings were had:

Subsequently and on the ___ day of ___ 19__ said fugitive delivered to the agent named in the within the warrant whose receipt for the said fugitive ___ is annexed hereto and made a part of this return. Dated the ___ day of ___ 19__

6-24-69-5C (9C-243)

STATE OF NEW YORK

COUNTY OF
CITY OF
I,
the agent of the State of ___
named in the within warrant do hereby acknowledge the delivery to me this ___ day of ___ 19__ by ___
the officer entrusted with the execution of the said warrant, of the body of ___ fugitive ___ from the justice of said State of ___
Dated this ___ day of ___ 19__

I was then handcuffed and swiftly taken out of the building and placed in an unmarked police car next to my son, who was screaming and crying, trying to get to me. The two detectives drove us to police headquarters in Yaphank. My son and I were taken inside, where I was told to keep him quiet. A female officer, seeing my son so upset, gave him a new toy, but it didn't change anything with him; he was in his stroller, his arms reaching out for me. I heard one detective say, "Call his mother to get the kid." It seemed to me the two detectives were in a rush to get me out of there.

I was taken away from my son back to Riverhead jail. Suddenly my parents were notified and they had to drop what they were doing to go and find my son and my vehicle, which was parked somewhere at the district court. My mother had to drive it home. Having been diagnosed years ago with sclerosis of the spine, all this stress and hardship was very difficult for her, and my son spent his elementary school years scared of the police. On one occasion he even became hysterical at the sight of a female uniformed police officer who visited his class to speak on child safety.

I was incarcerated as my mother wrote an open letter to the three governors from South Carolina, Pennsylvania, and New York involved in my case. The letter was sent via express certified return mail and each of the three envelopes contained identical documents, one for each governor, asking for help and for a federal inquiry. Not one word was delivered in response. Three governors remained silent in spite of the fact that the governor's warrant from South Carolina, supposedly signed under the great seal of the state, did not actually have any seal attached to it.

I ended up spending ten days in Riverhead Jail with no idea what was to happen to me next. It was the start of the worst days of my life. I was left in a cold limbo, separated from my family. They only let me out of the cell to shower. I had lost my appetite and was losing weight. There was nothing I could do to stop it or to take my mind off of the hell I was going through.

My mother did get the chance to visit me twice in this time. Each time, we sat at a table in the visitation room and discussed her efforts to clear my name. Unfortunately, nothing was forthcoming. I also asked her about my son and wanted to make sure he was being taken care of. When she visited, she put some money in my commissary account and gave me some magazines to read. This helped improve my mood a little. The magazines also gave me pictures of scenery and landscapes that I pasted with the help of a bar of soap to the upper walls of my strangely designed cell. Over the bed, in the back, the ceiling had two levels divided by a three foot wall, and I posted the nature photos on the walls of this ceiling in a mural so I could look up at them from bed to help pass time.

The tenth day began with a frightening surprise. Word reached me that I was going to be "extradited." I grabbed my things and was led towards one of the elevators, and descended to the ground floor. When the door parted in front of me, I was confronted by none other than Robert Frist. I was shocked beyond belief to see him in Suffolk. This was the very officer who had harassed me when I first moved to Oliverville, who had initiated my detention, who we had asked the DA to investigate after he held a loaded gun to my head, physically hurt me, and then participated in a police melee during my abduction to the basement of the Oliverville fire house basement. He was now responsible for my safety.

The other man apparently dispatched that day to pick me up and transport me was John Marsh, the Pennsylvania county detective who had persuaded out-of-state authorities that I was sentenced to eighteen months. He was also the one who seemed to be sending the altered photographs and records across state lines to the various locations where I had been in residence over the years in New York and South Carolina.

There was nothing I could do at that point, though. I was handed over to Frist and Marsh, who put me in chains and placed me inside a new police vehicle that replaced the one Frist had foolishly totaled at taxpayers' expense. I had no means of seeking legal support. There was no one there to question. One of the officials from the county sheriff's department did notice the emblem on the side of the vehicle that Frist used to transport me—the same vehicle he had clearly driven from Pennsylvania.

"Oliverville Borough Police?" the county officer had yelled out at the Pennsylvanians. "You're not from the Sheriff's Department." It should be on record, I feel, that the two Pennsylvania men who transported me had at least misrepresented themselves to the county jail officials. They must surely have misrepresented that they were personally authorized to take me across state lines.

Finally, it also became clear that the statements made to the jail officer by Frist and Marsh were meant to be deceptive, intended to persuade the jail officer that the Oliverville Borough Police Department actually existed – a falsehood given when there was still only one officer, hired part-time, and that was Robert Frist.

This was all clarified later in a local newspaper article discussing the retirement of one sheriff after ten years, and the appointment of a new one, but at the time it all seemed suspicious.

I was afraid for my life, although I was equally afraid to yell out for help as I was taken away. It didn't come as much of a surprise, though, that my cries would be ignored and that there was no one there to help me. The men I was dealing with seemed familiar enough with managing any collateral damage, so to speak. I was quite convinced that calling for help as I was taken away would only lead to further harm in Pennsylvania.

The governor had readily backed the police department and the DA's office from what I could see. The authorities had also backed the New York district attorney's office as well. There was no sense of justice among these people, so I was left to be taken in Robert Frist's vehicle, chained in the back like an animal.

When we reached the Long Island Expressway, Robert Frist stopped the car. We were near a hot dog stand and Marsh went into the trunk of the car to go through my belongings. It seemed that he was looking for my money, of course. I had none; it had been taken from me in jail. Satisfied that there was nothing, Marsh and Frist went off to purchase food before getting back in the car to continue the journey. As we passed the exit to my home in New York, I wondered if I would ever see my son again.

As we entered Pennsylvania, Marsh started going over some paperwork, which I could see quite clearly from the back. I noticed a warrant from Judge Robert Early. It was the first time that I had seen Judge Robert Early's actual signature on a document. Every other piece of documentation I'd seen from him contained only a printed stamp of the judge's name.

I'm not sure exactly how I felt about seeing the signature for the first time on a document relating to my case. Whatever stamp of officialdom there was upon these activities, it was nothing I could ever believe in. I do know, though, that as we stopped somewhere in Pennsylvania at a truck stop, both Robert Frist and Detective Marsh went and ate at a restaurant, and I was left in the back of the police vehicle, denied water and food and given no opportunity to relieve myself.

Chapter Twenty-One

I soon found myself in the darkest of my personal hells. That first night, I was delivered to the prison and mug shots were taken of me. I was admitted, observing all of the procedures for prison entry. I finally got to go to the bathroom, and then I had to strip off my clothes and change into an orange prison jumpsuit. I met a guard they called Big Bird, a really nice guy. He questioned Detective Marsh about what I was there for, because there wasn't any file handed over to him. Marsh said he would bring it the next day. I found out through Family Service there was a file with my name on it, but it was empty.

Every movement, every noise made me flinch. One of the corrections officers on duty that night entered my information into the NCIC system, expecting a hit. There was none. I was not there.

I was then made to sign paperwork to vouch for my belongings.

Exhausted and distraught, I was sent into solitary confinement, set up on suicide watch, and effectively watched on a camera system around the clock. It was definitely one of the most terrifying experiences of my life to date, comparable to the night of my first detention, some seven years before. I lost track of time. It was nearly impossible to bear the passing of time without any human contact at all, in a room of four terrible walls, cold and cruel.

After roughly three days, I was finally removed from confinement and taken out to be in the general population. I wasn't even sure what day it was or where I was by that point, but, when I was finally among the other prisoners, I quickly learned that there were many within that prison who had been victims, like me, of the judicial and law enforcement systems of that region. Indeed, I heard many people explain to me that the officials were keen to make money from their prison system, looking to fill up the prison as best they could, considering that the building was relatively new and profitable when it was full. What better way to profit from the new county prison than by filling it to capacity with desperate prisoners, men who could fall to the far-reaching power of the state?

In the first few days of exposure to the general population, there were also several inmates who warned me against accepting the service of the public defender, Carvelle. Many of the inmates incarcerated in the county jail insisted that they had used this attorney to man their defense only to find that, when they were convicted, Carvelle would flat out refuse to file appeals for them, warning inmates that the judge, in most cases, would "come down hard" in sentencing.

I had many conversations with these inmates and some with corrections officers, too. One prison guard I spoke to voiced his disgust with the officials and what they were doing to incarcerate individual people who, for whatever reason, were deemed troublesome or a *persona non grata*. Like me.

I learned, though, that many of the lawyers in the area were part of the so-called "clique" that worked with the district attorney. The lawyers mentioned included Marlin Bell. Several other inmates told me that Marlin Bell filed appeals for them only to withdraw them or discontinue them, just as he did with my appeal. I recounted the conversation between me and a Supreme Court clerk in Harrisburg. She went over my file and noted the violations committed by both the attorney and lower court, advising me that I should report the act to the judicial board of Pennsylvania, which I did, but nothing was done.

Some six days after my arrival, I made my first appearance at the courthouse, driven there by a county correctional officer who would later become a county sheriff. As I entered the room, there were many people talking away about one thing or another, only to fall into a dead silence as I began to draw attention, walking in with my hands cuffed behind my back. I saw a bald-headed man I didn't recognize seated at the same bench where I was put on trial some seven years ago.

I was seated on the left side of the courtroom next to several people I did not know. One among them introduced himself as Public Defender Carvelle. He was seated next to me, and he wanted to represent me. I told him that I already had an attorney and prayed that Carvelle would not be just another one of the many devices used against me to intimidate me and trip me up.

Despite my insistence that I already had representation, the next thing I remember is that Carvelle told me he was going to talk to Judge Early and two representatives of the district attorney's office. I couldn't believe that was Judge Early, remembering he had a full head of hair the last time I'd seen him during my sentencing.

Carvelle approached Judge Early and appeared to enter into a rather serious discussion. I thought it strange at the time, sitting there looking around the courtroom, that the DA who had made such a point of hunting me all of these years was nowhere to be found.

Then, when Early finally spoke loud enough for me to hear, what stands out in my mind was his statement, "He'll do his 30 days," with the only charge mentioned that day being a failure to report to prison. He said nothing about all the other trumped-up charges that had been thrown at me over the course of time—violating probation, being a fugitive from justice, an 18-month sentence, failure to appear for that aforementioned sentence that I was unaware of, and all the charges they had continually thrown at me and expected me to compensate for without my even being aware of them.

It was sometime during or after this confusing appearance that the chief detective of the county approached me and quizzed me about my legal representation before I was taken back to the county jail. He seemed to be very concerned who would represent me, mentioning Rosen, to which I responded, simply, that he was not my attorney. Apparently, there had been a deal made between Rosen and the DA before Rosen withdrew from my case. This apparent deal, though, helped me to understand why Rosen had worked so especially hard to try to get me to turn myself in. I would never have agreed to any such deal, though, even if I had wanted to. Rosen was paid more than $20,000 dollars by my family to represent me properly, something I felt he had not done. As for the DA, I would never make a deal with him; he was outright evil.

That was not the worst of it. One inmate who had been involved with drugs told me that attorney Marlin Bell had actually accepted such merchandise in lieu of money when he required the services of a criminal attorney. During our conversation I told him that I did not recognize Judge Early, who went from a full head of hair to outright baldness in seven years. This inmate, however, said simply. "That's what drugs will do to you." Statements like this, confessions like this from my fellow inmates, men who had nothing to lose, made me furious. Although I had no way of knowing whether these accusations were true or not, it certainly made me wonder if the men representing the justice system were involved in destructive things themselves, even as they were coming down hard on men like me while they flouted the law.

I told the other inmates I spoke with that I had paid Marlin Bell some $3,000 to represent me for the DUI defense. They were astounded. His usual fee was $1,500 for such a charge. "He robbed you," one inmate exclaimed.

Another inmate, a man who could hardly read and write, was incarcerated because his accuser, a relative, had told the DA that he had molested her daughter. Even though the woman who made the accusations had gone back to the DA and confessed that the molestation charges were made up out of anger when the inmate had punched the woman's boyfriend, there was no effort by the DA to even consider reopening the case, although clearly the charges of molestation and the charges of assault would be different and require different legal approaches. They just wrote this poor inmate off.

After I was released, I called this inmate's mother to verify the story and listened to her crying into the phone as she told me how she and her family had struggled to raise the money to defend him. This money was given to Marlin Bell, which only inspired him to delay the case, effectively refusing to file an appeal for his client, causing the inmate, now in state prison, to be sentenced to serve a minimum of twenty-five years according to a new law that just went into effect that year.

Horror story after horror story was related to me, and while, undoubtedly, there were some who embellished their struggles, enough of the inmates coming forward had stories similar to mine, involving the same people, and the same pattern of persecution to give one pause.

Some of the inmates also came forward saying that another of the attorneys involved, apparently in collaboration with the DA, would say that for $5,000 some of their charges could be dropped. For $10,000 dollars, "everything disappears." Hard to believe, perhaps, if I had not experienced the effects of this corruption myself, but there it was, right before me. Judges and lawyers appeared to be getting kickbacks through extortion, with the DA apparently taking the lead with the joint money-making scheme, a mutually beneficial arrangement for prosecutors, defense attorneys, and judges.

Another inmate had a story similar to mine. There had been a bench warrant out for him while he was working construction in Corning, New York. He was found at the work site and arrested; they grabbed him, handcuffed him, and forced him into a vehicle, driving him back across state lines. These law enforcement officers were under the impression, quite often it seemed, that they could do whatever they liked whenever it suited them. With their homes guarded by state-of-the-art security systems, as some of the inmates described to me, it is no wonder that these lawyers and officials feel so safe. The arm of the law does not even consider looking for them either.

When I had managed finally to make a collect telephone call to my parents, I had the name of a law firm in the next county. I had spoken to several of the inmates, asking for recommendations, because I did not trust any of the local attorneys. Before my next hearing, I asked my mother to reach out to Attorney Mark Hewitt, recommended by the inmates and located elsewhere in Pennsylvania.

Hewitt accepted me as a client and my mother paid a small retainer to start the process, allowing him to step in and effectively take over my case, instead of my having a decidedly untrustworthy public defender. The next step was for me to speak to Hewitt myself.

COPY

LAW OFFICES

, L.L.P.

May 23, 2000

VIA FAX TRANSMITTAL TO NO. (

Warden
County Prison
R.D. Box
boro, PA

Re: Joseph Waiksins

Dear Warden:

Please accept this correspondence as confirmation that I have been retained to consult with Joseph Waiksins who is currently an inmate at your facility. It is my understanding that upon receipt of this fax you will permit Mr. Waiksins to place a collect telephone call to me at my office at the following telephone number: .

Thank you for your attention to this matter and should you require any additional information, please feel free to contact me.

Sincerely yours,

mvb
cc: Mr. Joseph Waiksins

In the end, however, I spoke to Hewitt's assistant, who explained that he had received all of the information and paperwork from my parents. I would, according to her, be out within a week and put on probation for another two weeks. I was not to worry, she said, because I would soon be back with my son in New York. The courts were aware that Kelvin needed my care.

While I was still in prison and waiting to hear the outcome of the request for probation apparently made by my attorney, I was visited by the probation department. Their representative told me that there was paperwork filled out and that I would most likely spend the rest of my sentence on probation in Pennsylvania. The paperwork, he said, would not need to be transferred to New York.

While this surprised me, it was some time before I became decidedly perturbed by my new attorney's handling of my case. Around this same time, I met with a man named Joe whose role was to check up on inmates, including me, and ensure that I had everything I needed to be safe and above all healthy within the prison system. Since I was having some medical complications as a result of stress and chronic conditions such as stomach ulcers, these visits were especially important for me.

When I spoke to Joe, an exceptional gentleman, I told him that my attorney was securing my release and that I would be leaving the jail pretty soon anyway. Whatever my needs were, I intimated, they would not be his concern too much longer, or anyone else's at that place. Joe was amazed by my story, which I told him in detail, from its very beginning across the more than seven years of my marathon. Half the people in that jail, he said, did not deserve to be there, which I readily believed.

What I didn't realize, though, and what Joe did not know, was that my own sentence was far from over. The bureaucracy that had haunted me from the beginning, apparently adding to my sentence, stretching it out as far as possible, was still at work. A day or so after my 30-day sentence was over, I was called to the courthouse for another hearing. That is, I wasn't simply released as expected.

Because it was a court hearing, I fully expected Mark Hewitt to be in attendance and to represent me. He had been paid a flat fee to address the issue of my parole. My family would have paid more if told that it was necessary. We had been paying legal fees for the seven years of my struggles anyway. But there was no word from him.

When I arrived at the courthouse, I was told that the public defender, Carvelle, was representing me. Because of everything I'd heard, I requested that the hearing be re-scheduled, refusing to accept the representation I was being offered.

I was taken back to the jail and, when I finally got in contact with my actual attorney, Mark Hewitt, he told me that he knew nothing of the hearing. "You should have been released long ago," he added, echoing what many of my fellow inmates had been saying: that it was extremely strange for officials to so purposely delay my release.

Not only did I need to get back to care for my son, my health was growing increasingly poor. I had lost a considerable amount of weight and had acute stomach pains. I was denied medical attention for much of the time I was in the prison. I had started spitting up blood and somehow managed another collect telephone call through to my parents, telling them of my condition and insisting that they call Mark Hewitt and have him intervene with the prison authorities.

Mark Hewitt did contact the warden, and immediately I was taken to the hospital for medical attention which my parents were initially thankful for. However, the prison's own doctor proved to be little more than a prison guard with a coat, handing out pills and little else. I was given the wrong medication three different times, and it seemed that there was actually no effort to follow guidelines for the dispensing of medication for inmates per prison standards. After I was returned to prison, Hewitt also submitted a petition for parole. We received no information back.

When Hewitt sent various letters to the court and the prison warden, among the oddities was a reference to my apparently having been incarcerated for more than fifty days on a "second time DUI offense." This was a complete mystery to me.

Trying still to find out what I needed to do to be released and also trying to ensure that I had at least some chance of surviving my incarceration, I met again with Joe. As soon as he saw me, he confessed how shocked he was that I was still incarcerated. Indeed, he was very interested to learn about the particulars of my trial at that meeting.

"Let me look at your prison folder," Joe said, towards the end of our conversation.

When he returned some five minutes later, he insisted, "There's nothing in your folder at all. It's empty. This is a first for me." He also added, with conviction: "You shouldn't be here at all. You can walk out that door right now. How can the jail hold you?"

Joe became even more obviously upset by the situation when I told him that there had been an unscheduled hearing at the courthouse to which my attorney of record had not even been invited.

"What was the hearing for?" he asked, and I told him I did not know.

I described how I had been kicked out of my home in Oliverville, kicked out of my home in South Carolina, and even smuggled out of New York to Pennsylvania without being given any chance to defend myself before an impartial judge.

Joe was even more astounded when I explained that no one had helped me in the face of injustice—not the DA, not Judge Early, not the mayor, not the governor, not all the lawyers that I had paid. Joe certainly could not believe that I had gone through so much for only a misdemeanor charge, an unproven DUI that was brought on me. I explained that I had only wanted to protect myself and my family from these people; that I had realized, with the rumors going around, that the police officers wanted to force us out of Oliverville because the town wanted our Market Street home.

"I'll find out why you are still here and find out what that hearing was all about," Joe promised. Later that day, when I tried to call my family, the phone call was blocked, but other inmates could call out.

A week later, feeling more cut off than ever, I met with Joe again and he told me he could not find any information on my case at the courthouse. Officials were hiding something big, he insisted, convincing me all over again that my case was beyond unusual.

Although he had not found any paperwork about my case at the courthouse, what Joe did discover was that it had been a parole hearing that was scheduled without my lawyer ever having been informed. Yet, he added, how could a person go to a parole hearing when he had already served his time in jail?

I told Joe that while I was living in South Carolina, the DA sent down papers from his office advising the South Carolina authorities that I was sentenced to eighteen months and that the Pennsylvania governor was going to have me extradited. When I explained that we tried to have the DA investigated, though, all the information started to click. Joe put it together for me too, that my persecution, my handling by the law from the night of my detention onwards, was part of an elaborate scheme to beat me to the punch. The authorities of Pennsylvania had been out to get me before I ever had the chance to get them. All the while they were also covering up their wrongdoing.

It would be my last visit with Joe but before he left, he told me, in all seriousness, "When you get out, you need to get your story out, because these people are getting away with murder."

Hewitt, who was becoming extremely expensive, claimed to have properly prepared a petition for parole to the Court of Common Pleas, but not only was it not filled in, no copy was provided to me or my family.

Then there was more court hogwash awaiting me. I was driven again to the courthouse for a so-called parole hearing. I was seated, at last, next to Mark Hewitt. What followed was a lot of legal talk, a lot of it pointless, followed by, at last, my release on parole, even though my time was served.

When I questioned Hewitt about all this, though, he was very evasive. My questions went unanswered and he appeared very nervous.

There was nothing I could feel then but betrayal. I was also skeptical, since my attorney was insisting that I had been sentenced to eighteen months. With apparently no other choice, no way out, since my own attorney was apparently against me, obstructing my road to justice, I kept silent. I was terrified again, even with the man who was supposed to advocate for me sitting right beside me. I sat looking around for the DA but like before, he was nowhere to be found. I was certainly hoping this would be the last time I would have to see or hear Judge Early ever again.

As I held my peace, a court order was presented with the stamp-printed name of President Judge Early. It stated that "the court grants the request for parole from the original sentence in this matter and the defendant is released [...] effective Monday July 10, 2000 at 10:00 a.m."

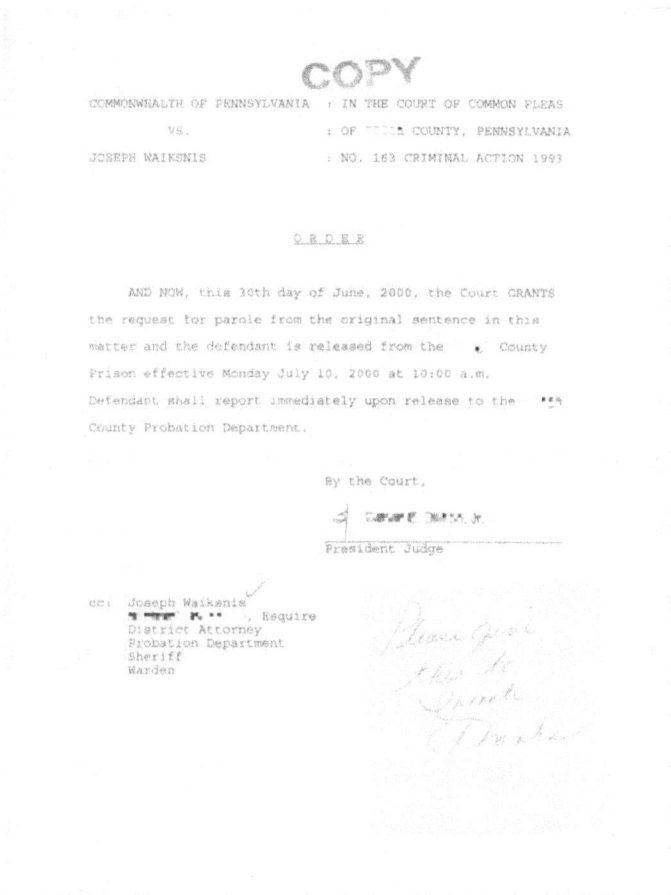

COPY

COMMONWEALTH OF PENNSYLVANIA : IN THE COURT OF COMMON PLEAS

VS. : OF _____ COUNTY, PENNSYLVANIA

JOSEPH WAIKSNIS : NO. 163 CRIMINAL ACTION 1993

O R D E R

AND NOW, this 30th day of June, 2000, the Court GRANTS the request for parole from the original sentence in this matter and the defendant is released from the ___ County Prison effective Monday July 10, 2000 at 10:00 a.m. Defendant shall report immediately upon release to the ___ County Probation Department.

By the Court,

_____ Jr.
President Judge

cc: Joseph Waiksnis
    _____ __ __ , Esquire
    District Attorney
    Probation Department
    Sheriff
    Warden

A couple of things were wrong for starters: the original sentence was, of course, 48 hours, altered then to 30 days. It was a third alteration to bring it to eighteen months. Then there was the fact that there was no written signature on this document at all.

There was also the problem that I had to report upon release to the probation department. I was paroled but having to address myself to probation, unsure even of what my sentence was or how I was to deal with it, or what the possibility of further incarceration was. There was no way to know.

I should have been released 30 days from the date of my imprisonment. Why, then, was I not? Why, when I was suffering from depression, losing weight, and, most of all, kept from my son, was I given no reprieve? According to my attorney, the reason I served extra time was because I refused the services of the public defender, which, he explained, would have expedited my process that day he couldn't be with me in court and Public Defender Carvelle had offered his services. Then I learned of all the restrictions that would be placed upon me.

I was to report by phone every two weeks until my files were transferred to New York. The document also stipulated that the transfer of my files could take up to six months.

The next item stipulated, however, that I was to pay a monthly supervision fee of $106, along with a monthly court cost of $53 dollars.

I was also to complete Act 122, about which I was told nothing, although I understand, by this time, that it is the requirement for the restoration of one's driver's license.

I was also told that I was not allowed to consume any alcohol, and I was told that I would need to conduct a follow-up drug and alcohol evaluation. To add insult to injury, I was also supposed to attend DUI school, although no further details on this requirement were ever provided.

In the end, my contempt for the system prevented me from ever following through on these things. I never called. I never heard a word about the transfer of my files from Pennsylvania to New York. I never reported to anyone in New York. I also refused to pay one cent, nor did I ever show up for an evaluation or a DUI training. I had only signed the papers they put in front of me to obtain my release. I received an order from the judge with a rubber stamp signature advising the probation department that they were relieved from collecting cost, fines, restitution, and supervision fees, dated January 26, 2004.

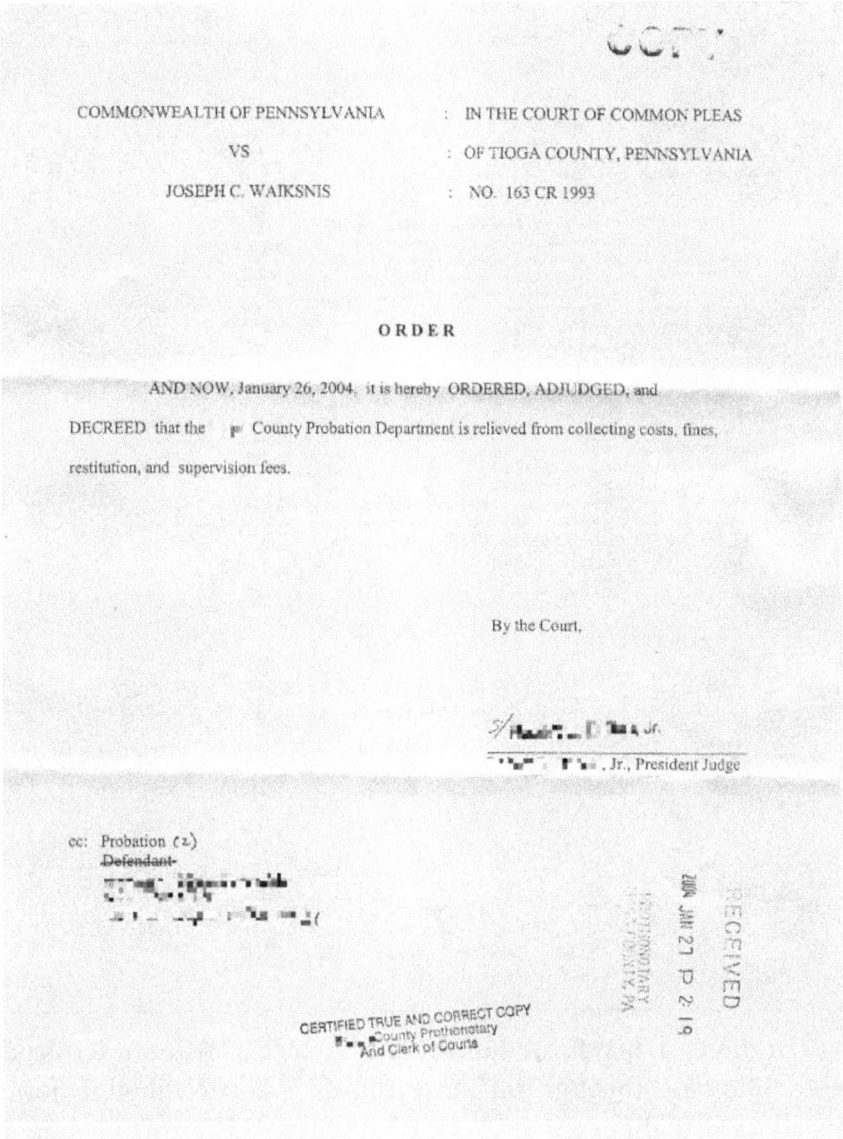

My mother, who had paid for the services of Hewitt, had wanted him to be present the day of my release to make sure everything was understood and aboveboard. As soon as she learned of the release from me via a prison call, she called Hewitt to beg him to show up, to make sure he was there to protect me. He refused, of course, and insisted that it was not necessary. He insisted that all inmates followed the same procedures when being released, even though she was absolutely furious, angered by all of his lame excuses and the fact that he had not provided any completed copies of forms that were to be filled out and supposedly filed on my behalf.

By the end of the day, I was finally free. Just before I was released, however, with all of the paperwork out of the way, I was threatened one final time by a detective who asserted that any violation of my probation would mean that I would be brought back to Pennsylvania to finish my time. I was also told that they were tired of me trying to have them investigated. If that happened, he'd added, "We don't need a governor's warrant." He implied that I would never see my son or anyone else in my family again.

I stepped out of the prison, finally, alongside another inmate who said, "This is one crooked county."

CHAPTER TWENTY-TWO

I didn't have a cent on me. My father-in-law, thankfully, drove from New York to pick me up. I was in such poor health by that point, there was very little I could do without help.

I ended up staying with my in-laws for a few days to recover. Meanwhile, my parents had sent funds so that I could begin to plan getting to Long Island. The journey eventually was undertaken; it involved boarding two buses and counting the innumerable hours until I could see my son. I had to fight down my desperate, visceral need to see him, which threatened to overwhelm me.

The closest bus stop to my parents' home was on Rte. 110 right off the LIE. Too weak to walk, I got off there and called my mother to pick me up. She was excited and delighted that I was back. I could hear her telling my son in the background: "Daddy will be home soon!"

I saw Kelvin for the first time in months. My mother brought him to the bus depot to pick me up, and I grabbed him in my arms the instant I saw him. He was ecstatic himself to see me. There was no better remedy for all the pain, fear, and horror of those last months.

My mother was stunned by my appearance and weight loss. She said I looked as though I had walked out of a Nazi concentration camp. I had lost so much weight as a result of being ill and denied proper medical care that my bones were almost visible. I needed to see a doctor. I made an appointment at the VA Hospital where I was placed on medication for depression and treatment for the ulcer I had developed. The psychiatrist at the VA Hospital was keenly interested in my story and extremely disturbed by my appearance and what it implied about the prison system.

Two weeks after arriving back in Long Island, I went to the law office of Albert Fisher, my old New York-based attorney, and demanded to see him. He had been there at my last court appearance, which I had thought odd since he wasn't present at the other ones. I had only talked to him through a speaker at the window from the enclosed soundproof room in the holding tank. He had done nothing to put a stop to what I deemed an illegal kidnapping.

Fisher was able to meet with me. He was surprised to see me and to hear about my experiences. I asked how it had been possible to get a governor's warrant for an extradition without a hearing. He didn't know what to say, other than that I had waived my rights somehow. I insisted that I had not. If I had waived my rights, there would be no need for a governor's warrant. That was his only explanation for the way I had been treated. It was a kind of reverse logic. He knew full well there were politics and illegalities going on, but there was little he could say or do besides advising me to just forget it and move on with my life.

Over the following year we sent letters to Fisher, trying to get answers and whatever additional documents he could get his hands on, but there was no response from him or his office. It was now March 2001, exactly eight years since I was kidnapped off the street and held in the fire house basement. We were getting no response to our letters, so my mother decided to send a certified letter to Albert Fisher about the fees and retainer. The response we got was a refund.

"Upon the receipt of your letter dated March 9th 2001, I retrieved your son's file and reviewed the retainer agreement," his letter said. "That review indicated that there was an excess payment of $1,000. Enclosed find a check returning that amount."

The additional $1,000 was only to be paid should the case go to hearing or trial. That never happened, so we got the money back.

After years of authorities hunting me down for something I didn't do, I was left with a pile of legal paperwork and a refund of $1,000.

I soon got a notice from the probation department stating that I was 30 days in arrears in paying them any money. Of course, I hadn't sent them anything, nor was I going to. The letter mentioned nothing about reporting to the authorities, either in New York or in Pennsylvania, as outlined in the parole conditions.

Although they were apparently keeping tabs on me and my whereabouts, there was no mention of my failure to report to the probation department either. I never reported to anyone. While I had initially had my concerns in ignoring their unlawful requests, by this time I was convinced the whole thing was a charade, a bid to get even more of my money `and to continue to make my life miserable, as if they hadn't done enough yet. I soon got an identical letter.

I received yet another notice, still stating that I was 30 days in arrears on the money I apparently owed to the courts. No one came after me for not cooperating with parole or probation conditions, whatever they were. It was a strange turn of events after I had been made to feel like Public Enemy Number One, and they had rolled out the red carpet at every opportunity to apprehend me. Now they were leaving me alone.

Or so it appeared.

Not feeling safe to go back to South Carolina, with all its haunting memories, I stayed on Long Island with my son for safety. Dawn eventually moved our belongings to New York before she left for her new duty station to serve out the rest of her enlistment in the navy.

Robert Frist didn't stay quiet either; over the years we were still receiving summonses mailed to my parents' address, including several made out in Dawn's name. The most notable was filed in January of 2005, the only documentation we received that wasn't forged or rubber-stamped. This continued until we finally sold my grandfather's house to our neighbor's son Richard Gutierrez for back taxes later that year; he had just gotten married and they moved in. He'd helped John when he was alive, and was also a close friend of mine. By then the house had fallen into disrepair; while I trusted Richard with the house, the sale stung me. I felt like I had lost one of the things I had been fighting for. Around this time, Frist ended up losing his job. I believe that the borough had gotten tired of his various antics and excesses.

COUNTY OF ⬚⬚⬚

⬚⬚⬚⬚ ⬚⬚⬚⬚
MAGISTERIAL DISTRICT JUDGE
District Court ⬚-⬚-⬚⬚
⬚⬚⬚⬚⬚⬚⬚⬚
⬚⬚⬚⬚⬚
⬚⬚⬚⬚⬚⬚⬚ ⬚⬚⬚

OFFICE:
TEL ⬚⬚⬚ ⬚⬚⬚⬚
FAX ⬚⬚ ⬚⬚⬚ ⬚⬚⬚

August 19, 2005

DAWN WAIKSNIS
C/O V SNYDER
40 E HALF HOLLOW RD
DIX HILLS NY 11746

RE: NON TRAFFIC VIOLATION – NT-23-05

Dear Ms. Waiksnis:

Enclosed please find a copy of the Warrant of Arrest that our office has issued for you for failure to respond. Our office has attempted to contact you and you have not responded. Please be advised that we have also sent a request to the Department of Transportation to suspend your driving privileges. Your prompt attention in this matter is highly recommended. Please contact our office immediately to resolve this situation.

Sincerely,

[signature]

⬚⬚⬚ ⬚ ⬚⬚⬚⬚⬚⬚⬚
District Judge ⬚-⬚ ⬚⬚

Letter address to Dawn stating a warrant out for her arrest

COMMONWEALTH OF PENNSYLVANIA

COUNTY OF ____

To any authorized person:

In the name of the Commonwealth of Pennsylvania, you are commanded to take into custody
(Name): WAIKSNIS, DAWN M
(Address): C/O V. SNYDER
40 EAST HALF HOLLOW RD
DIX HILLS, NY 11746

If the defendant be found in said Commonwealth, and bring the defendant before us at ____
(Address): ____

to answer the Commonwealth or ____ BORO
(Political Subdivision)
upon the complaint or citation of ____
charging the defendant with O §12 §§2021
SNOW AND ICE ON SIDEWALKS
and further to be dealt with according to law, and for such purposes this shall be your sufficient warrant.

With ____ hand and official seal of the issuing authority on this ____ day of ____

(Signature)

Ministerial District No.: ____
Citation No.: ____
FILED: 1/11/05
Docket No.: NT-____

Amount needed to satisfy collateral: $

Reason for warrant: **FAILURE TO RESPOND**

AOPC 417-98 **DATE PRINTED: 8/17/05 1:56:32 PM**

RETURN WHERE DEFENDANT IS FOUND

By authority of this warrant

☐ I took into custody the within named ____

☐ He is now at liberty on bail posted before ____

☐ in the ____ jail.

☐ before you for disposition.
☐ I accepted a guilty plea and collected $ ____ for fine and costs.

☐ I accepted a not guilty plea and collected $ ____ for collateral.

☐ I accepted the fine and costs due in the amount of $ ____

(Signature of Officer - Name & Title)

RETURN WHERE DEFENDANT IS NOT FOUND

After careful search, I cannot find the within named defendant

SIGNATURE

NAME

TITLE

WARRANT OF ARREST

WARRANT CONTROL NO.: ____
DOCKET NUMBER: NT-____

COMMONWEALTH OF PENNSYLVANIA

VS.

WAIKSNIS, DAWN M

OFFENSE DATE 1/10/05
CHARGE
O §12 §§2021

I acknowledge that I am voluntarily and knowingly pleading guilty. I paid to the officer the fine and costs stated in the warrant in the amount of $ ____

(Defendant's Signature)

I acknowledge that I am voluntarily and knowingly pleading not guilty. I paid to the officer the collateral for my appearance at trial stated in the warrant in the amount of $ ____

(Defendant's Signature)

Officer's costs:
Warrant ____
Miles @ c ____
Commitments ____
Miles @ c ____
Conveying to hearing ____
Miles @ c ____
Total ____

Arrest warrant dated August 17th 2005 with complaint from chief of police Robert Frist alleging offense failure to remove snow and ice on sidewalk on January 10th 2005.

My grandfather John's home, 2005.

Feeling helpless and thinking about what to do next, I came up with yet another idea to expose and get my story out. With the help of a friend and a new computer, I decided to build a website and post all of the documents, along with my story. This was all new to me. It took some time to build, but eventually it was up and running.

New York had elections, and I heard that we had a new head district attorney running the county. Hearing that he didn't put up with any corruption and also that he would prosecute to the full extent of the law, I thought: "What a better way to open up an investigation into the illegal extradition from New York to Pennsylvania?"

I sent a complaint letter along with my website address and even sent him a CD with all of the documents burned onto it. I did the same thing with the new attorney general we had in New York; my parents sent him their complaint too. Everything was sent certified return receipt, making sure they got it. Then we waited.

Weeks turned into months and we did not hear a word from either of them. What we did see was that at times, late at night, there was a police car sitting on our dead-end street, and our new neighbor who had received the police visits would go over and talk to them. The neighbor would be watching me at times, sitting in his truck in his driveway whenever I was out in the front yard. I felt like I was back in Pennsylvania, being watched.

After hearing nothing, my mother decided to take a ride to the DA's main office and meet personally with him. I wasn't allowed up to his office as I had left my ID back home. My mother was allowed in after signing her name to a log book. With copies of the governors' warrants in hand, she explained our story to a lawyer in the office, who turned my mother away. She was not allowed to speak to or see the new head district attorney. As we left his office, my mother was yelling out, "I'm a taxpayer, and this is how you treat me!"

From there we drove to the sheriff's office at the first district court, hoping to get some answers about those governors' warrants. Engaging two deputies in conversation, I handed them both governors' warrants from Pennsylvania and New York and asked a simple question: "Are they real?" They laughed, saying they looked real, but they pointed out a misspelled word "Mfarch" instead of March, which I already knew about. The one thing that did confuse both deputies, though, was the stamp of the Suffolk County Correctional Records Bureau on top of both warrants. How could that be? One deputy even ran my name in a computer, finding nothing.

This alone answered many questions I had. The reality was that the cops, the DA, the judge, and even the attorney general had faked an extradition to cover up not only what the police did to me that March night, but also the mock trial I had undergone and then the pulling of my appeal. I felt as if it didn't matter who I hired to protect my rights, because the person would run up against the system that had set its face against me and would throw up his or her hands and bow to the powers that be. I felt I had no rights in these United States; everybody I encountered was in the pocket of everybody else.

GOVERNOR'S OFFICE

THE GOVERNOR OF THE COMMONWEALTH OF PENNSYLVANIA

TO ALL TO WHOM THESE PRESENTS SHALL COME:

KNOW YE, That I have authorized and empowered and by these Presents do authorize and empower

⸱⸱ ⸱ ⸱⸱⸱ and/or agents

to take and receive from the proper authorities of the State of New York,

JOSEPH CHARLES WAIKSNIS aka JOSEPH WAIKSNIS,

a fugitive from justice, and convey the subject to the Commonwealth of Pennsylvania, there to be dealt with according to Law.

GIVEN under my hand and the Great Seal of the State, at the City of Harrisburg, this 31st day of Mfarch in the year of our Lord two thousand.

_____
Governor of Pennsylvania

By the Governor:

_____
Secretary of the Commonwealth

Pennsylvania governor's warrant sent to New York

I wasn't about to kneel to an evil power without a fight. Up to now my family and I had contacted numerous state agencies in the government, all the way up to the governor, as well as the ACLU and various media outlets. I even expanded my website and posted all of the documentation that was used against me to prove the conspiracy. The only thing I had left was to write this book.

I figured I would try the old approach with the media again after seeing some true crime and human interest stories on TV. Remembering what Edmund Depson had said to me a few years back, asserting that one of the news organizations would take on my story, and having nowhere else to go, this was my last stand to expose my story.

With an unbelievable story, but overwhelming documentation, I figured it would be best to see someone in person instead of mailing or faxing my story. My mother and I took the Long Island Railroad to Manhattan with copies of documents in hand and went to Rockefeller Plaza, hoping to meet with some representative for *Dateline*, only to be turned away. They explained that I had to mail my story to Story Ideas at Dateline NBC, which I did, just like the others, only to receive a postcard several months later in the mail saying that they apparently had to pass up my story due to the overwhelming amount stories they have. I had lost a major battle with the media and with it seemingly all hope of exonerating myself and ever living in my grandfather's home again.

Life as we knew it at my parents' home changed as well. Still living with my son at my parents' home on Long Island, I knew my troubles were far from over. My parents' home was once a safe and happy place, full of pleasant memories. It was where I grew up and went to school. Now it had turned into a kind of prison for all of us; it was not even safe to venture outside on our own property after all the unlawful things that happened to us and are still going on to the present day.

To this day my family and I are still living in fear of the police, the courts, and the next-door neighbor who was visited by the police. For a number of reasons, we suspect he is in cahoots with them, borne out by events in 2006.

I had met a new friend at a job I held at a home improvement store around 2004. She came to the store several times with her daughter asking for me by name before we finally met. She seemed nice and needed some help fixing things around the two houses she owned. I was doing side jobs to keep my head above water and I needed some extra money since the monetary judgments against me led to the county taking away half of my pay.

As I helped her out and befriended her, she was particularly interested in my life and in my issues with the legal system as I started to open up to her about my life. At first this just seemed like empathy from a friend, but in hindsight I find it probing. I began to be concerned about her obsession when one day I visited her and got no response from her when I called to say that I had arrived, which was what I usually did. There was a fancy Jaguar parked in her driveway, I heard the TV running, the door was unlocked, and she had expected me to come that day to work on the house, so I entered. I found her in her daughter's room, looking at my private website that I had been working on and wasn't public yet with a man who was apparently her lawyer. The lawyer was embarrassed, and quickly excused himself and left the house. I was flabbergasted that she would do such a thing without my knowledge, but it wasn't enough to end the friendship.

There was a second run-in with a woman who my friend introduced as a cop friend of hers named Allie. My friend specifically named her as an officer, and indeed that was who she truly was. I happened to be in the neighborhood where I was working and needed to pick up some tools I kept in the garage for another side job. My friend trusted me with a set of keys if I needed to work on the house when she was at work. When I pulled up to the house there was a cop car parked in front of her house. My friend was surprised to see me when I appeared at the front door. Just like her lawyer friend, Officer Allie made a quick exit and left. My friend said she knew her from when she used to do animal rescues with her husband and she just stopped by to see how I was doing.

The direct catalyst for the end of our friendship was over money. My friend owed me fifteen thousand dollars for the work I did and furniture belonging to my grandparents that I let her borrow until she found replacements.

One day she called me because she was having lock problems with her front door. When I showed up she had two sets of new locks for me to replace. I did as she asked but when I asked about holding on to a set of keys so I could have access to the garage she told me not now. Later that night when I was back home, she called me and said she no longer needed me and that I was not to come back to her house. I was shocked and in disbelief hearing this. I asked for payment but she refused to pay up and continued to act suspiciously. I told her that I'd settle for five thousand and that I'd pick up my tools and belongings and be done with her. Feeling betrayed since my parents and I helped her out so much, and since she continued to be obstinate when I called her later, I responded with some righteous anger.

On August 21st, 2006, I was arrested again at gunpoint in my parents' garage, again without a warrant, by Allie and another very young alleged plainclothes detectives who later turned out to be regular uniformed police officer as well, backed up by a uniform wearing officer whom my mother recognized as being one of the officers from the 2nd precinct. He had stopped them the night coming back from my grandmothers' looking for me, and now he kept his hand on his firearm like in an old western where I was wanted dead or alive. The fake detectives were from the first precinct, which was odd since my home is within the second. The alleged charge was that I had threatened to kill my former friend. They claimed they had evidence of eleven death threats on tape. My mother had to drive to the 1st precinct and post the $50 bail bond. I stood there, holding in my hand yet another summons, a desk appearance ticket to a court hearing at the same courthouse where I got those money judgments and where I was extradited. This time I was facing 25 years to life in prison, taken from my son once again.

At my first court date I was handed and had to sign a temporary order of protection. It stated IT IS HEREBY ORDERED that the above-named defendant observe the following conditions of behavior: Stay away from her and her home, school, business, and place of employment. It was also stipulated that I should refrain from communication or any other contact or by mail, telephone, e-mail, voicemail or other means, as well as third party contact.

The order was set to expire after a year. The date issued was October 16, 2006. I was told by the judge that I must hire counsel and was also given the usual spiel about how if you can't afford counsel, one will be appointed to you before your trial. He told me I was facing 25 years to life. I had no choice, of course, being threatened with this. I had to go to court with a lawyer or be taken away from my son again, put in jail, possibly for life.

I hired two more law firms to fight yet another trumped up charge, spending thousands of dollars on lawyers' fees over the next three plus years. The lawyers performed no better than the others I had hired in the past. As usual, I was told to plead guilty so the judge would go easy on me. For what? I demanded to see and hear the evidence myself over and over again. This went on for some time. My first attorney dragged his feet, claiming he was doing everything he could, but the DA was hiding the tape from us. On one of those early court appearances a young female DA I spoke to about my case did say to the judge that she listened to the tape and heard no such threat, even as my friend claims I said eleven times "I'm going to kill you, you just signed your death sentence" but the judge struck it down and my attorney didn't speak out stressing to me that the charge still stands because of her sworn statement she made to the police. "Friend, you are facing 25 years in prison. Let me handle it."

What could I do? I had been going to court every other month for about a year with the same results until it was time for the temporary order of protection to expire. Over that time period I spoke to my attorney about getting my belongings back and was told all I had to do was go down there and pick them up in person. I did not dare and tried to have them picked up by one of my coworkers but with no luck. I figured once the temporary order of protection ended, I would file a lawsuit and try to get my belongings back this way.

The year finally came and went. It was October 10, 2007 and the temporary order of protection finally ended. My mother and I were waiting as usual in the court hallway for the attorney. This time he was a no show. I called his office and was told by one of his associates that he was out at Riverhead on official business and that my case had been like all the others adjourned. We were told to go home, and that the attorney was going to contact me about the next court appointment so we left. Following this I was contacted by the Suffolk County Sheriff's Department to come down to the courthouse to be served not a temporary order but an Order of Protection. To my great shock, this new order read "Convicted for Disorderly Conduct P.L.240.20" and that this order of protection shall remain in effect until 10-10-08.

It turns out that since I wouldn't cop a plea deal, they simply cooked up a court appearance at which they marked me convicted for disorderly conduct on the 10th. I was not called in and as such was not present when they illegally "convicted" me for an unrelated charge out of thin air, and this is borne out by my lack of signature on the forged documentation. I believe that my attorney may have been in on this scheme at first, but got cold feet when the time came. After this, my bail was returned to me, in spite of the fact that my first bogus charge was still being tried.

I received another letter in the mail for my next court date. My attorney was always too busy to return our calls. Seeing him at my next court date, December 04, 2007, he apologized to me and the judge who was very upset with us, stating I was a no show in court. That's when my mother yelled out that we were here. The judge yelled out "If you and the DA can't come to a deal, I'm marking this as final for trial," which would involve a jury of cops rather than my peers. I yelled out "I want a Jury Trial," to which the judge whined about needing to call in actual jurors. From that day on all of my court appearances were marked "Jury Trial." I was keeping record of this by printing out all of my court dates from e-courts online. I was facing 25 years to life, then convicted of disorderly conduct when I wasn't even in court, and now this judge wanted to continue to push the first case without evidence.

I've talked about how police "overcharge" people and then plea bargain with them to get them to plead guilty to a lesser charge. If you are innocent and you stand up for your constitutional right to a jury trial by your peers, the prosecuting attorney and judge get angry because you are causing a bottleneck in the already overcrowded system. I had to play the game.

In any case, I replaced the first attorney with a different one, Badoglio, on January 22, 2008, who was if anything worse.

As things dragged on, Badoglio and his associate kept trying to convince me to go to my friend's house to pick up my furniture and tools just like my last attorney tried to. They kept claiming that I would be able to in spite of the order of protection hanging over my head. I didn't fall for their ploy, recognizing that they could use such a visit to make my legal situation worse, if not also as an opportunity to pull something diabolical.

Then on August 4, 2008 my mother and I were sitting in court waiting to be threatened by the judge once again when I heard a case similar to mine. This defendant was called up for his first court appearance, charged with an identical charge as I was, Aggravated Harassment, P.L.240.30 2nd. The defendant told the Judge he didn't have an attorney. The judge replied that the charge against him was not criminal but a minor violation, and that as long as he didn't violate the order he didn't have to return to court or retain an attorney. I couldn't believe what I just heard – here I was dragged through the legal muck and dealing with backstabbing counsel, when others like me didn't as long as they played by the rules.

I lost count of my appearances after three years of going to court; it felt like it would never end. I decided to make a trip to the city with my mother to meet a well-known lawyer to try to get some answers. Hearing our story and looking through all of the court dates I had, he recommended that I get a transcript printed out of all of my court appearances. He said it sounded to him like a good old boy thing was going on out there, and that he would love to read my transcripts to see what the story was. Both of my attorneys over the course of the case had told me that my transcripts couldn't be made available to me until the trial was over, but I finally resolved to get them from the courthouse anyway.

My quest for the transcripts was short-lived; at the courthouse, in spite of being shown my driver's license and case number, the court clerk couldn't find any transcripts related to my case at all. Typing in a similar name search, she did find two other case numbers related to my being arrested and extradited, but there was no court transcript for those either, because that case was sealed, she said. I asked the clerk if I could have a printout of that similar name report. She printed it out, saying that this was a first for her after thirteen years of working there, and that I should report this to my attorney.

Examining the similar name report, I noticed three different court case numbers: there was the court docket number for the current case, and another court docket number regarding when I was arrested at my parents' house, having three court appearances before being extradited on my last appearance in Room D11. Then there was a third court docket number 2000SU003682, showing me being arrested a month before I was arrested after coming home from getting a gift for my son's birthday. It showed I had three court appearances in January; the case was then sealed.

Top part of the similar name report (Sealed)

How could that be? I wasn't arrested at all in January and never made any court appearances whatsoever. It seems that Suffolk County had something in store for me, and it must have backfired, and that's why the case was sealed. I think the police were getting ready to kidnap me and smuggle me out of New York State, just like at my court appearance, when I had brought my son along, thinking it was going to be dismissed. It was all planned. It turned out that the local courts have been doing this for more than a decade, as revealed by the October 2 2016 *Long Island Newsday* headline "Hundreds of LI Court Cases Blocked From View, Signed, Sealed And Secret" (Please see http://projects.newsday.com/long-island/long-island-court-cases-improperly-sealed/) They also had a penchant for dragging other people through an expensive and protracted trial process alongside me. I met a Hispanic man who also retained Badoglio and had to pay him exorbitant amounts for over a year. Eventually, he ran out of money, and was as such forced to plead guilty.

Knowing there was no such thing as justice in the courthouse, I told Badoglio and his associates what I found out and that I wanted a copy of that supposedly incriminating tape where I allegedly had threatened someone's life. I finally did get a copy of the so-called evidence on tape. Listening to it back home, I found, of course, there was no threat; the tape was blank, like the DAs admitted. Of course, I knew it was all made up, but what could I do, facing life in prison now, all cooked up for the sole purpose of destroying my life?

The attorney in the city had advised us to file complaints to the grievance department, turning in the judge and our lawyers in the new case, which I did March 9, 2009. After a year and a half of waiting, I finally received a letter stating that they found no wrongdoing, even as they admitted that there was no warrant for my arrest. By then I had stopped going to my court appointments; I was just wasting my time and money, always being told to plead guilty. The two law firms were angry, and they had given up on me at that point, knowing they couldn't break me. Instead, they pretended that I still went to my appearances, and the transcripts bounced between calling them bench trials and jury trials. The very last e-court printout shows my last court appointment was held on March 30, 2009, given the labeling Motion; I found out later it was a motion to dismiss me as a client. I received a certified letter dated March 30, 2009 from my attorney stating "Due to your failure to appear in court on Friday, March 27, 2009 a bench warrant has been issued for your arrest". The funny thing was, there is no March

27, 2009 appearance on my e-court printout at all, so I took it as just a way to get back at me. After that the next time I tried to sign in there was no record found of me and nobody came around to pick me up. But they got their revenge in other ways.

It started towards the end of the trial when the pretend detective showed back up at my house. It was as I walked my son to the school bus one morning. She, back in plainclothes and in her own car, flew down my block towards us. I had to warn the bus driver to avoid her as she screeched to a halt within sight of me. She stared angrily out her window at me, as I returned the favor while wondering why she'd shown up at all, and in particular at the exact time of morning when the bus came. She backed out of the dead end and sped off northbound on the street that intersects with mine. Eventually I figured out how she knew when to come and threaten me.

We found out that one of the neighbors who lived on our block filed a complaint about our next-door neighbor, Balbo, at the town hall. One of their kids was almost run over by one of his dump trucks while waiting for the school bus. Fed up with the heavy traffic he was causing on our quiet street, the family went straight to the town hall and complained about it, but nothing was done. Wondering why nothing was being done, the family did further investigation on the Internet and found news articles that this same neighbor, whom we had seen being visited by the police, was also being investigated by the police and the F.B.I. This blew us away and seemed to present an answer to one of our many questions as to why the police only visited one neighbor in our area to ask about us. They had a rat in the woodwork right next door.

Something that many people don't know about the justice system is that they employ "confidential informants," otherwise known as C.I.s. Many times, these informants are recruited from among people who are facing criminal charges themselves. The informants are offered reduced charges, or even to have the charges against them dropped entirely, if they act as secret agents for the police. They are not usually trained in any way, and their sole motivation is to work off their own charges by spying on other people who may or may not be involved in criminal activities and "snitching" on them to the police. They are motivated to provide any kind of information, whether it is true or not, in order to seem useful to the police and to get their own charges lowered. It is a well-known practice in police departments, which may explain why someone who was in major trouble himself might be spying on us.

Keeping a close watch on the spy, we noticed that sometimes late at night Balbo would turn off his outside night lights. We wondered why he would do that. Night lights are for just that purpose—to provide light at night to discourage anyone from coming on a person's property for fear of being seen. Why would he plunge his property in darkness like that—and only on some nights? We found out one day. What we found out compounded the fear we lived in, ratcheting it up to terror.

It was September 28th 2008, a few days after I stopped appearing in court. I planned to take my son to the park the day that I found out my 1996 Geo Metro had been sabotaged. Thank God, the car shook violently before I reached a high rate of speed; I slowed down and drove straight back to the house. On investigation, I found that the front passenger's wheel had more than double the air pressure of 62 pounds per-square inch. Going anywhere fast would have caused a blowout and, quite possibly, a serious accident.

My family was shocked to see this dangerous vandalism to my car; this could have caused the death of my son, my mother's grandson. Needless to say, we never made it to the park that day.

My 1996 Geo Metro

I am pretty strict about car maintenance; I had purchased four new whitewall tires from Sears in East Northport not long before. I know very well that my tire was at the proper air pressure the day before this happened. I had no other way to interpret it but that someone was trying to harm me. I felt that someone had made an attempt on my life. I also figured I knew why: that month, I was scheduled for three separate court appearances as they tried to turn the screws on me. Since I ducked out, they wanted to send a message or even hurt me. After this, I stopped going out for walks and bike rides in the neighborhood as well. I could not feel safe there at all anymore.

Over time we found hidden cameras mounted on the outbuildings and the side of the house of that new neighbor. The way we found out was that my mother noticed in 2010 that some of our Rosa Rugosa bushes along her front property line either were dying off mysteriously or were being pruned. She asked me if I knew any reason for the sudden gaps in the bushes, and of course, I didn't.

When I told her that, she started keeping a close eye on things to find out what was really going on. Looking out the window one dark, rainy day late in the afternoon, she got her answer. She heard one of Mr. Balbo's dump trucks coming up his driveway. This happened each afternoon, but instead of driving straight back to his backyard property as was his custom, he parked along our front property line, and a driver and several workers jumped out of the truck and walked to Balbo's backyard. Assuming they were going to work on his property as they did at times, and not thinking much of it, my mother went to do laundry. When she returned, she happened to look out her bedroom window, and she saw Mr. Balbo's workers on her property, cutting down her Rosa Rugosa.

Running out in the rain in her slippers, she confronted the workers and yelled at them to get off her property. One just stood there, shaking his head and saying, "No English," but Mr. Balbo himself got out of the cab of the dump truck. My mother yelled at him, "Get your workers off my property! Why are you cutting down my bushes?" Mr. Balbo walked right up to her on her own property, stared down at her and said, "Why don't you people just move?" She fought back by saying, "I'm going to the town hall to report this." Mr. Balbo then removed himself and his workers from her property and drove the dump truck to his own backyard.

I heard about this after I came home that night, so the following day I went to inspect the area of the Rosa Rugosa bushes. I was standing in the driveway, observing the new damage done and wondering why Balbo was doing this. Then I happened to look up towards his house and noticed something that looked like a camera lens pointing straight down at me where I was standing in the driveway. It was a well-hidden security camera.

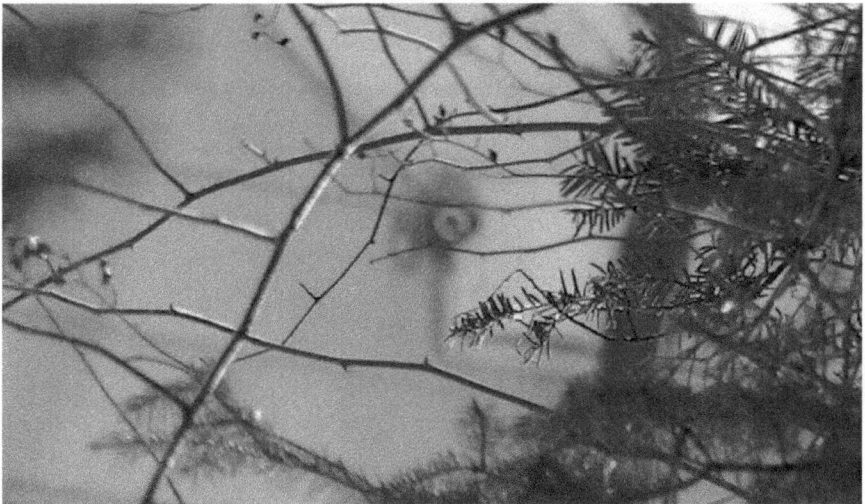

A camera pointed at our driveway

That was the reason for our Rosa Rugosa bushes disappearing; we were being spied on, and he wanted a clear view. On further inspection along the property line, I found yet another camera mounted on one of his buildings. It was pointing straight down into our pool and deck area where we sit and have our BBQs. Finding these spy cameras, I immediately told my parents, who looked for themselves. We decided to take photos of the cameras as proof. Because our driveway is so dark at night, I could see the front camera glowing an orange-red color at night. Apparently, it had infrared night vision.

Hidden camera, pointing to our yard

Our backyard, hidden camera to the right at property line

Why would this neighbor use security cameras to spy on us, watching every move we made? Who was he reporting to and why? The Confidential Informant explanation is the only one I can think of as to why someone being investigated himself would be in cahoots with the police.

Needless to say, not having any privacy either in front or in back, we stopped opening up the pool and having BBQs in our backyard. Our use and enjoyment of our own property was taken away, just like it was in Pennsylvania. We didn't feel safe or comfortable sitting in our own back yard, knowing we were being watched. My growing son suffered the most because he lost the use of the pool and the back yard. As I said, we became prisoners in our own home, afraid to go out on our own property.

Over a period of time we caught the neighbor trespassing again. Super Storm Sandy had hit right around Halloween, and in truly spooky style, the neighborhood was still in the dark from the storm. There were no streetlights; everyone was without power, and nobody was out trick or treating in the neighborhood—or so it seemed.

It was half past three in the morning on Halloween; I was fast asleep on the couch in the family room. I woke up, hearing something hit the side of the house outside the parking area. Looking out the window I saw what looked like eggs being thrown at the house and our vehicles. The eggs were coming from the front of our property. Going to the front window, I saw the silhouette of a person running across our property, going through the cut Rosa Rugosa bushes, and going onto Balbo's property. Staring out the window as I was, it didn't take long to figure out who it was. Balbo, who smoked, lit a match and his features were lit up in the glow of it. There was no other mischief on our dead-end street; our house was the only one hit that Halloween night. We spent the next day cleaning egg off the house and our vehicles. My mother was furious, saying our neighbor was nothing but a night creeper and wishing she could have a fence installed.

Money was tight for my parents after spending some sixty thousand dollars in legal fees for me. Eventually, though, they did gather enough money to hire a fence company. They hoped that installing a six-foot wooden privacy fence that ran along the whole east side of their driveway would fix the problem. The fence started at the street curb and ran all the way back to our backyard fence, some one hundred feet, for the sole purpose of protection from this intrusive, untrustworthy neighbor. The new fence was also high enough to block the view of the one front camera pointing down our driveway, so we had some visual privacy at last.

You would think a fence like this would put a stop to the mischief, but late at night, soon after it was built, we heard gun shots coming from the back of Balbo's property. The next morning my stepdad found his mailbox ripped out of the ground and lying in the middle of the dead-end street. Another neighbor came over and said he had heard the gun shots too, and had reported it to the police. The cop didn't want to hear about it all; he just took down information. It looked like it was going to go exactly nowhere from there.

My parents were tired of taking all the punches, so they tried a new approach and went to the town hall to complain about the illegal commercial business next door. It was similar to when the neighbor had complained about the gun shots; the police weren't interested. In fact, my parents were surprised to find that the town's inspector knew who they were, and he told them to just deal with it, as everybody has problems. My parents were shocked; my mother was complaining about all of the illegal structures he had built up to the property line, all without any visible permits. She told the town clerk that our family had been living here for over forty years, paying our fair share of taxes, living in a quiet residential area until this neighbor moved in with his business. She said we were tired of the noise, the pollution of breathing in the exhaust, the rumbling of trucks coming and going making deliveries in the illegal warehouse he built, the workers' vehicles, and the garbage that was being piled up along our property line, attracting rats and other rodents. Yet, to my parents' surprise, even after all this, nothing was done. Somehow, without notifying us or the surrounding neighbors, all of the illegal structures Balbo had built without any permits or variances, including the 30 X 30 X 30 warehouse that was built ten feet from our property line, were given a pass. On the way out a resident who had overheard the conversation advised my parents to turn that neighbor in to the EPA. Time will tell whether he is ever made to answer for the damage he did to the environment and to his neighbors' use and enjoyment of their own property. It seems that not only was the deal meant to get the police off his back, but the town inspectors too.

To get back at us, Balbo turned some of his spotlights to point down on our front driveway and back yard property. This went on for some time, and then in early 2017, Balbo got even bolder and added a new spotlight right outside my parent's eastside bedroom window, lighting up their bedroom and the whole side of the house.

New spotlight outside my parents' bedroom window

Yet even though my mother and stepdad made noise at the town hall to make him stop pointing his lights on us, nothing was done about it. How could someone who was being investigated by the police and the FBI have that kind of power? It seems the long arm of the law was proving to be no match for us; they knew how to keep things quiet. We felt we must be such a threat to law enforcement, they would do anything to disrupt our lives, even if it meant spying on us and unwarranted arrests. In fact, that's exactly what they did to get back at us. It has taken a lot of fortitude for my parents to choose to stay in their house of forty years.

As well, several years earlier I had applied for children's health insurance in the county, and we qualified for it. Over the years I always took Kelvin for his yearly checkups and reapplied each year with his case worker. Then right in the middle of the fiscal year, I received a letter in the mail from Suffolk County stating that my son's New York State health insurance had been dropped. No reason was given. My mother and I tried like hell to get it back, but with no luck. This was a low blow— attacking a child to get back at me. I wondered what was in store for us next.

Thankfully, that case was eventually abandoned and a little of the weight has been lifted from my shoulders. However the cooked up monetary judgment going back to the attempt to seize my grandfather's house in 1998, has continued to haunt me.

Sometimes I think it might have been better if they took the old house. I received several more money judgments not long after the first one from the same courthouse, today adding up to over a quarter of a million dollars. The person who forged those judgments against me some twenty years ago, is now a judge at the same courthouse where I was extradited out of New York. We feel that the reason for all of these judgments that keep on adding up will someday be used against me, possibly trying to pull off the same stunt on my parents' property, patiently waiting for the right time to pounce.

These monetary judgments I received years ago still stand, hanging over any attempts at gainful employment and have also kept me from acquiring a passport. Also, just recently as of

September 2019 my New York State driver's license was wrongfully suspended that is my right as an American citizen. I was sent a notice of the suspension that was lacking the needed signatures and rationale. I contacted the DMV, who confirmed that my license was suspended but couldn't figure out who did. Then adding insult to injury during the coronavirus pandemic, I never received any of the three stimulus checks. I'm guessing it was intercepted by none other than Suffolk County collections. Ever since I received that 65,000 dollar judgment, over the years Suffolk County has been taken my tax returns and seizing my bank accounts.

You'd think it would let up, that they would have had enough after twenty years and would leave me alone. I was arrested numerous times, extradited out of two different states, and monetary judgments that added up to a lottery winning kept coming at me like a whirlwind trying to pull me down.

After all my experiences, is it any wonder that I haven't retained a lawyer to fight these judgments? What I've learned from my crusade is that the people in law enforcement know how to keep things quiet and get things done. It doesn't matter if you're a lawyer, cop, a judge, or even the governor; they all work together to cover up their crimes. It spreads like cancer; they all reach agreements between themselves that serve the system, not the citizen. By this time, every hope and dream for justice I have had has been strangled. I just don't believe I can get justice anymore or ever living a normal life as an American citizen.

There are some who might say I should have just gone along with the system way back when, and sometimes I've even thought that. That I shouldn't have let it come to trial, as they sometimes punish a citizen for insisting on his or her right to a trial; they like you to plead guilty to get it over with and justify the arrest. Some might say I should have just taken the earlier punishments in hope that the whole snowball would have stopped rolling long ago. Some will say that my lawyers simply couldn't do more for me than they did; others may think I am paranoid about the corruption that pervades the justice system, where lawyers, judges, district attorneys, and elected officials all "drink tea together," as one bona fide policeman put it.

I could have gone along with the system at any point and perhaps lessened the impact on myself and my family by simply accepting what they said about me and paying their fines and doing their time.

There was a problem with that, though. I was innocent.

I know I am not the only person in the United States who has been convicted unfairly of a crime and whose resistance to that, however right or naïve, has been punished with ever-escalating legal problems. We already know that innocents are serving long, hard prison terms. DNA testing has exonerated a significant number of people behind bars who are serving time under terrible circumstances for crimes they did not commit. Where was justice for them?

I pray and hope that telling my story will help raise public consciousness that our justice system is often calcified by routine, red tape, bureaucracy, and apathy for the rights of citizens. As one of my lawyers said, "Bureaucracy runs itself." It grinds on its rusted wheels toward its destination of preserving the system and making it easier on those entrenched within it rather than taking the time and trouble to deal with individuals justly, leaving oh so many crushed beneath the corroded mill.

A retired Suffolk County Judge, Stuart Namm, published his own story about the legal system in Suffolk County entitled *A Whistleblower's Lament: The Perverted Pursuit of Justice in the State of New York.* He hit the nail on the head when he compared the legal system in Suffolk County to the Wild West. It truly is, and they have been gunning for me for a long time.

My nightmare goes on.

www.ingramcontent.com/pod-product-compliance
Lightning Source LLC
Chambersburg PA
CBHW021923040426
42448CB00008B/889